The Year without a Purchase

The Year without a Purchase

One Family's Quest to Stop Shopping and Start Connecting

Scott Dannemiller

WJK Westminster John Knox Press
Louisville • Kentucky

First edition
Published by Westminster John Knox Press
Louisville, Kentucky

15 16 17 18 19 20 21 22 23 24—10 9 8 7 6 5 4 3 2 1

Book design by Sharon Adams
Cover design by Barbara LeVan Fisher/levanfisherstudio.com

Library of Congress Cataloging-in-Publication Data

Dannemiller, Scott.
The year without a purchase : one family's quest to stop shopping and start connecting / Scott Dannemiller. — First edition.
pages cm
ISBN 978-0-664-26068-2 (alk. paper)
1. Consumption (Economics)—Religious aspects—Christianity. 2. Wealth—Religious aspects—Christianity. 3. Families—Religious life. I. Title.
BR115.C67D36 2015
241'.68—dc23

2015002767

♾ The paper used in this publication meets the minimum requirements of the American National Standard for Information Sciences—Permanence of Paper for Printed Library Materials, ANSI Z39.48-1992.

This book is dedicated to all those without enough.
May these words help us part with plenty
to make the world a better place.

Contents

Part Three: Growing in Faith Together

Part Four: Serving God's People

Part Five: The Results

Acknowledgments

I owe an enormous debt of gratitude to my wife. She is the one who makes me a better person, constantly refocusing our attention on God and on doing the right thing. Without her, this book would never have been finished. She is my most vocal cheerleader and critic, happily editing with her red pen and offering suggestions. Thank you for your dedication to me, our family, and this project. I also must thank our kids, Jake and Audrey, who are the pride that swells my heart, the muse behind my words, and the givers of my headaches. May these words one day remind you of your beautiful childhood and the love we share as a family.

And to my mom and dad, I could never repay you for all the gifts you've given me. I only hope my life makes you half as proud as I feel every time I remember that *you* are *my* parents. And to my brother and sister for setting the bar high and always showing love. Thank you.

I also acknowledge how my life has been shaped by my spiritual guides: Nancy Marroquin, Kristi Shay Moore, Rob Mueller, Alastair and Catherine Rundle, the Presbyterian Church's Young Adult Volunteer Program, and especially the beloved BAVs. Thanks for fortifying my soul.

And to our family in Guatemala: Martin, Graciela, Edwin, Francisco, Marlon, Eduardo, Josesito, and Yadi. Thank you for opening your home and your hearts and showing us what true generosity can be.

I thank our church family who supports and inspires, and our friends near and far who encourage and entertain. You provided us with both material goods to sustain us during the year and a fountain of inspiration to fuel my writing. I am so very grateful.

To Seamus McKiernan at the *Huffington Post* for being the first to publish my stories to a wider audience, to Lindsay Ferrier (Suburban Turmoil) for her encouragement and awesome video spot about our project, and to Glennon Doyle Melton (Momastery) for helping me go viral. Each of you has made a huge impact on my life with one small act of kindness. I only hope to be able to pay it forward someday.

And to Jessica Kelley and the good people at Westminster John Knox Press, thank you for your vote of confidence and your helpful critiques and feedback. It's been a blessing.

And finally, to our God who calls each and every one of us into a purpose greater than ourselves. May we always be listening.

Introduction to the Worst Book Ever

Thanks for buying this book. I hope you keep reading, but I suspect there's a good chance that you'll stop after the first couple of paragraphs. And it's not because you're not smart enough to decipher big, fancy words.

Words like *decipher*.

No, I think you'll stop reading because this book isn't for everyone. When we told people we were not buying anything for a year, we had mixed reactions. Some folks thought it was a great adventure. Others? Not so much.

My best buddy Marty simply asked, "Why?" The expression on his face was the same look he might give if, say, I had just told him I was moving my family to the Amazon rainforest to open a restaurant that sells nothing but corn dogs.

Complete bewilderment.

When I told my brother, he asked, "Are you going to write a book about it?"

I shrugged. "Maybe."

He paused for a moment, then added, "That sounds like the worst book ever. 'Chapter 1: Didn't buy anything today.' 'Chapter 2: I want a new shirt. Not gonna get it.' "

"Thanks," I said. "I'll make sure to quote you on the dust jacket."

Big brothers are full of awesome.

Sadly, I can't fault their skepticism. I feel the same way, but for different reasons. For starters, why would anyone want to write a book about not buying stuff? Anybody who actually buys the book would probably feel like a failure from the word "go." But I'm sure you picked up your copy at the local library.

Second, and more important, the vast majority of the people on the planet don't have excess spending money. Buying necessary items such as clothes, food, and shelter either stretches the budget or is completely out of reach. It's the global norm. According to a World Bank report, roughly 80 percent of the world's population lives on less than ten dollars per day . . . 10 . . . the equivalent of two pumpkin spiced lattes at your local Starbucks.[1]

Those struggling to buy the basics will find our challenge laughable at best, and extremely offensive at worst. And justifiably so. I would feel the exact same way if I heard of a family experimenting with my harsh reality just for grins. So feel free to throw this book across the room. Just make sure there is no one standing in your way when you take aim. We don't want anyone to get hurt, and we don't have liability insurance for that kind of thing.

Now, if you have made it this far, there is a good chance the concept of not shopping for a year has some appeal to you, but you're not sure why. You just know that a vacation from consumerism somehow sounds like a good idea.

That's how it started for us.

Our situation is the middle-class American dream. We live in a modest, three-bedroom, two-bath house in the suburbs of Nashville, Tennessee. We have two kids. Our boy is six, and our girl is five. Jake plays little league, and Audrey is in Girl Scouts. I'm a self-employed corporate trainer. My wife, Gabby, works part-time from home. We have a gym membership. We drive a fourteen-year-old Acura Integra that's paid off and a seven-year-old Honda Pilot that's not. Look up "Cheesy Suburban Doofus" in the dictionary, and you'll see a picture of me in my driveway. I'm the one trying to start the lawnmower, wearing Crocs and socks, and whistling a medley of 80s-hair band ballads.

But something is wrong with this life. And it's not just my poor fashion sense.

You have probably felt it too. The day-to-day stress. The busyness. The feeling that you can never get ahead. The worries. The anxiety. The want and the need. The giving in and the giving up. We feel all of this and more for no good reason. On paper, we are living a dream life, but in our hearts we notice an empty space is growing larger by the day. A hunger and thirst for something more.

And it's not about the money.

Don't get me wrong. Money is important. Money is what drives our economy. Money allows us to buy our basic needs and survive. But it goes deeper than that.

Preoccupation with money is a symptom of something larger lurking just beneath the surface. What is it that fuels our desire for money and the material goods it can provide? Why do we choose to struggle for "more" when simplifying would be so much easier? And what have we lost in the process?

That's what this book is about. I wrote it to try to answer these questions and more. It is written for the disconnected. The stressed out. The anxious.

And maybe.

Just maybe.

It's for you.

Maybe you're feeling pressure to keep up with the Joneses.

Maybe you couldn't care less about the Joneses, but you are concerned that your kids might be shunned or made fun of if they don't have what the Joneses' kids have.

Maybe you feel trapped in a job that drives you nuts. It leaves you feeling burned out, with only enough energy to snap at your spouse or your kids; but you can't change for fear of changing your lifestyle.

Maybe you're giving your family a better life than you ever had, but you still feel unfulfilled.

Or maybe you're just tired of buying crap you don't need, but you keep doing it anyway, and it creates a ton of stress in your life.

If any of these describe you, then you're probably feeling imprisoned by your life.

You want to know a secret?

It doesn't have to be that way.

Part One

Living with Integrity

How did we get here, and what's it all about?

Chapter One

Darth Vader and the Call from God

Love is patient, love is kind. It does not envy, it does not boast, it is not proud. It does not dishonor others, it is not self-seeking, it is not easily angered, it keeps no record of wrongs . . . Love never fails.

(*1 Corinthians 13:4–5, 8 NIV*)

Most ideas don't hatch overnight. Especially the questionable ones. They need time to percolate like a good cup of coffee. That's how it was for us.

You could say it all started ten years ago when Gabby and I started feeling disconnected—not from each other—but from reality. Gabby was working 50–60-hour weeks as an operations manager for a computer manufacturing company in Austin, Texas. When asked what she did for a living, her response was a simple, two-word answer: "Professional Nag."

She made money by staying on top of details and making sure other people did what they were supposed to do. Frankly, she was good at it. Her frantic days were spent bouncing from phone calls to meetings, dealing with crazy people. People who firmly believed that late computer shipments would cause the sun to explode and kill us all.

Unfortunately, she was becoming one of those people.

Gabby noticed her life becoming more transactional. Conversations were no longer meant for increasing understanding and building relationships. They were a means to an end. Just another task in an ever-growing to-do list, and this attitude was beginning to bleed into her personal life, blurring the lines between life and work.

My job wasn't much better. I was a recent transplant to Austin. I worked as a technical trainer for a technology company. I hardly knew a soul and traveled most of the time. When I wasn't traveling, I was working online, spending time with "virtual people." To compensate, I forged relationships in places where people were forced to interact with me.

If I felt the need for some conversation, I would just drive over to Kool Klips and share life stories with Belinda as she gave me an aptly priced six-dollar haircut. This worked well until our in-depth chatter served to be too much of a distraction, and my hair began to look like I had taken a nosedive into my kitchen blender.

Then there was the grocery store—a perfect place to pick up some crackers, spray cheese, and spot-on relationship advice. I began to call the checkout clerks my personal friends, learning about their families and social lives. I would hold up the line to ask lots of questions and delve into their personal business. It was an honest attempt to build community with those around me and create a more connected world. Unfortunately, my desperation turned this simple act of friendly conversation into something creepy. Shortly thereafter, they installed self-checkout lines.

Coincidence? Not likely.

On the outside, life was good for us. We had good jobs, a house in the suburbs, and vacations to exotic destinations. Inside, we felt as if we were stuck on a hamster wheel, pursuing activity for activity's sake.

Over dinner one night, we were both bemoaning our harried existence. We were becoming cogs in the wheel of a culture that was drawing us closer and closer to things that felt so very unimportant. We both felt the need to change the trajectory of our lives. We knew we wanted to focus on something different, but we weren't sure what that something different might be. That's when I blurted out, "Maybe we should just be missionaries or something."

They were throw-away words. A hypothetical question wedged in between bites of mashed potatoes and mac-n-cheese. In retrospect, I probably said it to get my wife to fall in love with me all over again by giving the impression that I was some sort of saint.

It didn't work.

In the time it took me to move my fork to my face hole, a smile instantly formed on her face, and she answered with an enthusiastic, "OK! Let's do it!"

I nearly aspirated my meatloaf.

I heard an audible "click" echo from inside her skull. My wife sprung into *work mode*. Ever the planner and organizer, she was frantically creating a mental Gantt chart of tasks, resources, and deadlines. She rattled off a list of "to-dos":

- Research potential locations
- Choose a destination
- Sell the house
- Sell the cars
- Find someone to take care of our dogs

The flood of words spewed forth as if a dam had burst inside her. It was like she had been planning this all her life. This idea of disconnecting in order to reconnect had captured her heart. It was a drastic change to kick start meaning, and she held on with both hands.

Meanwhile, I compiled a list of ways we might die as missionaries in a developing country:

- Impaled on long, sharp spears
- Cooked in a giant, black cauldron
- Thrown into a volcano
- Murdered by drug lords
- Ravaged by dysentery

Needless to say, I was not on the bandwagon. I have always been a fan of making the world a better place, so long as it means I don't have to change anything about my life. Like Martin Luther

King, I, too, have a dream. The difference is, rather than rally millions of people to put their lives on the line for truth and justice, I prefer to discuss my dream in very ambiguous terms over a plate of nachos.

So, there we were, battling it out. One of us motivated by love, and the other motivated by fear. A quick glance at history and the nightly news shows us that fear normally wins. Fear is strong. It has bulging biceps and ginormous pectorals. Fear admires itself in the mirror, grunting as it hurls weights the size of Volkswagens into the air with ease.

Love, on the other hand, is fragile. Love blows kisses and dandelion fluff into the breeze. Love bakes a batch of cookies for the school fundraiser and offers you a comfy seat on the bus. Normally, love doesn't stand a chance against fear.

But love is persistent. And this was a long-term battle.

As the weeks wore on, I began to wonder if the nagging in my gut had less to do with my eating some bad sushi and more to do with God, but I couldn't be certain. I was looking for a sign. I wanted it to be something obvious, like the voice of The Almighty echoing through my living room. To me, God's voice sounds like James Earl Jones' Darth Vader mixed with a hint of Charlton Heston.

Scott. I am your Father.

Alas, the celebrity voice-over commands never materialized. If God was sending signs, He must be using fine print. Maybe The Almighty Marketer was trying to speak to us through all those roadside billboards adorned with pictures of faraway lands? Or the advertisements that were in our faces twenty-four hours a day?

That's when I started to notice all the hints buried in the pages of newspapers and magazines. Laundry detergent. Potato chips. Hair Club for Men. It wasn't the *products* calling out to us. It was the *slogans*.

"A new formula."

"You want more."

"It's time for a change."

But I still wasn't sure it was a call from God. One evening, Gabby and I were discussing our options when the phone rang.

She answered. It was an acquaintance of ours. The woman didn't sound anything like James Earl Jones, but her words were a rubber mallet to my noggin.

"Hi Gabby. This is Katy. I know it's short notice, but I was wondering if you and Scott would be interested in joining a two-week mission trip to Guatemala next month."

God is funny.

We had been thinking of spending a year or more as missionaries, but the concept was terrifying. The uncertainty of such an experience was creating an avalanche of anxiety. Now, it was like God was pulling double-duty as a telemarketer, telling us, "Here's your money-back guarantee! Just try it out for two weeks, and if you don't like it, you can return to your mundane old life. But if you're satisfied, we'll give you a full year of mission service and even throw in this lovely set of steak knives!"

It's hard to say no to bonus steak knives.

We agreed to go on the trip as a way to test the waters of missionary life. What we didn't realize was that this simple decision likely sealed our fate. Love's persistence overcame the strength of fear, fueled by the same force that put us on the hamster wheel in the first place.

Peer pressure.

Yes. That force that made you wear a tuxedo print t-shirt to prom back in the '80s? The mysterious power that told you to streak the quad back in college? The one that caused us to give in to the expectations of others, trying to leapfrog the Joneses and losing ourselves in the process?

God can use it for good.

In much the same way you might tell your friends about a new gadget you just purchased, we innocently told friends and family about our two-week mission trip. Inevitably, this led to discussions about a possible year-long commitment. Which led to people asking, "Why?"

This is when the tone of our conversations would shift. We moved beyond chats about Lasik surgery and family vacations and dove into the deep end of the connecting pool, discussing life and its frustrations. We talked about stress and busyness. We talked about meaning. We talked about the false allure of manufactured joy. And the more we talked about these things, the more people would ask, "So when are you leaving?"

Now we were trapped. There was no good reason *not* to commit to a full year. Besides, if we told people we were going to look for meaning, we *had* to do it. What would they think if we didn't? We would be frauds, falling short of their expectations. But at least this time, we had a hunch that those expectations were pushing us in the right direction.

Chapter Two

Doing Nothing for God

Many are the plans in a person's heart,
but it is the LORD*'s purpose that prevails.*
(Proverbs 19:21 NIV)

We signed up to be part of the Young Adult Volunteer program through the Presbyterian Church (U.S.A.). We were over the maximum age for the program, but apparently there aren't a ton of people beating down the door to make a couple hundred bucks a month and live in "third world" conditions for twelve months, so they let it slide. We were filled with a mix of excitement and trepidation. While it was a scary leap of faith, we knew it was going to be a great adventure. And secretly, I had grand aspirations of selfishly saving the world in the name of God.

Prior to hopping on the plane to Guatemala, we spent a week in missionary orientation. It was like army boot camp, but instead of yelling, push-ups, and daybreak marathons, we did lots of singing, reflecting, and daybreak praying. It was less physically taxing but emotionally exhausting just the same.

The hardest concept to accept was the idea that we were to treat our year as a "ministry of presence." Our leaders said that our focus should not be on achieving any major goals, but rather, experiencing simplicity among God's people and doing our best to be living examples of God's love for all those we might encounter.

Wait. That doesn't sound very sexy.

We had grown accustomed to a fast pace of life. Calendars were crammed with things to do. We were incredibly active. Working extra hours, then meeting up with friends and their families. The weekends were full, too. Throwing parties for friends, running charity races, and serving at church. Now we were being asked to commit to being a vessel for God. Nothing more, nothing less. Which sounded like doing a whole lot of nothing.

In addition to being "present" we did have actual jobs to do. Gabby's role was to work as a liaison between local Guatemalan villages and mission teams coming from the States. She would help plan itineraries for the mission teams based on what the village leaders needed. Sometimes it was building a structure, such as a church or community center. Other times it was cultivating vegetable gardens or constructing composting latrines. It was a glamorous job, if glamour comes covered in diesel fumes and pees in a steamy outhouse.

My job was to teach leadership and project-planning skills to twenty-five pastors scattered throughout the southwestern part of the country. The hope was that they might use their places of worship as a centralized location to serve the greater needs of the community, starting nutrition projects or after-school programs to keep youth out of trouble.

Even though we understood this whole "ministry of presence" concept, it was still very hard to shake our corporate-American mind-set. And it was more than just the change in activity level. It was also a change in outcomes. I wanted to be able to share a list of accomplishments: how many schools we could build, how many projects we could complete, or how many lives could we save by the time our year of service was over. Maybe even get a certificate of achievement I could stick on the refrigerator. It didn't take long for my performance-minded mind-set to come face-to-face with missionary reality.

This year was not about achievement.

As soon as we landed, it was evident that we both had the Spanish skills of a nine-year-old with bad grammar. Imagine if some third grader from Nicaragua came to your city and claimed to have all the answers to your community's problems. Would you listen? Probably not. And even if we had been fluent in the language, we didn't truly understand the culture anyway. We were like a Texas rancher dropped in the middle of a housing project in Brooklyn.

Our expectations and focus quickly shifted. We learned that it's hard to measure meaning. Impossible, actually. It is, however, something that can be felt, and we felt it most deeply in our everyday interactions.

While we did accomplish some amazing things throughout the year, *by far* our greatest blessing was sharing a home with Martín, Graciela, and their six kids, combining lives from completely different worlds. They were a Spanish-speaking family of Maya Quiché descent, and we were suburban American DINKs (Dual-Income, No Kids). While we possessed a deep understanding of our own lives, we had no clue about theirs. They had faced hardships we would never fully understand. Extreme poverty. Civil war. Genocide.

As honored guests in their modest home, they offered us the best of what they had. Each night we would stand on the rough concrete floor around the warmth of the wood stove, watching Graciela pat out corn tortillas by hand and muffling our coughs as the wood smoke filled the room, floated up to the tin roof, and escaped through the gaps.

At mealtime we all gathered around an old wooden table surrounded by mismatched chairs. Some were plastic. Others were made of metal with peeling vinyl cushions. In a house without a couch or a La-Z-Boy, it was the best place to share stories of our upbringing, comparing lives and finding commonality in the midst of glaring differences.

We were humbled by their generosity, often receiving the only meat at the meal. It was a simple extravagance, but an extravagance just the same, because in Martin and Graciela's house, excess didn't exist. There were few conversations about new stuff, the latest movies, or techno gadgets. There were no material distractions at all, so all the conversations were about immaterial things—the things that really matter. Looking one another in the eye and learning about one another. Not what you have or what you do, but *who you are*. What made you who you are. What drives you. The hopes and the hurts. Fears and dreams.

It was a shock to the system.

In the United States, when you meet someone, one of the first questions asked is, "So, what do you do for a living?" How do you earn money? The answer defines who you are.

I am a teacher.

A doctor.

A nurse.

A postal worker.

In Guatemala, we were never asked this question. Not even once. In twelve months. This experience temporarily severed our connection to money. We no longer had any bills to pay. Our program paid our host family enough to cover our food, and we received a small stipend that was more than enough to pay for transportation on the chicken bus and an occasional trip to an Internet café to send updates to family and friends. So material goods stopped being an everyday concern.

Imagine for a moment that your very sense of self has been stripped away. You have no career. No culture. Everything in your immediate possession fits into four large suitcases. You speak with the simple words of a child and are constantly humbled by the kindness of a family who earns next to nothing. Meanwhile, everything you used to believe about security and accomplishment is disappearing like frost in the sun.

What would you do?

We started asking some hard questions. But it's not something we decided to do on our own. No. It was a task given to us by our mission supervisors eight months into our experience. They often gave us kooky assignments that were supposed to be good for us. Like spiritual brussels sprouts, these challenges were supposed to help us grow. And this time, they were right. The question they posed was, "If we aren't defined by our jobs and we can't measure the value of what we are accomplishing here, then what *does* define us? What is at the core of who we are? What is our purpose in life?"

Unfortunately, you can't cheat on this assignment. The answer isn't found in a fortune cookie. Trust me. I looked. You have to open up your soul to find it. Chisel through the childhood dreams, the voice of your mother, and the expectations of people you've tried to please who never really cared in the first place.

Beneath all of that, you find your foundation. It's a solid, white wall, scrawled with the words that reveal who you are. Your personal motto, written by God. We've just been too distracted to read it.

Gabby and I spent a couple of days face-to-face on our bed in our tiny adobe *casita*, asking these hard questions and massaging the answers. Even though all our distractions had been pruned away, it was difficult to distill our purpose into a short string of words. The end result was what we call our "family mission statement." The words are part actual, part aspirational. The mission may never be complete, but the idea is that the statement is meant to guide our every decision: *To tirelessly seek God's will each day by living lives of integrity, owning what we have, growing together in faith, and serving God's people to build a world without need.*

When we put these words on paper, we were a world away from our friends and family, we had no home, no income to speak of, and few creature comforts. We pooped into a hole in the ground. We bathed once a week with water that we heated by burning our garbage. We slept in a twin bed that resembled a sway-backed horse. Based on these facts, we should have felt disconnected. Miserable, even.

But we weren't miserable. Far from it. Instead, we felt a sense of satisfaction we had never before experienced.

Why?

We felt satisfied because, for the first time, we felt that we were *living with integrity*, completely aligned with that mission. Maybe you have felt that way, too.

Every day, we *owned what we had*. Everyone around us had very little, so we appreciated the little that we did have. We were truly grateful for the simple things, and we took care of them.

We were *growing together in faith*. We weren't worried about what others wanted us to *do*, but asking for clarity on what *God* would have us *be*. Away from all our distractions, we were having deep conversations about meaningful topics and connecting with people on a different level.

And we were *serving others*. Without a real salary, our jobs became about doing good for others. It was the easiest way to prioritize our actions. When trying to decide what to do each day, any task that helped someone else automatically floated to the top.

Our lives weren't perfect, but they were incredibly peaceful. We realized that experiencing a sense of connection was as much about connecting with your own purpose as it was about connecting with others. It was wonderfully illogical, and at the same time beautifully simple. For the first time in our lives we felt perfectly aligned. Tuned in to the stillness of our souls.

And then we ruined it.

Chapter Three

How to Screw Up a Good Thing

A pretentious, showy life is an empty life;
a plain and simple life is a full life.
(*Proverbs 13:7* The Message)

We arrived back in the United States with a fresh perspective. We had spent an entire year living a simple life and learning how the rest of the world lives. You would think that such an experience would produce clarity of vision reserved for monks and sages, but our experience was anything but clear. It was more like sleeping peacefully in a darkened room for twelve hours and then having someone wake you up by shining one of those used-car dealership advertising searchlights right on your face.

On our first trip to Target, surrounded by seventeen different brands of fabric softener and a kajillion choices of snack foods, Gabby and I had an argument in aisle seven over whether or not we needed Scotch tape. Not just a disagreement, mind you, but a genuine marital argument. One where perfect strangers stop and ask, "Is everything OK?"

Based on the intensity of our discussion, you would think we were trying to decide whether or not to put the family dog to sleep.

And then came Thanksgiving.

We stuffed ourselves on more food than we had seen in over a year and retreated to the living room for some conversation with our extended family. Talk turned to the upcoming Christmas celebration. Several people were discussing what an appropriate dollar limit should be for the gifts we would buy our six nieces and nephews. Twenty dollars? Thirty? Fifty? Before I could grab the words and shove them back into my pie hole, I blurted disdainfully, "I don't think any of us should get *anything*. Not even the kids. We already have more than enough."

Merry Christmas!

It got real quiet, real fast. Not a creature was stirring, as they say. Did I believe what I said? Absolutely. All the kids in our middle-class family had far more than they could ever need, especially compared to the children we lived with in Guatemala. But that wasn't what troubled me.

We had been through something that precious few of our peers had ever experienced, yet somehow we expected our photos and stories to change their lives. At the same time, we forgot that our family and friends had spent the past year changing and growing in their own ways, and we were completely ignoring that. We were caught between two worlds, and our attempt to honor those who were now far away put us at risk of alienating those closest to us.

So we did our best to balance being *in* the world but not *of* the world. We kept one eye on the concerns of those on the margins, and the other on the world before us. Slowly, we began to adjust to the accelerated pace of life. We adopted causes that kept us close to the plight of immigrants and hungry people in our country. We led fund-raising efforts. We advocated for change through the appropriate channels. We wrote to senators and congressmen. We made donations. We accomplished things!

At the same time, we were making a life for ourselves in the States. We got jobs. Then came two children, batteries not included. Their entry into the world helped us discover one of our out-of-whack values. We said that family was important to us, yet we lived nearly a thousand miles away from them. To remedy this, we moved to Nashville, Tennessee, to be close to our family. We bought a house in the suburbs with a picket fence. But things were still messed up.

We spent a considerable amount of time and energy buying piles of shiny junk. Most of it was purchased with the best of intentions. We wanted the best for our kids, and we had the means to provide a lot of it, so we bought burp-reducing bottles, educational DVDs, and dye-free laundry soap. Never mind that both of us grew up in an era when cribs were made with finger-pinching metal parts, and family road trips weren't complete unless at least one child napped on the ledge below the back window of a fake-wood-paneled sedan. Our kids were going to have a solid head start.

Slowly but surely, over a decade, our mission began to fade. We became focused on new things such as mom's clubs, little league, and church potlucks. Work hours were spent trying to get ahead. Free time was spent on home-improvement projects designed to transform our humble abode into the envy of the neighborhood.

Fast-forward five years. The change is gradual, but it eventually invades our everyday language. No longer are we bursting with the awareness that we have far more than we need. Instead, I catch myself saying, "I *need* a new pair of dress pants." Am I naked from the waist down?

Or, "I think we *need* to renovate our bathroom." Are we allergic to linoleum? Is there a verse in the Bible saying that God hates Formica countertops?

Today, when we look at our day-to-day actions, we are no longer certain that we're following our family mission statement—the one we paid $500 to preserve as a custom-made piece of shabby-chic artwork for our home. You can't make this stuff up. We're straying from our values, and there is tangible evidence on our wall to prove it.

Recently, our Sunday school class began studying the book *Firstfruits Living* by Lynn A. Miller. In the book, Miller talks about how faithful people put God first in their lives by giving away the best of what they have. Their *firstfruits*.[1]

Yes, the man is crazy.

But reading this book, I notice that I am doing the exact *opposite* of what it suggests is the path to fulfillment. I am essentially hoarding the best of what I have for myself and giving away the leftovers. If a Boy Scout comes to the door collecting canned food for a fundraiser, I am the guy who reaches into the very back of the pantry, pushing the chicken noodle soup out of the way so that I can snag that three-year-old can of hominy.

Because poor people love hominy.

It's ridiculous. And when I *do* give away something of real value, I don't part with it easily. Instead, I give it with the stipulation that the person must thank me profusely for the gift, acknowledge my awesomeness, preferably in public, and then proceed to use the gift in the exact manner I intend. It's an unspoken selfishness constantly lurking beneath the surface.

And I don't like it.

One evening, Gabby and I are discussing our general dissatisfaction with getting further and further away from the joy and fulfillment we felt ten years ago. It's one of those wonderful reflective conversations where you feel that you are really accomplishing something by examining the trajectory of your life, with the added satisfaction of making no real commitment to change anything for the better.

That is, until Gabby asks a hypothetical question.

"What if we didn't buy anything for a year?"

Shaken from the comfort of my own inaction, I respond as any good husband would.

Defensively.

"Wait. Are you saying that I buy too much stuff?" I bark at her, ready to challenge every frivolous purchase she has made in the past six months. A new dress. An art set for Audrey. Incredibly soft toilet paper.

"No. I'm just saying it would be interesting to see if we could do it. If we could get back to a simpler lifestyle. A life more connected to God. And one another."

Challenge accepted.

Reluctantly.

Chapter Four

The Rules

So here's what I want you to do, God helping you: Take your everyday, ordinary life—your sleeping, eating, going-to-work, and walking-around life—and place it before God as an offering.

(*Romans 12:1* The Message)

The thought of not buying anything is both intriguing and scary, but the wheels instantly start spinning in my brain. It would be a drastic change—a shock to the system to force a new way of living. Like teaching someone to swim by throwing them from the top deck of an oil tanker.

Just before year's end, I notice the commercials appearing on TV showing lots of happy, motivated people setting New Year's resolutions for themselves. Things such as weight loss and exercise. I sit, slug-like on the couch, pondering what annual goal I might set for myself that I could back out of a short time later. Maybe I could eat less junk? Or run a marathon? Or take a vow to keep bad smells and sounds inside my body instead of sharing them with the family?

Glancing up at the television, I see how each advertisement promises that the key to success is not found in the resolve of the person setting the goal but rather in the product being sold. Weight loss isn't accomplished by eating *less* stuff, you silly goal setter, you! No! Just eat *more* of *our* stuff! Getting healthy? You won't do that by exercising *more*, you poor, misguided soul! You actually want to spend *less* time working out. And our machine will help you do just that!

As I sit in my pajama pants and marinate in the stench of mass marketing, a wave of calm comes over me. The kind you feel when you are certain of what you must do. I'm tired of straying from our mission. And the signs are all in front of me. I think back to Guatemala. And the Sunday school book. And the outrageous ads shouting at me from my TV. In that moment I commit. It's settled. This next year will *not* be about slimming down, getting stronger, or smelling better. This will be the year of simplicity.

The year without a purchase.

I feel resolved. Invigorated. And like any good husband, I neglect to share my decision with anyone else in the family. I want Gabby to have ample time to share in my joy, so I corner her on or about December 27th at the perfect moment. Just as she is rushing to leave the house after finishing up an argument with our son on the value of wearing pants when the temperature dips below freezing.

As she slips out the laundry room door into the garage, I shout, "Hey Gabby, I think we should do it. Not buying anything for a year."

She turns to look at me, expressionless. There is a beat of silence, and then she answers, "OK, but we need to decide what this means. Like, what the rules will be."

Rules? We don't need no stinking rules!

A vow has been made, and I have created marital harmony by going along with my wife's original idea. I am one world-changing, smooth operator. We can work out the details later.

"Later" comes that same evening when Gabby plops down next to me on the couch. We sit staring at the shiny new 42-inch LED TV we bought for ourselves as an early Christmas gift to replace our 15-year-old set. We considered the new TV a "need." The old one would randomly print Spanish subtitles on the screen at odd times. In addition, the dysfunctional tube was cropping off about a quarter of the image all the way around. This was particularly evident when watching, say, an Olympic volleyball match where serves and spikes would come from invisible players located somewhere offscreen, and the score of the match was always a mystery.

Gabby's voice breaks through the digital audio coming from the new television. "So, are we really doing this thing?" she prods. "Not buying stuff?"

"Yeah." I apathetically reply, mesmerized by the clarity of the picture on screen. I can actually see Brian Williams's pores.

She digs deeper. "So what are the rules? I know this was my idea, but now I'm getting cold feet."

I am freakishly adept at avoiding conversations of commitment. Truthfully, I don't feel a huge sense of urgency to nail down any specifics, given that our refrigerator is filled with plenty of holiday leftovers. We can survive for over a month on Chex Mix alone, so I continue to flip channels and wait for Gabby to decide, therefore freeing me from any responsibility or accountability.

"Hello!?!?! You gotta engage here!"

"OK," I say, not taking my eyes off the TV. "If you can eat it, you can buy it."

"What about toilet paper?"

"OK," I quip, wanting the commitment conversation to be over as soon as possible. "Food and toilet paper."

"You're killing me, Dannemiller!"

She obviously wants more from me than I am giving. I increase my level of engagement. "OK. We can buy hygiene products. That seems reasonable."

"What about cleaners?" she asks. "Are those considered hygiene?"

This item had slipped my mind, as one cares about cleaners only if they are the one actually doing the regular cleaning. I constantly tell my wife how amazed I am that things in our house never seem to get dirty.

"I've heard you can use vinegar and water as cleaner."

She voluntarily retreats from our chat. I'm guessing it has something to do with the fact that I am not offering to do more of the cleaning but simply asking her to allocate some more of her precious time to making the cleaners themselves. By default, we table the "what's on the list" decision until a few days later when we embark on a road trip to visit family in Ohio. With the kids occupied in the back seat, Gabby and I have plenty of opportunity to chat.

I open the conversation by telling my lovely wife all the things that should be off-limits for her to purchase. Makeup. Clothes. Household knick-knacks. Party supplies. Unfortunately, in my haste to list these items, I fail to realize that we are now confined in a tightly enclosed space for the next seven hours.

The result of such recklessness is something like taking a sharp stick and poking a beautiful swan. A swan that prefers to participate in discussions instead of being told what to do. Initially very pretty to look at, but you don't want to be around when the feathers get to flying.

I see she is taking notes, so I wisely shift away from making proclamations and start to ask more open-ended questions to keep her from reaching over the center console and turning me into a shish kebab with her Bic pen.

"So, what are the essentials?"

Gabby answers with the obvious. "We have to buy groceries. We can't live off our summer tomatoes for a year."

"True. But what about gifts? You like to give gifts."

I hit her where it hurts. Gabby's whole reason for living is to remember every detail about what people like so that she can give the perfect, thoughtful, tear-inducing gift. She ruminates for a moment and then comes back with an idea.

"Maybe we set aside some money for gifts throughout the year?"

I counter, "No. We can't buy gifts. That's the point. That would be buying 'stuff.' I say we make 'em instead."

"But you have to buy stuff to make gifts."

"No you don't. You can use stuff you get for free."

"What do you mean?" she asks.

"Stuff that's free, that's just lying around."

"I think they call that garbage," she says.

"No, they don't," I retort. "There's lots of stuff you can get for nothing."

"Right. It's called garbage."

Silence.

She continues, her tongue dripping with sarcasm. "I haven't bought Christmas gifts for your niece and nephew yet. Do you want to make them gifts out of garbage?"

No fair. Leading question. After another long pause I offer, "Maybe they'd like a singing telegram?"

"Great idea. Every high school and college-aged kid I know loves a singing telegram."

After further discussion and the kids wondering "Why does Daddy look like he might start crying?" we finally negotiate the terms. What helps us most is coming back to our reason for doing this in the first place. Sure, it's about defining needs vs. wants, but that's not the main point. We lived for a year without a washing machine, dishwasher, heat, or clean running water. We now know that these are *not* basic human needs. The only true needs are food, shelter, and clothes to keep you warm. But this experiment is about so much more than that.

We have been living life by accident. Allowing our schedules and possessions to define us. Buying new stuff instead of owning and appreciating what we have. And through this, losing an honest connection with people and with ourselves. The time has come to live by a set of rules to help bring us back into balance, reconnect us to our mission. To live life on purpose, with purpose.

To tirelessly seek God's will by living lives of integrity, owning what we have, growing together in faith, and serving God's people to build a world without need.

But how will not buying stuff help us reconnect to our mission statement? Taking it piece-by-piece, we have some hypotheses.

Living lives of integrity. This one is easy. As a family, we talk a pretty good game when it comes to our concern for our fellow humans. But if someone followed us around with a video camera for a month, would our actions really match our words? Sadly, I think not. Integrity is all about words matching actions, and we hope not buying stuff will remove distractions and lead us closer to fulfilling our mission and God's purpose for our lives.

Owning what we have. Another easy one. We have an abundance of choices in this country. We also have an abundance of wealth compared to the rest of the world. This makes it easy to simply replace something when it breaks. We don't even have to spend a lot of money in the process, since it's easy to find a garage sale, Craigslist ad, or second-hand store filled with top-quality items that someone else cast off because they wanted something newer, shinier, and better. We believe not buying anything will help us both invest in and appreciate the abundance we already have.

Growing together in faith. This one is tricky. Aside from praying for a quick end to the year, our experiment will not necessarily guarantee we march toward God as a family unit. In fact, the frustration we feel may actually get in the way of our higher-minded goal of enriching our relationship with God. We need to be intentional in our approach. Like most families, we fill our calendars with activity. Sporting events, school commitments, and daily life take up the majority of our time, and as the kids get older, the time commitments increase. At this point, it would take a crowbar to create *new* space each day for dedicated family time with God. So our goal will be to find ways to be more mindful of God in our everyday schedule to create new habits that last.

Serving God's people to build a world without need. This is perhaps the loftiest, most impossible part of our family mission. Initially, we predict that going "cold turkey" on shopping might free up some funds to donate to worthy causes. From a strictly financial perspective, you would think that having more disposable income would make a family more generous. But after doing some digging, we find the opposite is often true. A number of independent studies show that those with more household wealth actually tend to give a smaller percentage of their income. *The Chronicle of Philanthropy* reports that families earning $50,000–$75,000 per year donate 7.6 percent of their income to charity, versus just 4.2 percent for those households earning over $100,000.[1] It's even more interesting at the extremes, as a recent article in *The Atlantic* shows, the wealthiest 20 percent give just 1.3 percent of their gross income, while the poorest 20 percent give 3.2 percent.[2] So this challenge certainly shouldn't be about saving money and storing treasure, though that might be a nice by-product. In the end, we hope that a decreased focus on material goods will help us redefine our needs and make it easier for us to share our material gifts as well as our time.

But it's all a crap shoot.

When it comes to rules, we keep it simple. We know that a shorter list will be easier to remember and adhere to on a day-to-day basis. So we settle on the following list and agree to modify it if we run into any glaring omissions:

1. **We can buy stuff that can be "used up" within a year**. Groceries, gas, hygiene products. No clothes. We have plenty of those. If there truly is a need (for example, not a single pair of our kids' shoes fit without causing irreversible toe damage), we will find hand-me-downs.
2. **We can fix stuff that breaks.** Unless the repair cost is greater than the replacement cost. Or, unless a suitable replacement already exists in our home.
3. **Gifts must be in the form of charitable donation or "experience gifts."** The idea is to build connections and memories by doing things such as going to dinner together, visiting the zoo, or traveling to visit friends and family.

As we look at the rules, we're reminded of a passage from John. Jesus speaks of his disciples, saying,

I'm saying these things in the world's hearing
So my people can experience
My joy completed in them.
I gave them your word;
The godless world hated them because of it,
Because they didn't join the world's ways,
Just as I didn't join the world's ways.
I'm not asking that you take them out of the world
But that you guard them from the Evil One.
They are no more defined by the world
Than I am defined by the world.
Make them holy—consecrated—with the truth;

Your word is consecrating truth.
In the same way that you gave me a mission in the world,
I give them a mission in the world.
I'm consecrating myself for their sakes
So they'll be truth-consecrated in their mission.
(*John 17:13–19* The Message)

I love this passage. Jesus is speaking of joy. A joy that lasts. And that joy comes from being *in* the world but not *of* the world. We are all seeking this joy. And Jesus alludes to the fact that we can find this joy and satisfaction by living our lives in this world under God's protection. Because the evil Christ is talking about is not a bogeyman hiding around every corner. Instead, this evil is our feeling of inadequacy and worthlessness that comes from not measuring up to the vision of success as the world defines it. Conforming to the world's desires is the perfect way to blind ourselves to the grace of God. That grace that is ever present, reminding us of how we are loved unconditionally.

And this is the truth of which Christ speaks.

So our rules are an attempt to be *in* the world and not *of* the world. Admittedly, this set of rules is not so outrageous. We're not winning any Nobel Prizes here. Not even close. We're still going to use the Internet. We're still going to watch TV. And in so doing, we know we're falling short of the example of Jesus. Sure, we could try to live exactly like him, but that would require wearing sandals and a tunic everywhere, feeding the multitudes with only a bucket of chicken and Value Meal #4, and learning how to make a table and chairs without the aid of power tools.

And that's just plain bananas.

What we genuinely hope is that living more in alignment with our mission statement will help fulfill our mission in this world. And if we have listened carefully to the call of Christ, we sincerely hope this will lead us to complete joy. The one that Christ promised. A joy that lasts.

Chapter Five

The Monster under the Bed

Submit yourselves, then, to God. Resist the devil, and he will flee from you. Come near to God and he will come near to you.
(James 4:7–8 NIV)

The night of January 1, Gabby and I are both lying in bed. The holiday hustle has subsided, and the kids are tucked away in their bedrooms, headed off to dreamland. I set my book on the nightstand. Optimistic, I am wondering what the first night of the year might hold for me. Would we begin with some romance? Half-smiling, Gabby prematurely lays her book down and turns her head toward me to look into my eyes.

Definitely romance.

I gaze at her. We sit in silence for a moment as I await our first "pillow talk" of the new year. Then she let loose with, "It's only January 1, and I'm already irritated with you."

Forget the "Year without a Purchase." Maybe we should call it the "Year Preceding Our Divorce."

I respond, "Why? What did I do?"

She looks at the ceiling.

"This year is going to be a lot harder for me than it is for you."

Apparently, when you decide that you are not going to buy anything for a year, thoughts of withdrawal pervade your every waking thought, and maybe even some of your sleeping thoughts.

But she's right, and there is nothing I can say to change it. It will be harder for her.

It's no secret that men and women have different purchase patterns. Look no further than my underwear drawer filled with boxer briefs held together with duct tape and dental floss. I tend to avoid the everyday needs such as soap and socks and buy big-ticket items like fitness equipment (AKA dirty clothes holders) or TVs instead. It's a guy thing. We don't shop often, but when we do, we buy big.

On the flip side, Gabby, like most women, makes small purchases to make life easier and to nurture the kids. It's a girl thing. They just shop more often. In fact, the Nielsen group estimates that women make roughly 70 percent of household purchase decisions, and when they do purchase, they tend to buy things that benefit the family, whereas men are more likely to buy things that benefit themselves.[1] Even so, I am dumbfounded at her ability to so quickly dismiss the purchase of a full-sized recreational vehicle converted into a backyard smoker capable of feeding the cast of *Braveheart*, and yet deliberate for hours over whether or not to buy the multipack of coconut-scented sunscreen.

For Gabby, it will be an in-your-face challenge all year long, and she will feel that she is denying not only herself material comforts but our family as well. Every trip to the grocery store will be a reminder of what could be. Not buying those little things that could provide moments of joy or continuous enrichment.

For me, I'll feel the pain on those random occasions when I have to resist the urge to plunk down a credit card to buy a mechanical bull that will entertain house guests at a Fourth of July party.

Still, whether male or female, there's one thing we hold in common. It's the lingering feeling that this twelve-month fast from consumerism will be a year of deprivation. Not only deprivation from new material goods, but also deprivation from something intangible—the mysterious force that compels us to acquire new stuff. It's a monster that must be fed. An addiction to the temporary gratification that comes from satisfying an urge, and the subsequent appetite that grows exponentially thereafter. It's something dangerous. You can feel it.

But you never see it.

In that way, these early days of our challenge feel a bit like a horror movie. You know the one where ominous music hovers over the actors for the first half of the film? The one where unsuspecting expendable cast members are picked off one-by-one by a monster lurking just off camera? You hear the screams and gurgles and disgusting sound effects that let you know something horrible is nearby. It's something dangerous. You can feel it.

But you never see it.

The prospect of meeting this force leaves us with a lot of anxiety. And a lot of questions:

Will it bring us closer together, or create more tension in our house?
Will our friends support us, or think we are nut-balls crazy?
Will we learn anything from the experience, or will it be a waste of time?
Will our kids jump on the bandwagon, or will they fight it?

Each of these questions could have a positive or negative answer. Given our feelings on this first day of the year, it becomes apparent that we might need a solid plan to end up on the favorable side. Otherwise our feelings of deprivation may diminish our willpower and cause us to fall victim to spontaneous impulses. So we sit down and agree on three specific actions in addition to "The Rules" that we believe will help us succeed. It's not much, but it's a start.

One: Don't tell the kids. I know. It's not so much an *action* as a *lack of* action. On the one hand, we acknowledge that the kids could help us in the challenge. We could involve them and help them become more mindful of purchases. They could also use their powers of annoyance for good, constantly reminding us not to buy stuff.

On the other hand, we selfishly don't want to deal with the complaints that would likely come if we told them we wouldn't be buying them anything for a year. And while our friends and family can give us the perspective of people "in the know," our children could be our measuring stick to see if we can do something different and still remain relevant. To truly see if we can be *in* the world but not *of* the world. Finally, it might be fun to see whether or not they would even notice. Given the trade-offs, we decide to keep it a secret from them.

Two: Limit our exposure to consumerism. The sheer number of catalogs and advertising emails we receive on a daily basis is mind-boggling. We figure that reducing the amount of advertising we see could likely reduce our urge to buy more things. While we won't cut ourselves off completely, which would require watching only public television and blindfolding ourselves whenever we leave the house, we will do our best to limit our exposure to certain forms of advertising.

Three: Do an appreciation audit. We read how people who spend time each day writing down five things they appreciate report increased levels of happiness and life satisfaction. This seems like a good way for us to avoid feelings of deprivation and perhaps fill that unseen void that we used to fill with new stuff. While we don't plan on doing this every day, we agree to set aside time to give it a try.

Looking back at our list of action steps, we instantly know that they will not be enough to lead us to success, but paired with the rules, they will certainly help. We also know that the next few months will bring up new issues, unintended consequences that we cannot foresee at this time, and rather than commit to a plan that we will have to abandon and that will leave us feeling like failures, we think that it's better to allow for some flexibility.

Still, the unknowns are scary, lurking under the bed. We just hope that when we expose them to the light of day we'll see that they are perfectly harmless.

But only time will tell.

Part Two

Owning What We Have

Coming to grips with who we are and what we own

Chapter Six

Our Little Science Experiment

A gift opens the way
and ushers the giver into
the presence of the great.
(Proverbs 18:16 NIV)

The first week back to school after the holidays, Jake comes home with an invitation to a birthday party. The girl who invited him is having her bash at a local karate school where the kids will spend an hour or two in a giant, padded room, rolling on the floor, punching foam-filled bags, and beating each other senseless. It sounds a lot like a room I would like to build in my house, but I would add a big drain in the middle so that we could just throw food in there at mealtime and then hose the thing down once the kids had stuffed their cake holes.

But we're not buying anything this year, so I must either let my dream die or build it out of garbage.

I look at the invitation and don't give it a second thought. Just another of life's events. I move on to thinking about important things, like wondering if I'm too old to be a member of a boy band. Gabby interrupts my daydream by reminding me that our little experiment will be reaching its tentacles into even the most mundane events.

"We need to think of what Jake can get Meredith for her birthday."

"Huh?"

The social convention of gift giving totally slipped my mind. If I were a single dad, I wouldn't remember a gift until we pulled in to the karate school parking lot. Meredith would receive some pocket lint and a handful of ketchup packets we have crammed in the glove box.

But what do you get a kid when you can't buy any stuff? This is something we didn't think of ahead of time when we created our rules for the year. The rules state that "gifts must be in the form of charitable donations or 'experience gifts'" to build connections and memories. But that's not what most six-year-olds want.

I think of the reaction Jake might receive if he gives Meredith the gift my mom bought us for Christmas. It was a donation to Oxfam, the proceeds of which are used to buy livestock for someone in a developing country.[1] In all honesty, we absolutely loved this gift. It's such a great concept! A gift that truly keeps on giving by helping to lift someone out of poverty. And it conforms to our rules. But I could see little Jake sheepishly (pun intended) handing a card to little Meredith.

"What's this?" she would ask.

"It's a goat."

"No it's not. A goat can't fit in an envelope."

"It's a card that talks about how I bought you a goat."

"Where's my goat?"

"He's not here."

"When do I get him?"

"You don't."

"Why?"

"He lives with some other guy."

"Why did he take my goat?"

"He didn't take it. I gave it to him. My dad says he needs a goat really bad."

"So for my birthday, you got me a goat and then stole it from me to give it to one of your dad's friends?"

"Pretty much. Happy birthday anyway."

I would be shocked if our son didn't receive a wedgie within ten minutes. I hear they teach that at karate school now. My brain starts to awful-ize the likely turn of events. First, Jake gives Meredith the goat. Next, the wedgie. The following week, he's not picked for the dodge ball game. Later, no one will accept his invitation to prom. He drops out of school. Can't get a job. Moves back in with us. Refuses to shower. Starts collecting cats—not figurines, but real cats. Dies sad and alone at fifty-eight, found sprawled on his couch wearing dirty sweatpants and eating generic cheese curls straight from the bag, watching Wheel of Fortune reruns.

It's a slippery slope.

After vetoing the goat, option two is to get Meredith an "experience gift," but that's not as simple as it sounds. A movie ticket doesn't cost much, but it fails the "build connections" test of our rules. A trip to a children's museum is good, but is it really a gift to give someone a ticket to something that requires their parents to buy two or three more tickets at twenty bucks a pop to accompany their kid? Sure, Meredith could go by herself, but I think Child Protective Services frowns upon that sort of thing.

A third option is to give no gift at all. I'm sure Jake wouldn't mind. The funny thing is, Meredith probably wouldn't notice either. Those of us with children know that kids can hardly remember what gifts they received last Christmas. Heck, we adults can hardly remember the gifts we received last month.

As we reflect on the choices before us, we realize that this dilemma is less about the kids and more about Gabby and me. We want to live out our values as best we can, but we know we are a walking contradiction. Stuck in our own heads, wondering how others might react if we don't get the right gift. Wanting to do the right thing, but not wanting to force our values on other people. Trying to overcome the pull that "stuff" has on us and the meaning we give to that "stuff."

And we wrap our kids up in this mess.

Case in point: I don't know if you've been to a kid's birthday party in the last ten years, but they are a bucket full of crazy pants. According to a 2013 report by Gigmasters.com, 70 percent of parents spend over $300 on a child's birthday party, and a whopping 14 percent spend more than $1,000.[2] One of the biggest bones of contention are the "goodie bags." For the uninitiated, these are bags full of stuff that your child receives for attending a party.

We had goodie bags back when I was a kid, too. We called it your "stomach," and you filled it with as much cake and ice cream as you could possibly cram down your throat during the festivities. The funny thing is, the majority of parents today report not liking the new tradition of goodie bags, yet 80 percent will give them out anyway.

It's insane.

When Gabby and I think back to our best memories of childhood, not a single goodie bag comes to mind. Or even a birthday gift. What we do remember is spending time with friends and family, doing something exciting. How can we give this as a gift without breaking the bank or the rules?

A quick search of the Internet gives us the answer. We find a boatload of science experiments that can be done at home using regular household items purchased from the grocery store. Since food and hygiene products are acceptable Year-without-a-Purchase items, this seems like a worthy compromise. So, we print up instructions for each experiment and the science behind them, and fill a plastic baggie with the necessary ingredients.

As we're packaging up the gift, I am surprised that such a simple decision can produce such anxiety. Maybe it's not really anxiety but simply a feeling of uneasiness. At first I think it may have something to do with our trying to keep our no-purchase challenge a secret from the kids. Would they think giving a homemade science experiment for a birthday gift would be odd, perhaps even tipping them off that we weren't buying anything? Then Gabby reminds me that young kids aren't accustomed to going to the mall to buy gifts for people, so there won't be a lot of questions from them about this slightly off-the-wall change.

Once we get past our concern, we allow Jake to choose which experiment to give away. His two favorites are the Ivory Soap experiment and the Mentos experiment. I won't spoil the results, but if you want to see for yourself, just stick a bar of Ivory Soap in the microwave for two minutes (yes, it has to be Ivory), or go outside and drop a sleeve of Mentos mints into a 2-liter bottle of Diet Coke. The soap is surprising, and the Mentos, well, just be prepared to run fast.

Jake selects the Mentos experiment for Meredith, so we put the bottle and the mints in a box and wrap them with leftover paper we found in the garage. On the outside, we tape a gift card to a local frozen yogurt shop that was good for one free cone—a gift that passes our regulations because it's food, and it provides a good opportunity for the family to share the experience of eating together.

Our second hand-wringing moment comes when Jake actually takes the package to the birthday party. He is obviously unfazed, but we wait with bated breath to see if there will be the faintest whiff that our gift is "different." We realize that it's preposterous to worry about being judged for what your kid brings as a gift to a child's birthday party. But *some* people do.

Some people like us.

We aren't questioning Meredith's reaction. That's a slam dunk. What kid doesn't like ice cream and exploding soda? We're anxious because this is the first time that our decision to not buy anything will affect someone outside our immediate family. Granted, we're just dipping our toes in the water, but it is a test-drive to see if we can do something unconventional while being *in* the world. Will they think it's inappropriate? Cheap? Weird?

That's when we realize that our uneasiness is self-created. Human beings are not born with an innate desire to "one up" one another when it comes to gift giving. It's all learned from social conditioning. We take a bunch of shiny junk and cover up the image of God that's been planted like a seed inside of each one of us, thinking we can improve on the original design. But it's impossible. So often our desires just ruin it all.

> *In the beginning was the Word, and the Word was with God, and the Word was God. He was in the beginning with God. All things came into being through him, and without him not one*

> *thing came into being. What has come into being in him was life, and the life was the light of all people. (John 1:1–4)*

And when I consider this, I am embarrassed that we even let such a trivial issue as birthday gift giving become a dilemma. And we do it so often that we don't even notice. Like breathing.

It's ridiculous.

There was never a need to worry, no matter what the outcome turned out to be. That said, Meredith's mom later commented that the science experiment was one of her daughter's favorite gifts. She kept begging to go outside and do the experiment *together* with her family. No, not a solo pursuit. An experience to be shared.

So based on this result, I think we're going to keep this gift-giving alternative as we progress through the year. It's a reminder to avoid getting trapped in our own expectations and insecurities. Though we should probably come up with something different for the adults.

I'm not sure that we can trust them with Mentos.

Chapter Seven

Darn!

"Keep your life free from the love of money, and be content with what you have; for he has said, "I will never leave you or forsake you."

(Hebrews 13:5)

Even though children make this year-long challenge a bit harder, with birthday parties and nagging in the checkout line, there is one benefit of going through this ordeal as parents of grade-school kids: We rarely leave the house after 6:30 p.m.

There may be an odd occasion when we are out after dark, but it's usually due to a mistake of some kind. Such as Jake's baseball game running long. Or my ill-advised decision to try a "short cut." Or an insatiable need to venture into the backyard to investigate a suspicious noise that is most certainly a rare suburban Sasquatch.

But most nights, we're very boring. We pay bills, do some leftover busy work, and then meet on the couch to discuss the day's events.

One such night in early February, Gabby calls me to the living room.

"Come in here, honey! I have something to show you!"

Her voice is excited, as if she just got a letter from a long-lost friend or read an article proclaiming bowling shoes were back in style. I immediately get up to see what the hubbub is about, anticipating what might be the most exciting thing to happen in our house since nearly electrocuting myself while hanging Christmas lights back in November.

"Look what I have for you!"

When I round the corner, her leg is extended toward me, and she is waving her toes in my face. With no bowling shoe attached. And no letter.

Her foot is covered with a paper-thin sock. On the back of the sock is a hole the size of a small melon. Her heel looks like it is 10 centimeters dilated, due to give birth to a bouncing baby bunion at any moment.

"I need you to fix my sock," she commands.

"I don't think so."

"But honey, you said that you would repair at least one item of clothing this year—maybe even darn a sock. So here's your chance."

When we discussed living out the "owning what we have" part of our mission, I committed to mending articles of clothing instead of letting them seep through to the bottom of the dresser drawer, never to be seen again.

"But I've never darned a sock before. I gotta start small. And look at that thing! That's like asking the school nurse to do open-heart surgery."

Consider the age of this sock. It looks like it may have been worn by Wilma Rudolph when she won the 100-meter gold in the 1960 Olympics. The hole developed shortly thereafter. At the medal ceremony. I'm not sure this is in the "repairable" category.

"You gotta learn somehow," Gabby replies. "We can't just be throwing things away."

She's right. The United States of America has become a "throw-away" society. The U.S. Environmental Protection Agency estimates that each American produces nearly 4.5 pounds of garbage every day, compared to just 2.7 pounds back in the 1960s.[1] Today, people in the United States toss roughly 400,000 cell phones every 24 hours.[2] And clothing? The average American household pitches 177 pounds of it every year.[3]

And it's not just "stuff" we're throwing away.

The USDA and EPA together estimate that the United States throws away 30–40 percent of its food supply, which is 50 percent more than we threw away back in the '70s. The waste in homes and restaurants alone amounts to $390 per person every year.[4] Enough to keep a college student alive with Ramen noodles for four semesters.

It's one thing to sit here and spout off statistics in a book, but another to actually do something about it. The truth is, when I look at Gabby's sock, I see something that needs to be thrown away. My grandmother would see something entirely different.

I tell my dad about the sock fiasco a few days later, and he shares a story of how he used to watch his mother darn socks while she watched Lawrence Welk on TV. It involved weaving thread together to essentially build a patch in a hole. This sounds difficult, but it was a necessary evil in his house. He was one of twelve kids, and they didn't have the luxury of buying anything they wanted. Heck, he had to fight for a seat at the dinner table.

But Dad worked a lot as a kid, either helping my grandpa with odd jobs or working on his own to help pay for his tuition at the Catholic school. He taught me the value of a job well done, and the satisfaction you feel when it's a job you truly enjoy. Dad didn't have mountains of toys in his house as a kid, so his friends and family were his recreation. To this day, it visibly pains my father to spend money on stuff, but it visibly fulfills him to spend time with those he loves.

I'm praying it's in the DNA, because my experience is far different from that of my father. I had only two siblings growing up. There were fewer mouths to feed, and we always had more than we needed. *Enough* was the norm for me, and that continues to the present day; the global economy allows my family to buy mountains of really inexpensive stuff from a country we've never visited, made by a person whose name we probably couldn't pronounce. Personally, I've counted the number of socks in my underwear drawer. I have thirty-two pair. I could go over a month without doing laundry and still not have to worry about wearing soiled socks. It's a far cry from the way of life my grandparents enjoyed when planned obsolescence didn't exist. While sock care and repair may be a fun diversion this year, it won't be a necessity for me.

Not long after our sock debate, I am scheduled to travel to Omaha on business. Gabby has since forgotten about the giant hole and moved on to bigger and better concerns. Namely, making sure I don't do something stupid. She gives me her mental checklist as I head out the door to the airport.

"I love you. Do you have everything? Your belt? Your computer? Underwear? Socks? Pants?"

My wife is *too* good at reminding me about things like this. It's such a part of my business trip ritual that the instant she starts running through the list, my ears transpose her voice into a muffled trumpet sound akin to Charlie Brown's teacher. It's all too familiar. I just don't hear it.

"Yep! Got it all! I'll call you when I land." It's my stock answer.

Six hours later I unpack my suitcase in my hotel room. I place my toiletries on the bathroom counter. I hang my shirts in the closet and deliver my workout clothes to their respective drawers. It is a perfect setup. Except for one thing.

Socks.

I rifle through my suitcase looking for footwear to carry me through the week. I search every nook and cranny of my bag, unzipping pockets and plunging my hand deep into the dark recesses of each one. I find a boarding pass from a trip I took three years ago, a collar stay from a dress shirt I no longer own, and a lovely crayon drawing my daughter made for me.

But no socks.

My first thought is, "It's only 8:30 p.m. I still have time to run to Target and buy some socks for tomorrow."

Then I remember the rules. We can't buy any clothes unless we're naked.

As I look down at my feet, I have to admit that my socks haven't disintegrated. They are perfectly fine, save for the fact that they smell like the dirty laundry basket on a Bering Sea crab boat. And

I'll be damned if I am going to bail out of this year-long challenge after only a month!

I recall our days living with our host family in Guatemala. There were no stores nearby. And no washing machine. There was just a large concrete sink behind our *casita* and a big bar of soap in the shape of a soup can.

I saunter up to the sink in my hotel room. It's not like the *pila* from our mission year, which had a rough-ridged bottom for scrubbing out stubborn stains and smells. It's not built for the job I am about to tackle. But there is a menagerie of scented soaps and gels within arm's reach, so I take full advantage.

I think of my grandmother as I fill the bowl with hot water and add a healthy blob of rosemary mint shower gel and moisturizing shampoo. I let the socks soak for five minutes and then get to scrubbing. I'm not wearing a heart monitor, but I estimate that it took three minutes and 300 calories of elbow grease to get rid of most of the stink. There is still a lingering foot stench, but the socks pass the wafting smell test—that one where you wave them quickly in front of your face to try and simulate yourself walking quickly past a stationary person. Happy with the result, I vow to avoid standing next to anyone for an extended period of time tomorrow.

The ambient temperature in my room is pretty chilly. I know the socks aren't going to dry by morning if I just leave them hanging on a towel rack, so I grab the hair dryer. I feel a bit foolish styling my socks with a Vidal Sassoon 1500 Watt blaster, so I turn on *SportsCenter* to try and add some testosterone to the task.

It doesn't help.

After sixty seconds, the aroma of overworked hair dryer mixed with warm, minty foot odor tells me that I need to try something else. Out of the corner of my eye, I spot the heating vent. I crank up the room temperature to 77 degrees. The heater kicks on. I wedge my socks into the grates and wait.

A half-hour later, with sweat beading on my upper lip, I go to check the socks. They are dry on one side but still need some cooking, so I tuck them back into the grates. After another thirty minutes atop the vent, the process is complete. I must not have done a very good job of rinsing out the shampoo, because the texture of the socks is like a pair of canvas tennis shoes—rough to the touch—but I'm not going to complain.

From an environmental standpoint, the whole ordeal is probably a wash. While my commitment to the rules did save the world from yet another unnecessary pair of socks that would someday end up in a landfill, I probably wasted $15 worth of the hotel's energy and two tiny bottles of shampoo over the next three days as I washed and dried by hand.

But this year isn't about money. It's about stuff. And feeling disconnected.

As I sit in seat 3A on my way home from Omaha, I feel more connected somehow. Connected to our Guatemalan host mom, Graciela, and all the other women in the village, who scrub socks and shirts every day without complaint. I feel connected to my grandmother who saved every penny she could to clothe her family of fourteen.

And, oddly enough, I feel more connected to my socks. Because all too often, rather than *making do*, I *make excuses* for why I deserve something. And this leads me to contribute to the throwaway society by quickly replacing something that's not broken, without realizing the value in what I have. So salvaging the socks is a small victory. It's a step in the right direction toward living our mission, but we still have a long way to go.

Chapter Eight

The Price Is Right?

Of course, there is great gain in godliness combined with contentment; for we brought nothing into the world, so that we can take nothing out of it; but if we have food and clothing, we will be content with these.

(1 Timothy 6:6–8)

It doesn't take long before our anxiety over limiting purchases begins to fade. The sensation we feel is reminiscent of our missionary experience. At the beginning of that adventure, our bellies were initially doing back flips at the thought of using an outdoor latrine for twelve months and bathing only once a week. But after a few weeks, it simply became a new normal, drifting from immediate consciousness. Especially when we were engaged in everyday tasks.

The same is true for our no-purchase challenge. Not telling our kids has provided a fun diversion, forcing us to get creative. Likewise, the occasional sock mishap provides a simple reminder to be more intentional about the way we're living. But overall, we're settling back into our regular routine of waking up early, doing some exercise, getting the kids ready for school, and then going to work. With your mind occupied on other concerns, it's easy to forget you're denying yourself anything.

My typical day starts with eating a quick breakfast while sitting at the computer to check my calendar. One morning, while reviewing my schedule and lamenting that there's no time blocked off for a nap, my computer signals that I have a new email.

If you're anything like me, you cannot rest until you find out who is corresponding with you. It's an addiction. I live under the false hope that every message could be the missing link, revealing my life's purpose. Maybe it's someone telling me I have been selected to be on the next season of *The Amazing Race*. Or revealing that I am a direct descendant of Frank Sinatra. Or that my fifth-grade science fair project on "parts of the eye" somehow led to a cure for blindness.

Alas, it's a message from my wife titled, "I Have My Work Cut Out for Me."

I open the email, half-expecting it to list all my flaws that she is expecting to fix in our remaining time on earth. Instead, all I find is a screenshot of her email inbox. The image shows a list of messages, and 90 percent of them are advertisements or coupons. Gabby captions the image with, "Let the deleting begin!"

Over the years, my wife has signed up to receive "deals" via email. It's an honest attempt to save money, since she is the main shopper of the family. Typically she will see some promotion for a product we normally buy and sign up to receive regular coupons that conveniently arrive in our email inbox. By combining these digital offers with Sunday paper coupons, we've been known to get a tube of toothpaste for 25 cents, which feels a bit like being knighted by Queen Elizabeth for shopping excellence. Our thinking is that if we use coupons only for the stuff we buy anyway, we can reduce the number of things coming into our house and reduce the cost of the "stuff" we're buying.

How naive.

Like most people, we view coupons as corporate charity. As if advertisers went to confession and the priest told them to say fifty Hail Marys and offer 50 cents off a package of Oreos to atone for their sin of encouraging people to buy stuff they didn't need.

Guess what. There is no such confessional booth.

Let's face it—if clipping coupons encourages us to spend *less*, then why would companies offer them? Global research firm GfK recently conducted a survey of over 40,000 consumers. The research was sponsored by Coupons.com. And the results show coupons are actually a bad deal for consumers. Why? People who use coupons spend more money per trip than those who don't.[1] And the difference is significant. Those who use digital coupons, for example, spend 42 percent more per year, because they tend to shop more frequently, and spend more when they do shop.[2]

But why is that?

I go looking for answers and stumble upon a group called Inmar. They are a market analytics company. Ironically, they have a report on trends in the consumer coupon marketplace that you can receive for free, so long as you give them your contact information, which they can then use to market stuff to you.

I'm not making this up.

Among other things, the Inmar report highlights that the number of items that must be purchased in order to redeem a non-food-related coupon has been trending upward over the last five years.[3] The result? A separate *Harvard Business Review* report from May 2012 shows that all stores and brands offering coupons experience a sales "lift" from the offers, which I find amusing given that the term *lifting* is a euphemism for stealing. What is most surprising is that the majority of this "lift" comes from people who *don't even use the coupon*![4] It seems the only ones safe from all the coupon madness are those who never set eyes on the coupons in the first place.

It all reminds me of my mother, a gold-medalist for the yet-to-be-created U.S. Olympic Discount Shopping Team. She would come home and report to my father, "Honey! Look at these two dresses I picked up at the store today! Originally $100 each, and I got them for 75 percent off!"

And my dad would reply, "What I hear you saying is that we would have saved 50 bucks if you hadn't left the house today."

Did I mention my dad also says "I'm sorry" a lot?

We knew that taking a vow to buy no stuff would be hard, but the truth behind couponing is a revelation to us. In order to overcome our psychological tendencies, we need to actively disengage from consumer marketing altogether.

Back in the home office, Gabby now sits at her computer, diligently deleting and unsubscribing. It is tedious work. In many cases, the "unsubscribe" feature doesn't work, so she has to create a special folder as a catch-all for our coupon junk, which she can delete *en masse*.

I help by going outside to check the mail.

I walk to the curb and reach into our box to see what has been delivered that day. I hope to escape the lure of marketing, but find myself surrounded once again. In my hand I hold a stack of mail, but only one bill. The rest are envelopes filled with coupons, and a couple of catalogs. One in particular catches my eye. I've seen it before. It's titled *Solutions: Products That Make Life Easier*.

Just what the doctor ordered.

I open to page 1, hoping to find numerous products that will "make my life easier," as promised in the title. Maybe things like:

"TidyTurf": Grass that automatically turns dog poo into compost.
"BuffStuff": Exercise substitute pill.
"HubbyBuddy Millennium Edition": Gives automatic correct response to wife's questions, such as, "Why did our five-year-old daughter wear a bathing suit and cowboy boots to church last week?"

Unfortunately, as I leaf through the pages, I can't find a single one of these products. Instead, I find a lot of false and misleading advertising in the *Solutions* catalog. The vast majority of the products actually make life *harder*. For instance:

Vista Stair Treads ($29.98 each): These are little "ruglets" you place on each individual step on a flight of stairs. Now you can worry about thirty-seven of these little guys staying in place, and then wash each one individually when they get soiled. Or, you can cut down on the washing by telling people to avoid stepping on them. There's nothing upstairs worth seeing anyhow.
Baking Soda Caddy ($5.98): A clear plastic box to hold your baking soda. No, you don't pour the baking soda out of its original box, you simply set the baking soda box INSIDE the second box, or "caddy," if you will. The caddy also has a ventilated lid, so you can keep the open

box of baking soda inside an open plastic box. Kinda' reminds me of a trip to Target last year when I bought a duffel bag, and the cashier put it in a plastic bag so I could carry it out of the store. Am I taking crazy pills?

Deluxe Petstep Ramp ($179.00): The picture shows a carpeted ramp that you put beside your bed so that your dog can easily get in and steal the covers. The side of the ramp is hard plastic, perfect for stubbing toes when you get up in the middle of the night to use the restroom. Such newfound ramp-climbing skills would only encourage your dog to join the circus. Then, it's nothing but sleepless nights hoping he doesn't run off to Vegas with the dancing bear or, worse yet, the half-person-half-wolf lady. The $179.00 price does not include doggie prenuptial agreement or counseling.

I walk inside and throw the catalog into our large, cardboard-box-turned-recycling bin. As I do, a thought flashes before me: *I'll bet the neighbors have a really nice, decorative recycling bin.*

I reach back into the bin to retrieve the catalog, hoping to find a solution to my inferiority complex. Maybe a recycling bin adorned with attractive stars or suns or moons. Leafing through the pages, I do not find such an item. However, I do find a big trellis that is used to hide your trash can or recycling bin. So I can buy another thing to cover up the thing I use to contain the things I already have but don't want.

It's a never-ending cycle.

In this moment I realize the products in the catalog and those advertised in our avalanche of emails aren't actually there to make my life easier. Instead, the products are intended to make my life more enviable. After a while, I start believing that my life satisfaction is wrapped up in having the latest new gadget and increasing my standard of living, not realizing that taking care of all this stuff is actually making my life more complicated.

The rules of life are broken.

It's like when you were in grade school and always wanted to go to playdates and sleepovers with the kid who had the coolest stuff. I was not this kid, but my neighbor was. Barry's house was filled with treasures such as a Nerf Gun, Slip-N-Slide, Atari, and an unlimited supply of Slim Jims.

The problem was, when visiting his house, you also knew who made the rules. Inevitably, at the end of any game, the rules could be changed by the Keeper of the Slim Jim, as it were. You could be on the cusp of victory in the "Who-Can-Disembowel-My-Sister's-Stuffed-Animal-Collection-the-Fastest" game, only to find that the object of the game was to go to the family room and put on a Village People record.

Who is making the rules now?

After watching TV, reading the paper, and listening to the radio, I get the feeling that people with all the shiny junk (and TV stations and advertising budgets) have decided that shiny junk is the goal. And they make these rules knowing they have already won the game. And we are paying the price for it. Ironically, Jeff Bezos, rule maker and founder of Amazon, puts it best when he says, "What consumerism really is, at its worst, is getting people to buy things that don't actually improve their lives."[5]

If only we could redefine success in life and pursue it with the tenacity of an Olympic athlete. We could change the rules of the game so that the winner wasn't the one who could accumulate the most the fastest, but rather, the one who understood *enough* the fastest and worked the hardest to make sure everyone had it.

I imagine life is a lot like the game show *The Price Is Right*. And God is the great Bob Barker of the universe, asking us all to get as close to *enough* as possible, without going over. Inevitably, the winner would be some grandma from Pomona named Ethel who bid $1.00 after she saw the rest of us overestimate how much we really needed to survive. She would then get to hug The Big Guy and play in the final showcase, while the rest of us were left holding our year's supply of Turtle Wax and Rice-A-Roni.

Parting gifts for the overindulgent.

So our prayer is that we learn enough to avoid the lure of stuff and have the wisdom and willpower to find the value in what is right in front of us.

Chapter Nine

The Businessman and His Baggie

Do not judge, or you too will be judged. For in the same way you judge others, you will be judged, and with the measure you use, it will be measured to you.

(Matthew 7:1–2 NIV)

We now see how coupons and catalogs can make us feel less than adequate and entice us to buy things we don't really need. Logic would tell us that eliminating these influences would keep us from purchasing worthless stuff. But there are other situations that tempt us to spend as well. Early in the challenge, we notice things in our house are getting lost or broken at a record pace. And we're not just talking holey socks.

The first thing to go is Gabby's travel cup. The insulated one with the straw and the screw top. This 32-ounce cup is like a family member. She uses it every day in response to the standard physician's advice to drink eight or more glasses of water per day.

Unfortunately, Gabby lost the cup at a church retreat, which affected her more than you might imagine. She says she left it by bunk #2 in cabin #9, but I hypothesize that she probably left it in a bathroom somewhere, since drinking that much water demands you never stray more than 50 feet from a restroom or portable toilet. She phoned the camp multiple times to track it down. It's a rustic venue with very few staff members, so her calls to locate her missing friend went unanswered. I half expected her to start plastering "lost" signs on telephone poles all over the county.

We consider buying a replacement, but consult our rules to see if this is allowed. Since lost items are not mentioned specifically, it's a gray area. I pontificate.

"Gabby. Our rules state that we can't buy a replacement if a suitable alternative already exists in the house."

"So?"

"We own roughly three gazillion cups. Surely one of them can hold water."

She bats her eyelashes at me like she's auditioning for the role of the leading lady in a 1920's silent movie. "Aren't you going back there soon? To facilitate the church leadership retreat?"

I see where this is going. "Honey. The camp has about twenty-five different buildings on one hundred acres. I doubt I can find it."

"I'm telling you, I left it in cabin #9. You *have* to look for it. And not the way you *normally* look for stuff. I mean *really* look. Move stuff around and look behind things. It's the only insulated cup I have, and I would hate to go the rest of the year without it."

I mumble something about it being "just a cup." She mumbles something about "just giving birth" to our offspring.

I guess I owe it to her.

So, while I am at the camp I embark on a grand quest. I ask every camp counselor and staff maintenance engineer about the cup. The search borders on the ridiculous. I am convinced that the next retreat will be about the sin of fetishes, and the speaker will tell a story about the "crazy cup guy." But I know I'll never hear the end of it if I don't find the darn thing.

Finally, in the dining hall, I sneak into the kitchen and look for it. *Really* look. I'm moving pots and pans around. Looking behind boxes of crackers and tins of flour. Finally, on a random set of shelves, I see Gabby's floral cup. I am elated! I feel like the shepherd leaving the ninety-nine to find the lost "one" (only without any spiritual significance whatsoever).

I walk toward the shelf to grab the cup and notice a problem. There is no lid. No straw. I ask around, but it's no use. The cup has been decapitated. Useless. It feels a bit like searching for your pet hamster all over the house, only to find that the cat left him on the doorstep in a heap.

It's a sad moment, but at least Gabby has some closure.

Not long after the cup vanishes, Jake loses his basketball. It was a Christmas gift, less than two months old. He loaned it to some kids at school who didn't return it. The poor kid is devastated, thinking his friends let it roll off into the woods at the edge of the school playground and then left it behind, distracted by the bell at the end of recess. Gabby takes him to search the trees after school with no success.

Unlike the cup story, the basketball story has a happy ending. After canvassing the school and asking around, Jake learns that a good Samaritan spotted it and took it to the lost and found in another classroom. Jake and his ball are reunited, and I don't have to play the role of dream crusher by saying, "Sorry, we can't get another basketball son, because your parents are psycho-idiots who don't think they should buy any new stuff for a year."

Two days after we find Jake's ball, our old refrigerator in the garage starts to make some funny noises. I look in the freezer and discover a bunch of popsicles are now solidified in all sorts of interesting avant-garde shapes due to a lot of thawing and refreezing. Since I am a complete-and-utter failure when it comes to appliance repair, I predict our family will soon be knee-deep in leftover chili and half-frozen peas when the fridge finally gives up the ghost.

The next day, a blinding light erupts from our toaster oven while I prepare breakfast. At first, I think it might be an angel of the Lord coming to settle a spontaneous debate between Jake and Audrey as to the gender of her favorite stuffed animal. But imagine my disappointment when it turns out to be a blown heating element. Not only will I never know whether Crushie the turtle is a boy or a girl, but now it takes four minutes per side to toast a single slice of bread.

I look back at our rules and see we are allowed to fix things that are broken, provided the repair cost is less than buying a replacement. Since a second refrigerator is not a necessity, I opt for a treatment plan that includes violently shaking the afflicted appliance, followed immediately by fervent prayer. If it dies, then perhaps it was God's will.

The toaster oven is a different story. I call Cuisinart to inquire about a possible repair. A very chipper customer service representative answers the phone.

"Cuisinart customer support. My name is Jill. How can I help you?"

"Hi, Jill. I have one of your toaster ovens, and yesterday it spurted what looked like fireworks from one of the heating elements. Now the top one doesn't work. How much does the part cost? And can an ordinary guy fix it?"

"I'm sorry. A blown heating element is not a repairable item. I think it's time for you to buy a new unit."

Apparently, Jill hasn't heard of our challenge. We part ways quickly.

While not ideal, eight-minute toast is now a regular part of our morning ritual. I am content to deal with these minor setbacks. Heck, I even embrace them. Half-frozen food, cold pizza leftovers, and eight-minute toast are daily reminders of our commitment, however small, to change the way we are living.

That is, until I get punched where it hurts.

Similar to Gabby's treasured cup, I have a treasured suitcase. "She" was a gift from Mom. An olive branch to make my constant business travel a bit easier. The bag is a rich brown color with four fully articulating wheels and a pleasant disposition. She has a telescoping handle with extra length to accommodate taller folks, like me. She is always at my side and happy to carry my burdens without complaint.

Until . . .

Irritated after a long wait on the jetway, I yank her handle a bit too hard. It cracks, and one of the telescoping arms rips right out of its channel in the back of the suitcase. Shoving it back in is a bit like trying to shove a Twinkie back into its wrapper—requiring patience and lots of mumbled four-letter words. I get the suitcase back into semi-working order using some tape and string, but I know it won't hold up under duress.

I look for other options. Gabby has a beautiful new red rolling suitcase she got the previous year. It's clean, sizable, and in perfect working order. She catches me eyeballing it and says, "No way, mister. That's my suitcase!"

I think this may be the cup grief talking.

"But honey, we're family. Families share."

"I don't think so."

"Why not?"

"Because your version of sharing involves you using my stuff, breaking it, and then giving it back to me."

She has a point.

So I dive into the bowels of the closet looking for an alternative. Ideally, I would like a very small suitcase that might fit in the overhead bin of the tiny jet I was flying this week, allowing me to avoid the long wait at baggage claim. After some rummaging, I find what I'm looking for. The perfect-sized suitcase. A bag that meets the simple requirement of holding my garments and keeping them safe and dry. But there is just one problem.

It's purple.

And no, we're not talking royal purple. Not even violet. This suitcase is lavender. If this bag had a scent, it would smell like an infant Liberace wearing your grandmother's perfume. No self-respecting businessperson would dare be seen with a bag like this.

But I have no self-respect.

And I'm not buying anything this year.

So I pack the bag and prepare for my trip to Denver. I stuff it full of workout gear, business casual clothes, and socks. Yes, I remember the socks.

I get to the airport and clear security. Everyone notices my bag. Their eyes dart around the immediate area looking for a thirteen-year-old girl. Finding none, they avert their gaze to save us both the embarrassment. It doesn't help that I am humming a Justin Bieber tune that was playing in the airport shuttle van just minutes earlier. I try to look cool. Eventually, I forget about my suitcase.

As I am standing in line to board the plane, I hear a voice behind me.

"Excuse me, sir."

I turn to see a businessman in his mid-forties.

"Yes?"

His eyes are burning a hole in my suitcase. He continues, "Please tell me I'm not the only one today to give you $#*! about your purple bag."

"You're the first to verbalize it."

Appearing satisfied, he offers, "Good. I was just checking."

I don't know what else to say, so I board the plane and look for my seat. I quickly shove the bag in the overhead along with my coat and settle into 14B. I fall asleep not long after we take off, one of my most admirable skills.

I wake up when the wheels touch down. The plane makes its way to the gate, and, as usual, everyone jumps to their feet as soon as the doors open. A blonde woman in the row in front of me gestures to the man standing behind me.

"Could you hand me my bag?" she asks, pointing toward the overhead bin. "It's the rolling suitcase right next to you."

Without missing a beat, the man reaches up and grabs the purple bag.

I stammer, "S-sorry. That's mine."

"Really?" He stops and stares at me in disbelief.

I confirm without hesitation, "Yes."

"Nice." He says, before grabbing the appropriately toned black bag next to my clown suitcase and handing it to the woman in 12C.

I want to explain why I am carrying the bag, but I don't want to be "that" guy on the plane that holds everyone up. So I say nothing more. I just walk off the plane carrying a lot of baggage.

And I'm not talking about the suitcase.

Chapter Ten

The Power of Stuff

And can any of you by worrying add a single hour to your span of life? And why do you worry about clothing? Consider the lilies of the field, how they grow; they neither toil nor spin, yet I tell you, even Solomon in all his glory was not clothed like one of these.

(Matthew 6:27–29)

"You are what you own." Deep down, we all know it's a big lie, right? At last count, there are over seven billion people on the planet, and no two are exactly alike. Like a bunch of snowflakes. With arms and legs and foot odor. And there is a soul at the center of every person on the planet that drives their behavior and gives them a purpose in life. We are all far too complex to be defined by the shirts on our backs. Such small-minded thinking reduces God to the size of a Tic-Tac.

However, when I get to my hotel, I can't help but think of my interaction on the plane. The comments about my purple suitcase from perfect strangers should have bounced right off of me, but they didn't. It's obvious the bag I'm carrying says something about me. What that *something* is, I'm not sure, but I can see it in the faces of the people I meet, and it makes me self-conscious.

I fancy myself a self-confident person, so this surprises me. I may not be able to kill a bear with my own two hands or even get next-to-last place in an arm-wrestling contest, but I do have some redeeming capabilities. Take my job, for instance. Public speaking is the number one fear of people, yet I spend my days standing in front of large groups of professionals talking about lofty topics such as leadership and influence.

But somehow, dragging a purple suitcase through an airport gives me butterflies.

I consider calling the office building where I will conduct my next workshop to see if they have a place where I can check my bag in the lobby so that I won't have to keep it with me in full view of those who expect to see a professional guy show up to deliver a keynote address and, instead, meet some schlub who travels with his daughter's luggage. As if the quality of my work is somehow reflected in the color of my luggage.

Then my mind starts to wander, which is dangerous, as awfulizing is not far behind, followed soon by poor decision making.

But what if I run into my clients in the lobby? What will I say then? I can always explain our challenge, which I believe is a worthwhile cause, but I won't always have the luxury of time. What to do? How can I still drag this bag and maintain credibility?

Propelled by this feeling, I sit down at the desk in my hotel room, pull a black marker from my briefcase, and write on a blank sheet of paper: "Yes, I am a businessman carrying a lavender suitcase."

I find some masking tape and affix the sign to the front of the suitcase. Then I sit on the edge of the bed and stare at the bag.

Will this sign spark conversation? Most certainly. Will it encourage me to talk about why I carry the bag? Absolutely. Will it help relieve my discomfort?

Not a chance.

I come face-to-face with a harsh reality and one of the biggest lessons of the challenge thus far. As much as I preach that we are all more than the stuff we own, I have to admit that the twinge of nervousness I feel is based on something deep inside me. Why would I be concerned that other people judge me based on the suitcase I carry or the socks I wear?

Because I am guilty of the same judgment in my life.

I would be lying if I said there weren't times when I see a tatted-up, fully-pierced, leather-drenched guy on a motorcycle and say to myself, *Ummmm, he probably wouldn't be my first choice for babysitter.* Or better yet, I express surprise at people's occupations based on where they live or what car they drive. Thinking to myself, *Oh really? He's a doctor?! I wouldn't have guessed that.*

Apparently, I'm not alone. Luckily, we can (conveniently) blame society. In his book *Requiem for a Species*, Clive Hamilton discusses how attitudes have shifted over the past century. Hamilton writes about how we used to be a *production society*, focused on producing goods to meet needs in the marketplace, igniting the investor's confidence. But over time we have become a *consumer society*, focused on the process of acquiring things, igniting the consumer's confidence. This causes us all to focus less on what we produce and more on what we own, drawing more of our identity from the latter. A quick survey of advertisements over the past century tells the tale. Marketers used to tout the functional aspects of stuff, but gradually, they have shifted to focusing on what that stuff says about the owner. As Hamilton puts it, "It is virtually impossible today to buy any product that is not invested with certain symbols of identity acquired by the buyer knowingly or otherwise."[1] Our stuff becomes a kind of shorthand language for us to learn about one another and connect.

But it's all wrong.

We want to buy stuff to differentiate ourselves—as a reflection of our personality. The problem is, mass-produced stuff is the antithesis of "one of a kind." At best, it signals that we are part of a group. And here's where I lost my way.

When I travel, I want to be a part of the "professional businessman" group. I believe this gives me credibility. This allows people to form an opinion of me in a split second. There is something comforting about being part of a group. You can blend in. Fade into the background. You discourage questions. Discourage real connection.

But you know what?

You don't fade into the background when you're a businessman with a lavender suitcase. You stick out. You're an anomaly. The business suit and the child's suitcase don't add up. It's complex. Unknown. So people get curious. People ask questions. People connect.

And that's a good thing. Right?

The next morning I get ready for work and hop on the elevator to head downstairs for breakfast. I leave the sign on my suitcase. Still a bit self-conscious, I drag the purple bag behind me, glancing in all directions. I'm sure people are going to stare at me, but I see people milling about, trapped in their own worlds. Buried in a newspaper or a smart phone, just as I am prone to do when traveling alone, too distracted to notice the guy in a sport coat who is attached to what looks like a giant princess makeup bag. I park my things by a two-seat table and head to the breakfast buffet.

When I return, a woman is seated at the table next to mine. She has an impeccable hairstyle and wears a dark grey business suit. Instead of sitting facing her breakfast, she has swung her legs in the direction of my bag. She's bent over at the waist, holding her reading glasses in place at the temple as if they are going to fly off her face. She sees me move out of the corner of her eye.

"Oh! Sorry!" She says, giggling. "Is this your bag?"

"Unfortunately, yes." I answer. "If you like it, we could work out a trade."

She leans back and removes her glasses. "That's OK. I'll pass."

Apparently, business *women* are also allergic to my suitcase.

I place my breakfast on my table and slide into my chair. I adjust my napkin and pour milk into a bowl of Raisin Bran. She interrupts.

"So, are you going to tell me the story behind your bag, or are you going to make me ask?"

I normally refrain from chatting with strangers on the road. I don't know if it's a defense mechanism I have built up over time as a response to travelers who tend to "overshare" or if it's my way of preserving energy so that I can engage an audience and do my job when the time comes. But this is different. This woman is genuinely interested.

I tell her about trying to go a year without buying any stuff, and some of the roadblocks we have hit thus far. Namely, my suitcase.

"I bet you'll save a lot of money," she interjects. Judging from her appearance and her handbag (yes, *judging*), I assume that money is not a big concern of hers. She shifts ever-so-slightly to focus back on her newspaper.

"That remains to be seen," I say. "I hope we save money, but the main reason we're doing it is to try and get back to what's important. Connecting and sharing experiences with people. We've noticed that stuff sometimes gets in the way. At least for us."

She pauses. "Interesting," is all she offers. I notice her shoulders drop a quarter inch, as if she had been on alert and now decided she could relax.

I wait.

"It's funny," she says, without a hint of laughter. "I'm on the road a lot, so I miss out on time with my kids. I feel bad about it, so I usually pick up a gift or some trinket in the airport on the way home to remind them I'm thinking of them while I'm gone. But just last night I was thinking I need to stop doing that."

She explains how her kids often ask her why she travels so much, and she tells them she works so that they can afford the nice things they have. And in her eyes I see her silently questioning the value in what she provides. She doesn't say as much, but I recognize the look.

Like gazing into a mirror.

We talk about travel. Life on the road. We talk about the craziness of parenting today. We discuss the way things are marketed to kids and how hard it can be to avoid consumerism. As we finish our food, talk drifts back to the bag.

"Your project is interesting, that's for sure. It's got me thinking. My son's birthday is coming up. I was going to get him some video games, but he has dozens of those already. Maybe we should just do something together? Just the two of us? Alone?"

"Maybe so," I say. "Maybe so."

And that's where the conversation ends. We say our polite good-byes, but we don't exchange numbers. Don't even get each other's names. I'll never know what her son got for his birthday. Never know if she is traveling any less.

But in that one moment, we dove beneath the surface of everyday chatter to uncover the story behind the stuff. Stripping away the facade. Discovering.

We are so much more than what we own.

Chapter Eleven

Filling the Void

But those who want to be rich fall into temptation and are trapped by many senseless and harmful desires that plunge people into ruin and destruction.

(1 Timothy 6:9)

When this experiment first began, I imagined I would spend each day craving stuff I couldn't buy, but that hasn't been the case. Aside from washing socks in a hotel sink and dragging around some lavender luggage, this is not nearly as hard as I thought it would be. Fulfilling the "owning what we have" part of our mission has been fairly simple and straightforward. But there is another problem emerging.

One evening after preparing dinner, I yell for the kids. They wash their hands and set the table, we say a prayer, and everyone sits down to eat. I try to start some conversation by mentioning a story I read earlier in the day about a family mealtime ritual that President Obama and his family have at the White House.

Apparently, they play a game called "Thorns and Roses" where everyone shares a thorn and a rose—a bad part and a good part of their day. While my thorns and roses may not be as exciting as those of the leader of the free world, I think our family could try the game. After all, this year is about focusing on what's important, and this seems like a great way to invest some quality time with the kids. When I bring it up, everyone agrees that it sounds like a good idea, so we play.

The game is a smashing success. The usual bickering of "Stop staring at me, Audrey!" and "You're not the boss of me, Jake!" is replaced by thoughtful commentary on the happy and not-so-happy parts of our day. I am amazed at how such a simple game can help us reconnect as a family. Audrey even adds the categories of "Volcano" and "Tree." "Volcano" is something sad (for example, Audrey is sad because her stuffed animals aren't real), and "Tree" is something funny (for example, someone at the table admits to liking to fart in the bathtub on purpose because he or she likes the bubbles).

We each take turns sharing our perspectives on the day. The process takes a good twenty minutes with the extra categories. We agree we should add this to our nightly repertoire to build a new habit. Aside from a few dinners where the kids were so sleepy we had to force them to make noise and use tongs to help them open and close their mouths to chew food, we can't remember a mealtime so tranquil and civil.

When we finish eating, the kids ask if they can have dessert. After such wonderful dinnertime behavior, we can't refuse. And, per our rules, food is something we can purchase in bulk if we wish.

Jake asks, "How about some ice cream, Daddy?"

I scan my recent memory and remember finishing the carton the previous night. "I don't think there is any left, Jake. Sorry."

Audrey chimes in, "But what about the pink stuff?"

Jake clarifies. "That's cherry ice cream, Audrey!" waging his continued war on ambiguity in our house.

I deliver the bad news. "Yeah, honey, that's all gone."

I look over at Gabby, and her mouth is wide open in disbelief.

The kids continue, "But Daddy! We just bought it!" Audrey speaks as if I intentionally ripped the stuffing out of Dumbo. A mixture of disbelief and betrayal.

"I only had one scoop! How can it be gone?"

Gabby jumps in to save the day, "It's OK kids, we still have some Rocky Road."

I make a guttural noise, since saying the words out loud seems worse somehow.

Gabby turns to me and gives me her trademark "Look of Mild Disapproval."

"Don't tell me . . ."

More grunting from my pie hole. I prefer to confess with my mouth closed.

"But that's my favorite!" she cries.

"Sorry?" The questioning tone in my apology acknowledges that I didn't necessarily expect immediate forgiveness.

Gabby stands up, points at me, and shouts, "THORN!"

The kids are half-laughing, half-crying. As Gabby moves toward the freezer to verify, I try to support my status, "Gabby, that's not how the game works. I don't think Michelle Obama calls Barack a 'Thorn.'"

"She would if she folded all his laundry and he paid her back by eating all the ice cream!"

My wife reaches into the freezer and grabs the carton of Rocky Road. As soon as she feels the nearly empty carton, she turns to me and burns a hole in my skull with her gaze. Placing the carton on the kitchen counter, she opens it, revealing a half scoop of Rocky Road left inside. The ultimate slap in the face.

Like a police dog on the trail of the criminal's scent, she moves to the pantry where she pulls out a gallon-sized Ziploc bag, once filled with oatmeal raisin cookies.

"Why do we have a bag full of crumbs in the pantry? Where did all the cookies go?" But she already knows the answer to her hypothetical question.

I hide my head in shame. Gabby uses the moment as an opportunity to hold a family meeting and teach the kids a new word—*self-control*. It's a constructive conversation, much like "Thorns and Roses," but I can see the hidden agenda. The meeting has a dual purpose. Practical teaching as well as public shaming. And I deserve it.

The next morning I go to the gym, having nearly forgotten my transgressions completely. Prior to picking up lots of heavy things while trying not to soil my pants—aka Scott's strength-training session—I step on the scale. I put the large sliding weight at 150 pounds. Then I slide the smaller one along the beam toward the right.

A little more.

A little more.

I keep moving the little weight to the right until the scale finally balanced. But the reading is incorrect. WAAAAAAAY off.

It must be weighing heavy today.

Time to recalibrate the machine. I hop off the platform and zero out all the weights. With me off the scale and the weight set at 0 pounds, the scale is perfectly balanced.

Hmmmmm.

I notice the sweat towel slung over my shoulder. Figuring it's made of something ultra-dense, five pounds of cotton fiber, I throw it on the ground. I step on the scale again, but it continues to lie to me, telling me my five-pound towel weighs only four ounces.

Later that morning, Gabby says, "I think the scale at the gym is broken."

"Me too!" I echo. Happy with her validation.

"Yeah. I think it's two pounds off," she says. "There is no way I lost three pounds last week."

"*LOST* three pounds!?"

And then it hits me. I now understand why this challenge has been so easy for me. Apparently, every time I wanted to buy something new—a shirt, a drill, socks, pants, suitcases—I ate them instead.

I have gained seven pounds since our challenge started. The pleasure rush of new purchases has been replaced by a gluttonous, snack-tacular gorge-fest that can be described only as disgusting. I ate two half-gallons of ice cream in four days. Three bricks of mild cheddar cheese and two boxes of Wheat Thins in a week. Prior to our toaster-oven meltdown, I consumed three bowls of cereal and two Eggo waffles as an after-dinner nosh. If I keep this up, I will personally begin to resemble the USDA's nutrition pyramid, with the "cinnamon roll and French toast" food group giving me a wide-yet-jiggly foundation.

This is definitely an unforeseen consequence of this challenge. And quite troubling. If we simply replace one vice with another, can we truly call ourselves successful?

Something's gotta give. Right now, that "something" is the elastic waistband of my pants.

Chapter Twelve

Coach Burgess and the Brainiacs

Better is the sight of the eyes than the wandering of desire; this also is vanity and a chasing after wind.

(*Ecclesiastes 6:9*)

The episode with weight gain got me to thinking. Our whole reason for starting this challenge was to focus on what we believed to be important in our lives, so we developed a list of rules to help build commitment and focus on the right thing. A yardstick to measure failure or success.

But the rules aren't enough. They remind me of Coach Burgess, my seventh-grade PE teacher.

On the surface, Mr. Burgess was a motivator. His uniform was a white knit shirt and incredibly tight, polyester coaches' shorts that doubled as an anatomy lesson. Every day, sixty of us would sit on the floor in pristine rows as he barked orders at us while seated behind a six-foot wooden table.

"Alright, dog wipers! Line up against the wall!"

Dog wipers?

The coach's mission in life was to "toughen up" every middle-school boy within shouting distance. His method was simple. There were two boys in our class fortunate enough to sport a five-o'clock shadow at age twelve. Each day, he would handpick one of them to hurl a giant rubber ball at super-collider speed toward a cowering mass of pre-pubescent boys. Our job was to avoid openly sobbing in protest.

He called it "dodge ball."

The P.E. teacher failed in his mission to turn boys into men. I guess God and puberty are the ones who are supposed to take care of that. Thanks to Coach Burgess, I enjoy participating in contact sports almost as much as experiencing a breakout of teenage acne.

Almost.

Like the infamous coach, our rules are an extrinsic motivator, but they aren't building true commitment. I'm waiting impatiently for this year to fly by faster than seventh grade. My outward behavior says I'm not buying stuff, but my inward impulses are still there. The rules are treating the headache, but not shrinking the tumor. I have to understand the root cause of my impulsive behavior. Why do I crave stuff the way I do?

My first thought is to blame my mother. As the youngest of three kids, I was always a frequent sidekick on her shopping excursions. Under her tutelage, I learned to make a bee-line for the clearance rack and ask the manager for additional markdowns. She would keep things interesting by encouraging me to strike up conversations with mannequins to tell them how nice they looked. It turns out that this was not only good for keeping me busy but doubled as a good rehearsal for marriage. We would typically bring home an armload of shirts and pants marked "irregular," and Mom would teach me how to "fix" a defective item by distracting the eye with an accessory. For the record, I was single-handedly responsible for both starting and ending the short-lived "male brooch" trend of 1987.

But my cravings aren't Mom's fault. My desire to acquire stuff is deeper than a sense of nostalgia for days gone by. Those shopping trips built a love for my mother but not necessarily for the items we purchased. So what motivates someone who already has enough to want to buy more stuff? I go in search of some honest-to-goodness brainiacs to help me answer this question.

I find a study by some really smart folks at Penn State titled "Retail Therapy: A Strategic Effort to Improve Mood."[1] In this study, scientists surveyed people entering a mall and asked about their mood before shopping. The survey shows that some had come to the mall to celebrate. Others were just there because they had nothing better to do. Still more said they had come to the mall in a bad mood.

The researchers then interviewed the same people as they were leaving to find out if they purchased anything. So what did they find? Poor mood was the biggest driver of impulsive behavior. Sixty-two percent of those who had come to the mall in a funk walked out with a shopping bag. And for good reason: all but one of the respondents reported feeling happier when they left. And they had no regrets about the experience, even several days after the fact. It turns out "retail therapy" is a real thing.

This explains a lot, but it doesn't explain everything, because I sometimes buy stuff when I'm in a *good* mood. Or in no mood at all. What about that?

Searching deeper, I find that it has a lot to do with how God has wired our brains. I am not a doctor, but I did play one in a Neil Simon play my sophomore year in high school, so allow me to oversimplify for you.

Your brain is your body's Magic 8 Ball. It's where decisions are made. These decisions are a result of complex communication between different areas of your melon, each with something to contribute to the process at a given time. One of these areas is called the *nucleus accumbens*. You actually have two of them. One in each half of your brain. It's a small spot tucked away just a couple inches behind each of your eyeballs. You can touch it by jamming your pinkie into your eye socket, but I wouldn't recommend it.

The *nucleus accumbens* plays a big role in how you interpret pleasurable experiences. Think laughter, winning, sex, etc. Science tells us anytime we experience something that feels good—like when I decide to eat an entire sleeve of Thin Mints—a chemical called *dopamine* gets released into my *nucleus accumbens*. The dopamine helps stimulate connections between neurons in this area, like giving them all a beer to help loosen them up at a party. The result? This pleasure center lights up like the Vegas Strip, and we feel really good.

And the brain learns.

So the next time I see a third grader from Girl Scout Troop #514 selling cookies in front of my local grocery store, my brain anticipates a party in my mouth and starts the dopamine release a bit early. If I decide to buy them and eat the entire box while standing in the cereal aisle (not that I would ever do such a thing), I reinforce the connection. This is the beginning of addiction.

But here's the interesting part: Researchers, such as Stanford's Robert Sapolsky, have found that after a while, it's not just the reward itself that lights up the *nucleus accumbens*, but the anticipation as well. So, hypothetically speaking, if a guy was writing a book in a coffee shop and started thinking about a box of Thin Mints hidden in the pantry at home, the peak dopamine release wouldn't occur when the cookies touch his tongue, but some time before (again, hypothetically speaking). And research shows that when subjects are given the reward only 50 percent of the time, their dopamine levels shoot into the stratosphere.[2]

So what gives?

The reason shopping is so addictive is not the acquisition of the item but rather the anticipation. We crave something and imagine ourselves having it. This creates tension that we resolve with some retail therapy and a Visa card. The bigger the craving, the bigger the release.

But notice the big lie here.

Your brain doesn't actually want the object of your desire. It wants the chemical release. It wants to end the wanting. This explains why last December 25, my daughter spent a whopping twelve minutes playing with the stuffed poodle that had been on her Christmas list for eight weeks. The *girl* may have wanted the poodle, but her *brain* just wanted the chemical rush. So once the dopamine was released, the poodle was released as well. Into a giant basket of dozens of other stuffed animals just like it.

And we get stuck in an endless loop. I get a new car. I enjoy it for a time. But I want something newer. Why? So I can ultimately end the wanting and get my shot of feel-good juice. Then I'm happy with the new car until I start fixating on another. Then the wanting starts, and I won't stop until I get it. And most of this is happening subconsciously.

So what do I do about it?

Again, the answer might be buried in the brain God gave us.

My search for answers uncovers another fascinating study from the folks at Stanford, MIT, and Carnegie Mellon. They wanted to see if they could determine what's at work when a person craves an item but resists buying it anyway.[3]

People in the study were given $20 they could spend on "stuff" during the trial. Each subject was shown a picture of an item on a computer screen for a few seconds. Next, they were shown a drastically discounted price for that item.

So, let's say Darren is our test subject. Researchers show Darren a picture of a box of gourmet chocolates. These chocolates normally cost $50. But Darren's price is a mere $7. If he wants to buy the chocolate, all he has to do is push a button and the chocolate will be shipped to his doorstep. Any money left over at the end of the study is his to keep.

Sorry. The study is not accepting any new subjects at this time. I checked.

As subjects shop, their brain activity is measured using MRI (magnetic resonance imaging). The researchers notice that certain pictures tend to cause the *nucleus accumbens* to go nuts, indicating that the subjects really want whatever is on the screen.

But even though their cravings are going haywire, not all the people purchase the items they want. Why?

It appears there is another area of our brain that counteracts the pleasure center. It's called the *insula* (sounds like "insulation" to me—protection). The *insula* is the part of your brain that anticipates pain. It's the area that saves us from ourselves. The part that lights up in that moment between tripping on the curb and face planting on the sidewalk. Or between seeing a coveted purchase and actually parting with your cash.

For some test subjects, the *insula* lights up the instant they see the discounted price of the item. For others, it is as dark as hell's basement. Every time the *insula* takes a vacation, the subjects purchase the item they crave. The findings are so conclusive that, based on what they see in the early part of the study, during later trials the researchers are able to predict whether a person is going to purchase the item even before they make the conscious decision. They just watch the process in slow motion to see what the *insula* does, and freezing that moment in time, they know what the subject will do with 100 percent certainty.

I seems only fitting that God would build our brains in such a way, with both the seed of temptation and the compass of free will planted deep inside. But what does this mean for me?

This challenge is more than just a fight against advertisers. I'm fighting human nature, and simple rules just can't help with that. They may help guide our behavior, but right now following the rules feels like deprivation, and deprivation won't get my dopamine flowing. It's heightened anticipation with no reward.

Lasting change is going to require that we shift our mind-set. There must be some way to "trick" our brains so that we can feel pleasure in resisting. Or better yet, perhaps the pleasure is found in completely ignoring what we're missing and focusing on what we're getting instead. That's really the crux of "owning what we have," isn't it? Not just *owning* it, but *valuing* it.

Chapter Thirteen

Two, Four, Six, Eight, What Do I Appreciate?

Let the word of Christ dwell in you richly; teach and admonish one another in all wisdom; and with gratitude in your hearts sing psalms, hymns, and spiritual songs to God.
(Colossians 3:16)

The whole concept of outsmarting your own brain sounds as crazy as trying to keep a secret from yourself. How in the world would you do something like that? It seems impossible. I am afraid the simple act of trying to reason against myself could be so metaphysically paradoxical that it might open up a wormhole that will swallow me whole and transport me back in time.

Either that, or it will give me a raging headache.

In an effort to change our brains and truly "own what we have," Gabby and I decide to try something called an Appreciation Audit. The exercise was developed by a guy named Dr. Martin Seligman, who is often called the father of the positive psychology movement.

Years ago, Seligman was dismayed at the state of psychology. An overwhelming majority of practitioners were dedicated to studying depressed people to understand what was wrong with them so that they could ultimately develop therapies to get them all back to some level of "OK."[1] In fact, *USA Today* reports that in the mid '90s, scientific journals published roughly one hundred studies on sadness for every one study on happiness.[2]

Noting this imbalance, Seligman dedicated his efforts toward finding out what brings people genuine satisfaction in life. Ironically, many of Seligman's colleagues thought he was nuts. But over time, other researchers joined his efforts. Over the past two decades, their studies have uncovered some beautiful truths about the human condition. For instance, one question the movement sought to answer was, "Does money buy happiness?"

The answer is yes.

Sort of.

Harvard psychologist Dan Gilbert, a positive dude himself, sums up the research in his book, *Stumbling on Happiness*. He writes that psychologists have conducted countless studies over the years to discover the relationship between money and life satisfaction and have "generally concluded that wealth increases human happiness when it lifts people out of abject poverty and into the middle class but that it does little to increase happiness thereafter."[3] So the lifestyles of the rich and famous may be richer, but they are not, in fact, happier. It's something we've all known for some time, but it's nice to have scientific backing for the belief.

This news provides some solid logic to help us rewire our minds. Our family is already in the middle class, so there's not much to be gained by purchasing stuff, even if it is just food. So when we start to crave that "retail high," all we have to do is tell ourselves that it just doesn't make sense to try and buy our way into feeling better. It won't work.

So what's the alternative?

Luckily for us, Doctor Seligman and his cronies discovered something completely controllable that boosts feelings of satisfaction and minimizes feelings of loss or depression. And the best news of all?

It doesn't cost a dime.

Together with his colleague Dr. Ed Diener, Seligman found fifty severely depressed people and asked them to write down three things per day that they were grateful for and to explain why they were grateful.[4] They called it a "gratitude journal." Meanwhile, to make sure the act of keeping a journal wasn't the key to satisfaction in life, they asked other patients to keep a journal of childhood memories. Good or bad. It didn't matter.

After fifteen days, the group journaling childhood memories showed no measureable improvement in their depressive symptoms. Conversely, 94 percent of the people in the gratitude group showed marked improvement in symptoms, equivalent to what is normally obtained with medications or psychotherapy. Better still, these improvements were realized much more quickly than with the traditional methods of treatment.

When I learn of this strategy, I am immediately energized. Not buying stuff creates an itch that I can't quite scratch. There is a hole that leaves me feeling unsatisfied, and here is a potential remedy that costs absolutely nothing. In fact, it doesn't even require changing anything about my lifestyle or routine, save for simply noticing things I'm grateful for and documenting them.

Sign me up!

Gabby and I vow to take a month to record the things for which we are thankful. Five items every day. It will be a fun experiment to see if it makes a difference. We don't have a real measurement tool like the depression assessment Seligman used, but we can rely on anecdotal evidence. If we feel less impulsive and more satisfied at the end of the month, we'll call it a worthwhile endeavor. If nothing else, taking the time to write stuff down will leave less time for shopping or watching a TV show littered with ads for products we aren't allowed to buy.

On day one, I sit down at my computer with a bowl of cereal to record my gratitude while eating breakfast. Rather than write my list by hand, I choose to record it all digitally, since my handwriting looks like two ferrets got trapped in a spiral-bound notebook and began fighting over an ink pen.

So I type:

Things I'm grateful for . . .

1. A computer to type this list
2. Frosted Mini-Wheats

3. Pajama pants
4. My uncanny ability to win stuff
5. Work that I love and make money doing

Everything I list is very immediate. I can look around me and see dozens of things to be thankful for. Like the portable cell-phone charger I just won at a conference, which made me feel absolutely awesome-sauce. The lazy part of me is excited by this. The first week of my gratitude journal is either sitting on top of my desk or draped on my body. This is going to be a piece of cake!

(Note to self: remember to be grateful for cake.)

Unfortunately, one thing I am not grateful for is my inability to stick to a schedule. On day two, I forget to journal. Day two! So on day three I double up on my entries, identifying ten things. I mindlessly type the words on the page, and as I type, it starts to feel like cheating. I'm picking out items at random that happen to be in my immediate view. Sure, I am grateful for, say, my pen that never seems to run out of ink, but what value is that really bringing to my life? Is this really something I want to include in my journal? A convenient pen?

I allow my mind to wander around the house. I hear the sound of a vacuum coming from our bedroom. Gabby is doing some quick morning housework after a trip to the gym, so I type, "I have a wife who likes to vacuum." I know. She's strange. Something to do with seeing progress by looking back at the patterns she left in the carpet really elevates her mood.

But I appreciate it.

My mental excursion around the house generates a list of stuff comparatively more meaningful than what I listed on day one. It includes an insanely comfortable bed, a warm fireplace on a cold night, a strong roof to keep out the rain, a refrigerator full of food, and a hot shower.

I wish I could say that writing this list every morning leaves me with lasting glow of contentment that stays with me throughout the day, but it doesn't work that way. The contentment is fleeting, quickly giving way to the hustle of life. There are things to do. Problems to solve. Kids to yell at.

But I am proud of my list and feel my mind is now in the right place. I'm moving in the right direction toward owning what I have instead of craving what I don't. I feel as if I am outsmarting my brain, basking in the warmth of thankfulness for the things in my life. After a few days, however, I glance back through my list and notice something. Something disappointing.

My list is just a bunch of things.

Stuff.

While my satisfaction with my life is increasing, my focus is still misplaced. Sure, there are some intangible items on my list, but the majority of my gratitude is wrapped up in things that can be purchased from a store. Subconsciously, stuff still forms the foundation of my satisfaction.

Ick.

I think I need a shower.

Upon realizing this, I vow to change the rules of my own audit. No more tangible stuff. Only intangibles, whether mundane or profound. On the days that follow, I pronounce my gratitude for music and for talented taste buds. I also give thanks for my flexible job that allows me to chaperone school field trips. For safety. For children who are capable of showing their love to me. For a healthy wife and a healthy marriage.

At the end of the week, I look back through my list, and two things come to mind.

First, reading a list of thirty-five fantastic things in your life brings about a flood of gratitude. It's like opening a box of ice cream sandwiches and knowing you can eat every single one. An overwhelmingly beautiful sensation. Drowning in thankfulness for the blessings of life. I highly recommend it.

But the bigger learning comes later.

I return to Nashville around midnight after a long few days working out of town. Unfortunately, our second car is having trouble, and Gabby has taken it in for repairs. I'm not about to have her wake the kids at midnight to drag them to the airport to pick me up, so I crawl into the back of a cab and settle in for the ride home.

In this situation, I am normally quiet. After spending all day speaking to large groups of people, the last thing I want to do is strike up a conversation. Even ordering off a drive-thru menu is taxing. But I am buoyed by my recent conversation with the woman at breakfast about my lavender luggage and see an opportunity to build another connection I may not have made before.

"So, what's your name?" I ask the driver.

He says his name is Alex. He's from Somalia. As he drives me toward the suburbs of Nashville, we talk about his home—a home far different than mine. Alex tells me life has been a mixed bag for him. He has fond memories of growing up in a small village. Playing soccer with friends. Hanging out with family.

That is, until a civil war erupted.

Simplicity gave way to danger. Alex's father wanted no part of it. He took the family on a journey to safety. They eventually made their way to a U.N. refugee camp in Kenya. There, they spent a year living in a tent with a dirt floor, where temperatures frequently eclipsed 100 degrees. They received food rations once per week. There was very little to go around, and there were precious few opportunities for employment. So they spent their days waiting in lines, surrounded by dust, filth, and despair. And on the off chance they could talk to an official, they would beg for any chance to get back to a sense of "normal." But the response was always the same. A brick wall. Day after day spent in purgatory.

To me, this sounds completely miserable, but Alex has a different take.

"We had hope," he says.

"So what did you do?" I ask. I'm on the edge of my seat, happy that Alex is driving well below the speed limit and extending the length of my ride home.

He explains that he could read and write English, which was a relatively rare skill in the camps, so he started hanging around the Red Cross medical clinic in the camp, helping people fill out forms and translating for patients and nurses. It was his way of finding meaning and worth. Seeing his initiative, the clinic eventually created a job for him that paid $30 per month. Slowly but surely, Alex's family moved out of the tent and into a room with four walls. Then into a very small house. And eventually they found a program through the Catholic Church that allowed them to leave Kenya and come to the United States.

His story is far different from mine. I can't fathom going through such hardship myself.

"How did you keep going?" I ask. He answers in his labored English.

"I had faith." He hesitates. "I still have faith. I still go to the Catholic Church. They took my faith and made it real."

Faith made real.

The conversation with Alex sticks with me. Hearing his story is one of those brief moments where the space between heaven and earth narrows and we catch a glimpse of the divine in another human being. When I get out of the cab, it is well past midnight. He helps me with my bag. I extend my hand for a shake and say, "Thanks for sharing your story. It's been an honor to hear it."

He grabs hold and leans in. We give each other a safe, one-armed guy hug, communicating respect and connection without being too creepy. As he hops back into the driver's seat, he says "Blessings to you, my friend," and drives away.

I walk into the house, and it is silently still. Everyone has gone to bed. I peek in on the kids and watch their little chests move up and down with the rhythm of their breathing. I steal into the bedroom where I lean in to kiss my wife on the forehead.

Blessings, indeed.

I am still not ready for bed, so I retire to the couch, turn on my laptop, and look back through my list. Thirty-five things to be thankful for. Ice cream. Family. Friends. And as I look through both the tangible and intangible, I realize something.

Even these things can be taken away.

I know it's a morbid thought, but an important one. We don't know what the future holds for us. We all know that "stuff" is fleeting. It can vanish in an instant. But so can those things that are most important to us. I look back at my list and ask,

What am I grateful for that can never be taken away?

And that's when it hits me. We all have a choice no matter the situation. We can choose to be victims of circumstance. We can choose to be passive. We can choose a mentality of scarcity and fear, where we hoard and worry and stress our lives away.

We can choose despair. Despair is easy and suffocating all at once. But there is another option.

We can choose abundance. We can choose gratitude. We can choose hope. Because gratitude and hope are possessions that can never be taken away. And they are strengthened by faith. Like the love of God. Ever-present, no matter the circumstance. This is what drives us. This is what sustains us.

And for this, I am truly grateful.

Chapter Fourteen

Christ Is Risen! Let's Go to Arby's!

I have come that they may have life, and have it to the full.
(John 10:10 NIV)

Easter is here! It's one of my favorite times of year and perhaps the best reason of all to feel grateful. There's an energy in the air as winter dormancy explodes into new life. Christ is risen! He is risen, indeed!

But he still isn't buying anything at the Dannemiller house.

One of our favorite Easter traditions comes from Mexico. In the towns along the U.S. border, people make *cascarones* around the holiday, hollowed out eggshells filled with confetti. Tradition dictates that families gather to honor the agonizing death of Jesus and his triumphant resurrection by breaking the eggs on one another's heads—just as the disciples did at the Last Supper (at least that's what it says in my Jerry Lewis Standard Edition of the Bible).

In years past, we purchased a few dozen of these eggs at HEB, the famed grocery store in Texas named after Howard E. Butt. This year is a different story. Unable to buy the *cascarones*, we are making them ourselves. To accomplish this, we spend the better part of five weeks eating eggs every day for breakfast and watching my cholesterol spike. But it's not the egg *consumption* that's so fascinating. It's the egg *preparation*.

To ensure that we preserve the shells intact, each morning I am *tap-tap-tapping* on the pointy end of the egg with a paring knife until breaking through like a baby chick, then gently prying off a small piece, and violently shaking the egg out into a bowl. We must look like the most OCD bunch of chefs in the world. Several shells fall victim to *cascarone* research and development, but a couple dozen hollow husks make it to the top of our refrigerator where they sit to dry for a week or so.

The next step in the painstaking process is coloring the eggs. The thought of taking on this type of messy craft project gives me the shakes. I'm not sure why. Perhaps it's the fact that the kids have yet to master the use of their opposable thumbs. Or maybe I nearly drowned in a large vat of Paas color solution when I was young. Whatever the case, I leave this part of the work to Gabby and the kids. My job comes afterward, when I take a blow dryer to get rid of any moisture in the shells once they are colored. I put on some oven mitts to insulate against the heat, and wield my blow dryer like a champ. By the time I am finished styling them, every single egg looks like Donald Trump's toupee.

Next, we finely chop some old chunks of tissue paper that Gabby has saved from gifts and craft projects long past. There is a mountain of it in a variety of colors. It's as if she was saving it in case we needed to cover a dozen parade floats after the Apocalypse. We combine the tissue paper shavings with some finely diced financial documents we had recently put through the shredder. Sure, there is some risk in using confidential documents to fill confetti eggs, but we figure it's worth it, given that it would take a really nasty person to steal your identity on one of the holiest days of the year by resurrecting a document from a squillion tiny cutlets of paper. Still, we spread each document evenly among each egg to minimize our exposure.

Once finished, we have two dozen homemade eggs ready for smashing. Three dozen more are added to the inventory when our friend Mary Beth, hearing about our *cascarone* sweat shop, grows concerned and purchases them for us at the local Wal-Mart. It's such a kind gesture. We feel grateful for our friend's generosity and for the extra time we spend together as a family preparing for Easter. We never would have made this a DIY project had we not been tackling our year without a purchase.

So our egg-smashing fun fest is all set to go, but there is one big thing we lack.

Easter baskets.

While Santa has sweatshops full of elves to assist him in toy production, the Easter Bunny is a loner. The poor guy has to rely on Target to fill the baskets. But this year, no can do. Our bunny can't buy any stuff.

In years past, we put small toys and little knick-knacks in the baskets. This year we have to devise a different plan. In lieu of toys and fancy Easter grass, we stuff the baskets with more shredded mortgage documents and throw in some plastic eggs from Gabby's stash that seems to multiply in the garage. Apparently, crepe paper is not the only thing that will survive Armageddon. We will also have a trash bag full of multicolored eggs that can be used as makeshift change purses or something.

We cram the eggs full of jelly beans and fun-size Snickers bars to appease the kids' sweet tooth. We try to think of what else they might enjoy that's not stuff. While it's not a requirement to buy gifts for the resurrection, it was a tradition in our houses growing up, so we feel weirdly obligated somehow. After some debate, we decide to get Audrey a gift card for an Arby's roast beef sandwich and Jake a gift card for a Cool Ranch Locos Taco from Taco Bell.

We sincerely apologize to Michelle Obama for our poor food choices.

When Easter morning arrives, we hide the baskets and send the kids searching through the house to find them. We figure the thrill of the chase will be a nice substitute for the lack of tangible stuff they'll receive. We anticipate that they will likely notice the change from the previous year, so we don't even mention the Easter Bunny by name. We don't want to throw the poor fella under the bus.

We never would have guessed how excited the kids would be. They must put moon dust and Fun Dip on the shell of the Cool Ranch Doritos Locos taco, because Jake can't stop talking about them. He's thrilled with the gift card. It makes him feel like a "big kid." Either that, or it's the sugar rush talking.

And Audrey?

She looks at her gift card curiously. She can't yet read, but she recognizes the logo of her favorite fast food establishment. Once we tell her that the card is worth five dollars, she asks excitedly,

"Can I take Nana out to lunch?"

Holy cow. This is not the reaction we expected. We do a quick double-check.

"You want to share your gift card with Nana?"

"Yeah! Can I call her?"

We give her the phone. She's nearly breathless as she tells Nana all about her Easter basket. Then she asks Nana if she can use the gift card and treat her to lunch. Based on my mom's enthusiasm, you would have thought that Audrey had invented calorie-free chocolate. Both of them nearly wet their pants from excitement.

When the day comes, Audrey picks out a special outfit. Nana arrives to pick her up. They sit across the table from each other, sharing roast beef sandwiches, curly fries, and a mint chocolate shake. Audrey tells us all about it later that evening.

"It was delicious!" she shouts.

More satisfying than the meal, however, was the thrill of giving back to the woman who had given her so much. You could see the joy on her face. She knows the greatest gift was not the card itself, but rather sharing an experience with one of her favorite people. It never would have happened had we filled those baskets with a mountain of trinkets. It's a precious memory that's way too big to carry in her tiny Hello Kitty change purse. No, this one she'll be carrying in her heart for years to come.

Chapter Fifteen

True Confessions

Jesus said, "Father, forgive them, for they do not know what they are doing."

(*Luke 23:34 NIV*)

I grew up Catholic and am proud of my upbringing. I learned a lot about social justice from the teachings of the church, and I'm sure my Catholic guilt is at least partly responsible for the current austerity measures in our home. The Catholic vow of simple living is always top-of-mind, with priests living minimalist lives and nuns living with even less. Even the new pope is getting into the act. In his first few days at the helm, Francis refused the usual flashy fur-trimmed cape and bling-tastic gold cross that pontiffs wear at their unveiling. Instead, he opted for a simple white robe and iron cross. And for transportation, he's keeping the ultra-cool pope-mobile in the garage in favor of a basic Vatican sedan.[1]

It's like he's allergic to stuff.

I was never a very good Catholic. Most kids do their first confession in the third grade. Me? I skipped mine. Faked an illness or something. Then the guilt got to me, and I voluntarily elected to remediate many years later, as a freshman in high school. This created some real angst for me. By the time I finally mustered the courage to release my face-to-face, tell-all biography to Father Mikliska, I had moved way past stealing a few cookies and into regularly taking the Lord's name in vain and entertaining a constant stream of impure thoughts about the varsity cheerleading squad.

While we are still living in accordance with our "no purchase" guidelines, I feel as if we're finding loopholes, which causes my guilt to surface. We're not falling off the wagon, mind you, but our feet may be dangling off the back, dragging the ground, and kicking up dust.

Surprisingly enough, Jake's birthday wasn't a problem. At first, we worried that not buying stuff would make his birthday inferior, but drawing on our creative juices for our sports-loving kid, we had a wonderful party. Gabby made an awesome basketball cake. I found out that Kinko's, an official sponsor of the NFL, was giving away free team posters, so I went by and begged for a dozen or so, which they were happy to provide, as favors for the party. We made all sorts of sports games out of borrowed hula hoops, sidewalk chalk, and masking tape. We even created a "Hockey Goalie Jake" out of cardboard by printing a blown up picture of his face and pasting it on a cardboard cutout body. All his friends had a great time trying to shoot a foam puck through his fake legs.

For a rules-approved "experience gift," we lucked into some tickets to a Nashville Predators hockey game that a friend wasn't going to use. Jake invited a buddy and his dad to go along, and we all had a ball. We yelled at the top of our lungs. The home team won. And we gorged ourselves on candy I smuggled in buried deep within the pockets of my cargo pants. The good news is, Jake never once complained about not having a tangible gift to open, and we now share a great memory. The bad news is, I think I have to tell Father Mikliska about the contraband Sour Patch Kids.

For big events like a birthday party, some creativity and effort creates enough fanfare to distract the kids from the fact that there isn't a shiny gift at the end of the rainbow. In addition, it's nice to be able to savor the experience and talk about how much fun we had, rather than complaining that they don't play with the new toy we bought them. But the smaller things are still a bit of a challenge.

For example, Jake is registered for little league baseball and has fallen in love with playing catcher. At his age, the kids can't throw accurately, so to keep concussions to a minimum, they employ a machine to hurl balls toward the plate when kids are up to bat. Each pitch travels at about 40 miles per hour when released from the Iron Maiden, so the coach suggested Jake get a cup to protect his nether regions.

A protective cup isn't something you typically want as a hand-me-down. It's not like I can tell him to turn it inside out and use the "clean" side. I wrestle with the decision. A cup is definitely not a biodegradable, consumable item. Cups are made of indestructible plastic to withstand frequent blows. In fact, I'm guessing they'll be the only things left when future civilizations unearth our artifacts to try and understand who we were as a people. A scary thought.

I spy a recycled, single-serve yogurt container on our kitchen counter and wonder aloud if Jake could use it as an alternative. Before I can mold and shape it into something useful, Gabby intervenes, saying, "No way. We are not trusting our son's reproductive future to Dannon."

Her practicality and desire for grandchildren wins the day so we buy an honest-to-goodness cup, considering it a necessary item to ensure safety.

One Hail Mary.

Jake's tennis shoes are another issue. They are in such bad shape that each night instead of putting them in a closet, we have our son take them to the ER where they can be placed on life support and monitored by a physician. The soles are ripping off, and the side is developing a gaping hole, as if Jake has the feet of an eighty-seven-year-old man with huge bunions and an extra pinkie toe protruding.

One morning he asks, "Can I get some new shoes after school today, Daddy?"

I reply, "But son, you *have* other shoes. The black ones."

"But I don't like those shoes."

"You don't have to like 'em. They are not your best friend. They are shoes. And the job of shoes is to protect your feet. "

"But they aren't the *right* shoes. They are summer shoes."

"Summer is coming fast."

"Not until June. June 21st. You said so."

I love my son dearly, but in this moment, I am not excited about his ability to remember the exact date of the summer solstice as if he's channeling Rain Man. But the tennis shoes have now become more hole than shoe, so we coax him into wearing the summer shoes, even though they are technically "water shoes" made of synthetic material and pocked with holes to allow for quick drying.

It's not long before the elastic cord used to tighten the shoes snaps, causing them to flop around and slip off whenever he runs. I rig a solution by tying the broken ends together, but the fix lasts less than a day. We check with a few relatives and post on Facebook to find some hand-me-downs without any luck. The only other shoes in his closet are from his cousin Tyler, who is only a year older but has feet the size of Thanksgiving turkeys.

So we savor the flavor of failure and buy him a pair of tennis shoes.

Five Our Fathers.

Then there is the boy's lunchbox. It's one of those soft canvas varieties. Though less than a year old, the zippers that seal the pack broke this week, which doesn't seem like a big deal, but apparently public-school regulations require an insulated pack so that kids don't eat room-temperature bologna sandwiches and turn the place into a salmonella factory. While Jake's lunch pack is barely functional, we have another one he can use. The problem is, it's a paisley-floral print that looks like a grandmother's purse, which would be a bold fashion statement for a second-grader.

Lucky for Jake, his mother knows the exact location of the receipt for any purchase she has made since Milli Vanilli won a Grammy. Gabby quickly finds the original purchase slip and takes the defective lunchbox back to the store where we originally bought it. They give her a full refund, which we use to buy a replacement.

Pray the rosary.

The final straw is the Scholastic Book Fair. If you are unfamiliar with this event, it's a traveling road show of books, which visits every elementary school in America promoting reading and prepubescent capitalism. Kids are encouraged to chat with their parents about the books available and discuss whether they belong in their home library.

Our kids are very excited about the Book Fair. They keep talking about it. Audrey is very interested in *Skippyjon Jones*, a story about a Siamese cat that thinks he's a chihuahua. And Jake keeps hinting about a new sports almanac book; the new version of last year's book, which is now as worn as Pope Francis' childhood Bible.

In response, we remind the kids about this really cool place that's filled with books. You can actually go to this place, pick out some books, and give a card to an old lady who smells like moth balls and fresh-baked oatmeal cookies, and she stamps the books with a big rubber stamper and lets you take them home.

It's called the public library.

Audrey, unamused by our sarcastic description said, "What if we buy them ourselves?"

I search my memory for any of Audrey's pay stubs from her job as an imaginary unicorn trainer. Recalling none, I respond, "But honey, how are you going to do that? You don't have any money."

Jake noses in to the conversation, "Yes we do! We got money for Christmas last year!"

Sabotaged by Santa.

This is not something we had anticipated. Even though our kids never signed up for this experiment, we still consider them as active participants. It's a family challenge. So, much as our own parents "volun-told" us to enjoy countless acts of forced family fun, we're dragging our children along for the ride. There's no shame in that.

However, we do feel a little guilty. They each have ten dollars they received as a gift from a relative last year, and neither has spent a dime. The gift was given with a generous heart, meant to be enjoyed by the kids. Prohibiting them from spending the money is like taking away the gift and saying, "I hope you like what Aunt Lisa got you, but I'm sorry, you can't play with it for another nine months."

Who *does* that?

In the end, we tell them they can use their money to buy the items they want, provided we can read the books together on the couch before bed. This technically meets our "experience gift" mandate. Much like a sin of omission, it still feels like cheating. But we're not sure if that's because we feel guilty for making them use their fun money to buy something we otherwise would have been glad to buy them or if it truly is a failure, since God invented libraries to avoid such a purchase.

Two more Our Fathers, and bring the main dish to the next church potluck.

Whatever the case, it's obvious that this is still a learning process for us. It is in these moments that we realize this consumer challenge is very much a metaphor for our lives as Christians. We seek to model our actions on the way of Christ. The Savior's life becomes our litmus test. So we wring our hands and beat ourselves up anytime we fall short of his example. Unfortunately, in doing so, we forget about the gift of forgiveness.

And it is in this forgiveness that we find our strength.

In many ways, our challenge is just an outgrowth of falling short. While our intent may be noble, we are manufacturing a year of self-denial in response to our years of over-indulgence. And in doing so, we risk patronizing those that live without purchases every day due to a simple lack of resources.

At the same time, I believe God delights in our repentance. That moment when we recognize our actions don't match our intent to follow the call of Christ, whether we are bending the rules of life or breaking them. And while this may be evidence of fault or failure, it's also the first step toward finding our way back home.

Chapter Sixteen

The Worst Parents Ever

Can a mother forget the baby at her breast
and have no compassion
on the child she has borne?
Though she may forget,
I will not forget you!
See, I have engraved you
on the palms of my hands;
(*Isaiah 49:15–16 NIV*)

After our questionable purchases, we vow to be more diligent about adhering to the rules and honoring our intent. Exploiting loopholes just feels icky. We even come clean to some of our friends to gauge whether or not they felt that we cheated. Being that they are all still shopping freely, we know the answers before we ask for their opinion on the matter. It's a bit like asking a pastry chef if it's OK to indulge in a cream-filled cupcake or two while on a diet. Still, we want the accountability of community.

It takes a village.

Our friends agree that a protective cup and children's shoes are a necessity. And the lunchbox? They are all fine with exchanging a broken item, since it technically isn't *more* stuff, and fixing the zipper would have cost more money than the refund. The Book Fair brings a similar reaction. Since we never told people they couldn't buy gifts for our kids, our friends agree that allowing them to use their own gifted money to buy reading material is perfectly acceptable. Especially since the gift was given last Christmas before our challenge even started. But the most common thing we hear is, "It's for your kids, for goodness sake!"

These words hit us like a 2 x 4 to the forehead. It reminds us of all of the vows we made when we first brought those crazy, tiny people into this world. Before they took their first breaths, we decreed that we would never let them listen to annoying kid music. Or eat McDonald's in the backseat. And we would never think of doing that cliché discipline tactic where you yell, "I'm going to count to three, and then I'm going to (insert horrible, irrational, overblown punishment here)." It was simple plan. Foolproof.

And, as the old Yiddish proverb states, "Man plans, God laughs."

Foolproof plans such as ours often fail to take into account the ingenuity of fools. Today, you would think The Biscuit Brothers are the next Beyoncé based on the airplay they get on our car stereo. We have the Golden Arches value meals memorized. If we are ever trapped in a roadside avalanche, I know we could survive for days on the petrified fries my kids have stashed away beneath their car seats. And though I have an advanced degree, my children think three is as high as I can count.

Our kids make us do silly things. Bend the rules. Even when we do it to our own detriment. And theirs. We have to break this cycle. We silently judge other parents when we see them catering to their kids in public, yet we are guilty of the same thing, and it has to stop.

So we vow "No more!"

No sooner do we strengthen our resolve than we face another test. Jake's school backpack is broken. It was supposed to last the rest of the year, but the zipper gave out (yes, a sorceress cast a "zipper pox" curse on our house) and we can't fix it. The edges are far too frayed. We also can't return it, as it had been well-loved over the years and any attempt to claim product malfunction would be laughable.

Luckily for Jake, we have a backup on hand. Gabby got it as a giveaway at a trade show over twenty years ago. You might not think backpack styles change over time, but this one could qualify as an antique. It might as well be made of wood. It's a faded black canvas model with a wild orange design on it. Also, to assist the chronologically challenged, it has the date written right on the front to easily identify the vintage: 1989.

We held on to the pack as a storage place for dog toys, but our dog went to "live on a farm" a couple of years ago. Perhaps we're keeping it in the event she somehow gets reincarnated, finds her way back to our neighborhood, and wants to play fetch. So it hangs on a hook in the garage, strewn among a number of bags and baubles we infrequently use yet somehow find it necessary to retain.

This is how we learn that "owning what you have" often means "using what you have," so Gabby empties the bag and throws it in the washing machine. Once dried, it looks pretty good, save for the obnoxious design. I stuff it full of Jake's school gear and lay it in the hallway for him to find the next morning.

After getting ready for school, it's time to leave the house.

"Time to go, kids! Grab your backpacks!" I command.

Jake sees the clean, black replacement lying where his former bag used to reside.

"What's this?" he asks.

"It's your new backpack, Son."

"But I didn't pick it."

"I know. Mom did."

After twenty questions about the coolness of the pack and a debate over the definition of the word *new*, he loses interest in arguing the point and changes the subject, heading off to school with the new pack on his shoulders. I wonder if any of his friends will notice. *Of course they will notice*, I think. Sure, it's no purple suitcase, but most of the kids have Spiderman backpacks or something similar, and our son is sporting a retro pack from when George Bush Sr. was inaugurated. I pray no one makes fun of him when we drop him off at school.

Later in the week, things get even more challenging during the March Madness basketball tournament. No, we're not talking about the one that generates squillions of dollars of revenue and makes Vegas odds-makers giddy. We're talking about the no-holds-barred basketball slug-fest at Montessori Academy in

Nashville. The one pitting first grader against first grader to establish worldwide bragging rights for generations to come. NBA scouts in attendance. Corporate sponsorship deals going down in the hallways. Or so you might think if you saw me yelling like an idiot in the stands and going absolutely overboard during a six-year-old's basketball game.

As a fun way to celebrate the end-of-season tournament, the other kids' parents purchase some really cool red, Air Jordan socks for their players. Normally, we would reluctantly buy a pair for Jake. But the socks aren't protecting our child's reproductive future like the cup for the upcoming baseball season.

Gabby and I struggle with the decision. We don't want him to feel left out. It's hard being a kid sometimes. But the socks aren't part of the standard uniform. And they cost thirteen dollars. You read that right. Thirteen dollars! For socks!

So Jake becomes the only kid on the team without cool socks.

Please understand that we know how silly it is to wring our hands over these miniscule issues. Literally billions of people across the globe would gladly trade our dilemma of "socks or no socks" over the "food or no food" reality they face on a daily basis. It's almost not even worth mentioning. At the same time, we know that we are not the only ones who carry some heavy guilt over these decisions.

I ask myself, "Is this cruel? Have we gone overboard?" I don't respond to either question because I'm not sure I want to know the answer. We've all lived through childhood and know how cruel kids can be. We've all shed tears after taunts. We were left feeling inadequate. We didn't have the latest shoes or the latest style. We looked different. Acted different. Laughed different.

And it sucked big time.

But sometimes owning what you *have* also means owning what you *don't have*.

When we tell others about our decision not to make the sock purchase, some are very upset. One woman in particular says that, in the age of bullying, to deny our children and intentionally set them apart as "different" puts them in a position to be the butt of jokes. She says we are being irresponsible. And maybe she's right.

Even the U.S. government's "Stop Bullying" website lists social isolation as a risk factor for bullying.[1]

So the question we're wrestling with is this: If we have the ability to buy a few things and protect our kids from heartache and choose not to, are we the one doing the scarring?

Ultimately, I believe the answer is no.

Maybe this is only justifying our choice, much as we justified letting the kids buy a book, but I believe using purchasing power to protect our kids from disappointment only helps to perpetuate the idea that *what you own* is *who you are*. We cover our kids up with so much shiny junk that it's virtually impossible to see the person inside. And we drown out the God-voice inside each and every one of them. The voice that says you're uniquely and beautifully made.

When we "protect" kids in this way, we are actually depriving them of disappointment. Disappointment that forges faith in something bigger than today. Bigger than the present or the presents. A resolve that bubbles up from deep within, making us stronger day-by-challenging-day.

I am taken back to a time in junior high when all the kids were getting those cool, new, puffy Reebok high-top sneakers with Velcro at the top. I wanted a pair of those shoes like I wanted oxygen in my lungs. But my family simply couldn't afford them. At least that's what they told me. So my mom bought some knock-off Fast-Baks. They were not what I wanted, and they definitely fell far short of "awesome."

Still, I wore them to school.

But not before I wrote "Reebok" on a piece of paper, cut out the makeshift label, and taped it gaudily to the side of my sneakers.

And I owned them.

I showed them to everybody, saying, "I got these new Reeboks yesterday, but something seems a bit weird about them? Can you help me figure out what's wrong with 'em?" And no one cared. It didn't matter.

And you know what?

When we ask Jake about his day at school with the new backpack, he tells us his friend Yusef said his backpack looked like a "leprechaun bag," due to a strange, clover-like symbol in the 1980s graphic, but Yusef played with him anyway. And by the time the next basketball game rolled around, stubborn stains, stinky kids, and laundry schedules had all the other players in mismatched pairs once again. And our son never said a word about it.

Because that's how it is with kids. Often they are blissfully blind to the social land mines in their midst, and we parents are the ones who make mountains out of molehills, shepherding them through the dos and don'ts of living in the world—*and* of it.

At the same time, there are situations where our children may face teasing and taunts that can bruise their fragile egos. And it is heartbreaking. In these moments, we can try to protect them by purchasing the armor of name-brand clothing or the latest gadgets. Or, we can leave them to fight the battle with only their character and intuition. In most cases, I believe we should opt for the latter.

I realize that we may be rationalizing away the guilt of watching our kids struggle, forcing them to adopt a mind-set of simpler living, but maybe . . .

Just maybe . . .

What we're doing is taking their lives out of our own hands and placing them in God's.

Back where they belong.

Part Three

Growing in Faith Together

Before we can grow together, we need to be together.
It's all about connecting.

Chapter Seventeen

Yoga Pants and Jock Straps

The reward for humility and fear of the LORD
is riches and honor and life.
(Proverbs 22:4)

We hoped the backpack and basketball socks ordeal would end our angst about not buying anything for our kids, but that was just wishful thinking. The reality is that when two of the four people in your household are tiny, the purchase opportunities grow exponentially. It starts when they are babies and never seems to let up. When a kid is first born, there's a multitude of items you can purchase for convenience and safety. Think of the strollers, bouncy seats, high chairs, diaper bags, swaddle blankets, nose suckers, pack-and-plays, crib sheets, and sleep swings.

As kids age, the demands just get bigger, starting as early as grade school. I take some comfort in knowing that this is not just a modern-day problem. My parents tell me that they dealt with the same issues we do, as did my grandparents and their parents before them, all the way back to the prehistoric parents. Rumor has it that when Grug, the prepubescent cave dweller, asked for the latest custom-made loincloth all the cool kids were wearing, his parents were the ones to coin the phrase, "If all your friends jumped off a cliff, would you go too!?"

We made it through the backpack and sock debacle, but temptation doesn't take vacations. We took the kids to the YMCA pool for a much-needed energy burn, and while we were there, Audrey asked if she could swim in the "big pool."

Gabby answered, "You have to pass a swim test to be in the big pool."

"Can I take the swim test?"

Not seeing any harm, Gabby gives her the green light. "Sure honey. Knock yourself out."

The next thing we know, Audrey runs to the lifeguard to announce her intentions. She jumps into the water and swims a nearly flawless length of the pool. And the judge is generous.

"She passed. Congratulations! Now let me go get your wrist band."

While the lifeguard retrieves the ceremonial band, Gabby leans in close and says, "You know what this means, don't you?"

"Yeah. She can swim on her own. That's pretty cool." I am looking forward to a little less stress at the pool.

"No. Not that. Now we have to buy her some swim fins."

"What?"

"Yeah. Swim fins. And a mask. We bought some for Jake last year when he passed the test, and I told her she could get some when she passed *her* swim test. We have to be fair. We can't play favorites with our kids."

Gabby makes a solid point, but I'm not sure this is a done deal. I ask, "Do you think she'll even remember?"

No sooner had I spoken the words than Audrey approaches with her wristband in place and asks, "So can I get my swim fins now?"

Three dollars and a mountain of guilt later, Audrey has some new swim fins and a mask. No loopholes this time. It's our first official fail.

The emotionally draining exercise of raising children is simply a fact of life. There will always be the debate about what constitutes a *necessity*. The only thing that changes is that scientists and safety experts sometimes add new items to the list of *Stuff Kids Need* as they figure out what helps keep our tiny people alive—such as ergonomic car seats, hypo-allergenic crib sheets, and padded rooms.

I don't mean to alarm you, but today the U.S. Department of Agriculture estimates that it costs $241,080 to raise a child to the age of eighteen when you factor in housing, food, transportation, clothing, health care, day care, education, and toys.[1] It's a scary thought. Incidentally, this does not include the expense of college, which could cost more than a quarter of a million bucks. Unless you're raising a superstar athlete or Mensa whiz kid.

To be fair, these figures aren't equal across the country. It costs a lot more to raise a child in the urban northeast ($446,100) than it does in the rural Midwest ($143,160). Even so, it's enough to want to make you cry "uncle." As in, "Uncle Rick, can you please loan me your truck? We're packing up and moving to Evansville, Indiana."

Prior to this year, Gabby and I had seriously considered whether or not we wanted more kids. Initially, Gabby was hesitant, and I was the one pushing for a bigger family. However, after seeing the financial realities and considering our own levels of patience (or lack thereof), I backed off too. I reasoned that if God believed we should have more children, then he would have given us a sign, such as sprouting several extra arms from our bodies in the middle of the night and/or dropping an orphanage on the front lawn. (Note to readers: Please don't drop an orphanage on our front lawn. We don't have enough arms.)

To demonstrate my commitment to our decision, I slipped a note in Gabby's stocking this past Christmas. It promised that I would take the necessary steps to ensure we wouldn't have any more kids unless a stork dropped one on our doorstep. I know giving gifts is supposed to make you feel all warm and toasty inside, but in this case I felt queasy, like I just ate a funnel cake and then rode the Tilt-A-Whirl for an hour. In contrast, Gabby reacted as if she had been given her own pony when she learned that Santa's elves would be performing minor outpatient surgery on her husband.

It's the gift that keeps on giving.

Now the leaves are sprouting on springtime trees and the gift still hasn't materialized. Something about my fear of needles. And pain. And doctors. I secretly hoped Gabby would forget about it, but the year without stuff brought it all back to the top of her mind, what with the cost of kids and all. When you spend your days reminding yourselves about big promises, others float back to the surface.

My wife corners me this morning, her voice filled with tenacity, "Honey. Speaking of purchases, when do I get my Christmas gift?"

"Christmas is over," I bark.

"I know. But you promised me you would go see the doctor. To get your . . ."; she looks downward near my waistline and makes a *snip-snip* motion with her fingers, adding a sound effect for good measure.

I wince, "But that's a purchase, right?"

"I would call it an experience," she corrects. "And a gift to me. Perfectly acceptable. Besides, we have insurance to cover it."

A few days later, I go to the clinic to discuss "slashing our costs." I sit in the waiting room with a lot of other very nervous-looking guys. There's no small talk. And no eye contact. We just sit there, reading old issues of *Us Weekly*. The music in the office is soothing. Like you might hear in an elevator. Only instead of gently lowering you to the lobby, this elevator ride ends with a vicious blow to your manhood.

After a painfully long four-minute wait, I am ushered into an exam room where a nurse asks me a bunch of questions. As I finish my responses, the doctor comes in to tell me about the procedure. He has a very laid-back, calming demeanor, which I appreciate since I don't want a Dr. Shakes McJitterstein getting anywhere near my bits and pieces.

He hands me a brochure that looks like something you might pick up in an Orlando hotel lobby *circa* 1981. If the pictures on the cover are any indication, I will emerge from the surgery with a smile on my face, blonde flowing locks, and an out-of-style cardigan draped over my shoulders. Luckily, the brochure covers all the details of the procedure and recovery. I am happy to have this resource to remind me of the details of post-surgical care, considering that my panic has rendered my short-term memory useless.

The doctor explains that the "budget cuts" I am about to receive should be considered permanent. As he dispenses his sternly worded warning, he gestures to the document in front of me. On the page is a list of bullet points on ways I can make this whole ordeal easier. Namely, I should "shave expenses to the bare minimum." In addition, the packet suggests I purchase a couple of bags of frozen peas to help "cool down the market" after experiencing volatility. This is welcome news, since buying frozen vegetables is permissible according to our rules.

Finally, the doctor recommends I wear some very snug underwear for five days following the surgery to make sure to keep "tight controls" over my assets and prevent discomfort. After a quick review of my inventory of unmentionables, I realize that I don't have any such item.

Uh oh.

I have sworn off buying any clothing this year. And I have plenty of underwear. Just not anything really tight. I consider creating a loophole and calling it a medical expense, but I imagine that men have likely endured this surgery and lived to tell the tale without assistance from such garments before. When I also factor in the potential discomfort we caused our son by making him live with different socks and a disintegrating backpack, I feel it is time to make a sacrifice of my own.

When I get home, I tell Gabby all about the details of the procedure, complete with a diagram that would make any fifth-grade sex education teacher proud. Looking for sympathy, I also mention my lack of proper undergarments.

"How about my yoga pants?" she asks, smiling.

"Yoga pants?"

"That's right. I have a pair that are a little baggy on me. You could try them. They would be plenty tight enough on you."

A purple suitcase is one thing. Yoga pants is something entirely different. I appreciate my wife having my best interests at heart, but skin-tight pants have never been a good look for me. In fact, I think there is a U.N. sanction stating that Mick Jagger is the only man on the planet allowed to wear such a thing. But this is a medical emergency.

"OK. Hand 'em over."

Gabby reaches into the armoire and hands me a pair of pants that look like they are made for a five-year-old Hell's Angels groupie. I struggle to get one leg in. Halfway into the process I am begging for some axle grease. After five minutes, my lower half is fully ensnared in its nylon prison. I am bound up so tightly that if I were to accidentally bump into the corner of the dresser, the pants would split like a can of Pillsbury biscuit dough, revealing my right buttock to the masses.

Gabby is doing her best not to laugh. I look behind me to see my reflection in the mirror and do a double take. From this angle, I look quite attractive. However, when I turn to face the mirror, it's evident that this is not going to set any new fashion trends. I look much better leaving than I do approaching. What's more, the pants are very hot. Not *hot* as in, "Wow he's so attractive!' But *hot* as in "Yikes! I'm steaming my vegetables here!"

It's a definite no on the yoga pants.

Gabby is quite amused and can't help but share the joy. She happily relays the details of my doctor visit to her sister, Kerri. I hear her giggling over the phone. I appreciate their closeness as siblings, but this may be taking it a bit too far.

How little did I know.

One week before the procedure, a box arrives via standard post. Unbeknownst to me, Kerri has compiled a care package to celebrate my upcoming "austerity measures." It is filled with items I would never buy for myself whether or not we had made the "no new stuff" vow. Browsing the contents of the package, I am a bit embarrassed to realize that my sister-in-law has been spending a lot of time considering my nether regions, which Gabby finds hysterical.

At the bottom of the box I find a paper bag. When I open it, I see a slightly used athletic supporter inside with a note that reads, "Love, Owen."

"P.S. It's washed."

It's not every day you receive another man's underwear as a gift. It's a confusing experience to say the least. Here I am, holding perhaps the most practical gift I have ever received from my brother-in-law, yet questioning whether or not I'll use it. However, one thing is certain. I will definitely have to compile a custom-made thank-you note for the occasion, and not just because we aren't buying anything this year. Hallmark doesn't have a big selection of "Thanks Brother-In-Law for Sending Me Your Used Jock Strap" cards.

A couple of weeks later, I survive the procedure. Gabby drives me to the appointment and brings me home, where she has a bag of frozen peas lovingly prepared for me. I lay on the couch and surf channels for the better part of the morning. The discomfort from the procedure is far less than the discomfort of watching daytime TV. I think to myself, *this isn't so bad.*

Then I stand up to go to the bathroom.

By that point, the valium has worn off, and I have all my faculties. It feels like the urologist sewed a kangaroo pouch onto my groin and stuffed a bowling ball inside. And now, I would like some help carrying said bowling ball.

I stumble over to the care package. I stare at the jock strap and consider my predicament. A prideful man would carry his bowling ball alone. A humble man would seek the "support" of family.

Literally.

Funny enough, looking at this athletic supporter reminds me of the whole reason we are attempting the year without a purchase in the first place. It's not only about stuff. It's about how that stuff gets in the way of building relationships with people.

And now it's time to truly connect.

Reluctantly.

Even though the underwear is washed, it still feels a bit odd to wear someone else's skivvies, so I decide to put them on over my boxer briefs. Obviously my mind is not firing on all cylinders, but my purchase-deprived, post-op brain believes this should somehow help me avoid any awkwardness the next time I see my brother-in-law. As if that were still possible at this point.

In hindsight, it's a perfect metaphor for how we are constantly putting up artificial barriers between ourselves and others. I can honestly say I have never felt more connected to my brother-in-law Owen than in the moment I put on his underwear. And it's not just because our nether regions have shared the same cotton. No, there's something intangible about this pride-swallowing endeavor. Dare I say, something *beautiful.* And it's something I want to understand more deeply.

Chapter Eighteen

Naked in the Flat

> *Do not store up for yourselves treasures on earth, where moths and vermin destroy, and where thieves break in and steal. But store up for yourselves treasures in heaven, where moths and vermin do not destroy, and where thieves do not break in and steal. For where your treasure is, there your heart will be also.*
> *(Matthew 6:19–21 NIV)*

The understanding I crave comes soon enough. Not long after my procedure, Owen sends me something else. This time it's an email with a link to a video snippet from the documentary film, *Naked in the Flat* about a guy in Finland.[1] Owen's message simply said, "Kick it up a notch."

As if borrowing his jock strap wasn't "kicking it up" enough?

Curious, I click on the link and watch the four-minute clip. It tells the story of a documentary filmmaker named Petri Luukainen who, after a tough breakup with a long-term girlfriend, becomes a bit disenchanted with life, its superficiality, and his own obsession with stuff.

This all sounds very familiar to me. All except the girlfriend part.

In response, Luukainen decides to put all his possessions, including clothing, in a storage unit and retrieve only one item per day. The thought is that through this process he will learn what his true "needs" are, and what are simply his "wants." He starts the project during the middle of winter.

In Finland.

Not surprisingly, the first item he grabs from the storage unit is his coat. Apparently there is a lot you can do with a coat when you have absolutely nothing else. Besides helping you look creepy and enticing police officers to write you a ticket for indecent exposure, it can be a blanket, a curtain, or a pillow.

After the coat comes shoes. Then a blanket. Then a pair of jeans. As I watch, I notice Gabby looking over my shoulder, no doubt attracted by the image of a naked man's keester on my computer monitor. Luukainen describes his transformation, and I become ever more intrigued with the concept. While our year seemed like a radical idea at the start of the experiment, we have simply grown into a new normal. But Luukainen's idea would be a complete realignment of our lives. So I turn toward my wife and say, "Maybe we should do this?"

"Do what?" she asks, wanting me to clarify my pronoun.

"This!" I said, gesturing toward the screen. "Put every last thing in storage. Every. Thing."

I see her consider my suggestion for a brief moment before emphatically stating, "Naked? You do realize your skin tone is . . ."

She hesitates.

"Yes, Gabby?"

"It's . . . um . . . reflective. Might not be the best look for you."

She's right. And I suppose we should all breathe a sigh of relief. Otherwise the first item our family would retrieve from storage would be sunglasses to cut the glare from my body. Gabby and I continue watching the video to see the outcome of the experiment. What would this guy learn by starting off naked and adding to his collection of stuff one item at a time?

We discover that one of Luukainen's biggest takeaways is the idea that you don't own your stuff—your stuff owns you. After a few months and bringing roughly a hundred items back into his flat, he reaches that critical point where he doesn't really need anything else to comfortably survive—the tipping point where the value that a thing brings to your life is less than the effort required to maintain that thing.

For example, when Luukainen compares the effort required to bike around the city versus the effort required to own a car (earning money to pay it off, fill it with gas, purchase insurance, find parking, plus the time and effort required to maintain it and fix it when it breaks), it's no contest.

Strap on a helmet and get pedaling.

When I look at our own lives, I can relate. Stuff can put a lot of weight on your back, both literally and figuratively. Just peek inside our house for a glimpse at the *literal* part of the equation.

It's a well-known fact that the size of toys in a house is inversely proportionate to the size of the children inside that house. One look at our garage would make you think it's a breeding ground for giant plastic toys. A ten-year research project conducted by UCLA anthropologists studied thirty-two middle-class families in southern California for ten years. Of the families surveyed, three in four were unable to use their garages for parking cars due to excess stuff stored therein.[2] It's as if the Big Wheel is mating with the Little Tikes Kitchen during the cold winter months, producing a litter of wagons, portable slides, and Hippity-Hops by springtime. And in our case, very few of these things were actually purchased by us. Most are simply hand-me-downs from other parents who once had five kids but could only find three of them on a regular basis because the two weak ones were lost under a mound of colorful junk most of the year.

Don't get me wrong. We are thankful for both the means to purchase such a boatload of toys and grateful to generous friends and family for showering gifts on us. But this blessing can become a burden. And we're not just talking about toys now. Or even just families with kids.

It's all of us.

It starts innocently enough. We add to our collections piece-by-piece, not noticing how the things are encroaching on the livability of our lives. For instance, when those of us with small homes don't have the space to store our stuff, we wind up piling it in the garage behind an invisible line that designates the boundary between "storage area" and "space for the car."

But when we want to use our stuff, we have to move the car, along with the other boxes of stuff that are inevitably in front of the stuff we want to use. This takes up a lot of time and space. The tipping point occurs when the time and effort required to access the stuff becomes greater than the value the stuff provides. Then the worry begins. We start to second-guess ourselves.

And our worth.

I'm so disorganized! We really need to get a handle on all this stuff! Do we need more shelves? Cabinets? When can we set aside time to organize all of this? Do we need a three-car garage? More storage? Is our house big enough? Can we take on a bigger mortgage? How about an extra job to bring in more money?

Pretty soon that extra Cozy Coupe in the garage has us taking on a second job and tripling our stress. We literally cannot contain it all. The Self Storage Association (SSA) is a trade group for those who own and operate storage buildings. Their website states that public storage is the "fastest growing segment of the commercial real estate industry over the last forty years and has been considered by Wall Street analysts to be 'recession resistant' based on its performance since the economic recession of September, 2008."[3] Apparently, no matter our financial situation, we're still overwhelmed by stuff.

The SSA's website is a treasure trove of facts on excess. Roughly *one in ten* families is currently utilizing a storage unit. And 65 percent of those who have a storage unit also have a garage at home. There are so many storage units in the United States that the SSA estimates there is enough space (2.3 billion square feet) to accommodate every man, woman, and child in America with seven square feet to call their own. The problem is, we couldn't live there, since 87.4 percent of that space is already filled with boxes.

All this stuff creates a burden for us. And it's not only a physical burden but psychological as well. We live under the misconception that all this stuff will make us happier. It's a big, fat lie. One that Dan Gilbert, our favorite Harvard psychologist, believes is hard-wired into us.

Gilbert's research into happiness shows that human beings are notoriously bad at predicting what will make them happy. For example, many of us would likely believe that an exceedingly positive event, such as winning the lottery, would lead to huge gains in happiness, while an exceedingly negative event, such as becoming a paraplegic, would cause a huge drop in well-being. In truth, after several months, the lottery winners are only marginally happier than accident victims and no happier than a control group of everyday people like you and me (assuming your scratch-off ticket is a dud).[4]

Gilbert shares in a *New York Times* interview that the biggest predictor of happiness is our human relationships and how much time we spend with the special people in our lives. He says, "We know that it's significantly more important than money and somewhat more important than health. That's what the data shows. The interesting thing is that people will sacrifice social relationships to get other things that won't make them as happy—money."[5]

This brings us to the second thing that our naked friend in the flat discovered when he got rid of all his stuff. In an interview, Luukainen reflects in somewhat broken English: "When I look back at my year of experiment, the more I remember the things that I did with my friends than I remember what specific item I got." He remembers how his buddies helped him prepare meals when he had nothing. He remembers his brother coming over to wake him up every morning when he had no clock. Even the simple things, such as doing laundry with friends. These are the things that stuck with him.[6]

Simple moments shared with special people.

Looking over the past few months, we see how our priorities have shifted. And it wasn't necessarily intentional. People ask us what we have done with the money we have saved, and honestly, some of it has been used selfishly to connect with those we love. We have attended out-of-town funerals, reunions, and a one-hundred-year-old's birthday party we may not otherwise have had the opportunity to experience. We have visited friends who moved thousands of miles away. Officiated and photographed weddings. Laughed and cried with old friends from college whom we haven't hugged in years. Sharing old memories and making new ones.

While we can't say for sure that this wouldn't have happened had we still been shopping, we *can* say we would never have had the means to do it all. And in this day of email, text, and social media posts, every human being knows a face-to-face presence is the greatest gift of all. This rekindled connectedness to family and friends has made us feel lighter. Both in a *figurative* sense with a decrease in stress and a *literal* sense with my finally overcoming my propensity to use ice cream as a replacement for the retail therapy high.

This joy is not limited just to sharing time with those closest to us. We tend to think of what we are missing when we don't have something, but forget what we gain. As Luukainen observed, an unexpected blessing was allowing others to help him. In our own quest for independence and autonomy, I can now see how we had lost our sense of community.

In the past several months, our local network, like Luukainen's, has blossomed. A church member approached us with a backpack when she learned Jake's had broken. Parents of a boy on Jake's baseball team loaned us a bike rack for an out-of-town trip. Others are offering suitcases and lunch boxes and shoes. My buddy, Matt, is getting married soon, and Gabby's friend, Mari, is loaning her a fancy dress for the occasion. All these are such kind gestures. And they benefit both the giver and the receiver. Because, as Gilbert notes, another major factor in any measure of happiness is altruism—how much we give.[7] And in this case, the givers all know that their stuff would have sat on a shelf unused, like an old jock strap. But instead they are put to use to fulfill a need.

And the sad thing is, we often fight this generosity.

Our country was founded on its bootstrapping principles. A person needs only determination and wit to succeed. This mentality has made this country great. We are the wealthiest nation on the earth. But we've lost something in the process.

Patricia Greenfield, a doctor of psychology at UCLA, recently completed a fascinating study. Using Google Books NGram

Viewer technology, she was able to search the text of 1.5 million books dating back to 1800. What she found was interesting. The use of the word *give* decreased significantly between 1800 and 2000. Conversely, the use of the word *get* increased significantly between 1800 and 2000. The only time the word *get* declined in usage was around the time World War II began in the early 1940s, before creeping up again beginning in the 1970s.[8]

In our quest for individual gain, giving becomes less of a focus. And I don't believe it is because we are inherently selfish. I honestly believe this individualistic nature breeds people who are afraid of receiving help, because it requires admitting you cannot do it all by yourself. Feeling vulnerable.

Feeling naked.

But God made us to be in community. We need one another. We can't do it alone. It reminds me of a passage from Ecclesiastes:

> *Again, I saw vanity under the sun: the case of solitary individuals, without sons or brothers; yet there is no end to all their toil, and their eyes are never satisfied with riches. "For whom am I toiling," they ask, "and depriving myself of pleasure?" This also is vanity and an unhappy business.*
>
> *Two are better than one, because they have a good reward for their toil. For if they fall, one will lift up the other; but woe to one who is alone and falls and does not have another to help. Again, if two lie together, they keep warm; but how can one keep warm alone? And though one might prevail against another, two will withstand one. A threefold cord is not quickly broken. (Ecclesiastes 4:7–12)*

There are times when we need to lean on friends, family, or the kindness of a stranger. The one who was created in the image of God. Because sharing comes from the image of God that is buried deep within each one of us, that unselfish love that springs forth at the expense of ourselves. It's a beautiful thing. And it's something we've been missing without even realizing it.

It's certain we could "kick it up a notch" as Owen humorously suggested when sending us the video. We could dump everything and live naked in the suburbs. And we would surely learn a lot of lessons about faith, materialism, and the importance of liberal application of sunscreen. But in many ways, we are already seeing some of the same benefits with less-than-radical strategies. Our village is coming to life. And so are we.

Chapter Nineteen

The Purge

But since you excel in everything—in faith, in speech, in knowledge, in complete earnestness and in the love we have kindled in you—see that you also excel in this grace of giving.
(2 Corinthians 8:7 NIV)

If you are lucky enough to live in a place where seasons change, you can tell what time of year it is by looking at the trees. Light green buds signal spring. Canopies drenched in the color of an Irish meadow tell you that you are in the midst of summer. Brightly colored leaves falling to the ground and being kicked into the air by passing cars are an indicator that fall is upon us. And barren branches signal the dead of winter.

But there is another season that doesn't necessarily correspond to weather patterns and deciduous tree cycles. No, this season is marked by watching my wife buzz about the house with random bundles of stuff in her arms and a Sharpie marker tucked in her shirt collar. The stuff is destined for an organized pile somewhere. The Sharpie is used to label the stuff.

That's right—it's yard sale season.

This time, the event is not our usual neighborhood garage sale. Instead, our church has decided to host a community yard sale to benefit Alzheimer's research, and Gabby is excited to participate, not only because her father battled the disease for years but also because she loves any excuse to de-clutter. It's the perfect way for her to feel a sense of contribution while cleaning out our junk, and she is perfectly giddy.

I corner her as she is sifting through her closet, a roll of masking tape dressing her wrist like a bracelet. She tears off a piece and writes "$1" on it and attaches it to one of her old shirts.

"What are we doing today?" I ask.

"We're de-cluttering," she says matter-of-factly. "It's a great excuse to get rid of excess stuff and simplify. Isn't it fun?!"

My wife and I have very different ideas of what constitutes fun. When Gabby de-clutters, it inevitably turns into much more. The last time she mentioned clearing a few unnecessary items out of the garage, I found myself spending an entire day rearranging shelves, emptying every cabinet, and sweeping every nook and cranny in the place.

You know, having fun.

This time, in an attempt to avoid the inevitable, I tell her I will tackle my man-space in the garage while she deals with the closet. She agrees the "divide and conquer" tactic is a logical approach and blesses my decision. I hurry off to thin out our collection of tools and outdoor toys before she can come and lay eyes on our painting supplies and decide today would also be a good day to "freshen up" the eaves on the house. And the garage door. And the living room.

In a span of about forty-five minutes, I make a small-but-significant dent in our garage clutter. We have lived in this house for only five years, but I am still surprised at how much excess junk we have accumulated. While we can park a car in our garage, we are one lawn tool away from becoming one of the families in the UCLA research project.

Some of the stuff in my newly created donation pile is made up of things we purchased. Others are hand-me-down toys for the kids that are no longer age-appropriate. But a large portion are items we have boxed up and moved from house to house but still haven't used for the past decade or more.

I set aside well over two dozen things to give away. Basking in the glow of accomplishment, I continue helping Gabby by retiring to the couch to watch a rerun of *Deadliest Catch*.

I can hear my wife in Audrey's bedroom now. She and my daughter are sifting through the massive collection of stuffed animals Audrey has accumulated over the years. I wander over to the bedroom and listen to the debate. To demonstrate the outrageous supply of stuffed animals, Gabby has dumped the giant basket on top of Audrey and covered her in an array of unicorns and teddy bears in every color of the rainbow. My five-year-old is giggling and rolling around in the soft mountain, thoroughly enjoying herself.

The two eventually get down to business when I enter the room. Gabby tells Audrey she should consider which of the animals she wants to keep and which of the animals she would like to give away to another child who may not have as much to play with as she does. There are nearly a hundred stuffed animals in the pile, and Audrey quickly pulls out a half-dozen to give away. I notice she selects those that were freebie giveaways from a birthday party or old tattered animals she inherited from a cousin.

That was the easy part.

Still surrounded by a mountain of animals covered in synthetic fabrics and love, my wife encourages Audrey to consider how much she plays with each of them and suggests that perhaps those she hasn't played with for a long time, like the ones from the bottom of the huge basket, could be the ones she considers giving away. As soon as the words exit Gabby's mouth, Audrey's face contorts into a mixed bag of worry and sadness. Even if she hasn't seen some of these stuffed animals in months, or even years, you can tell that she feels connected to them somehow. They hold memories of good times that have come and gone.

My wife grabs two of the animals. One is a blue teddy bear she picked up on a trip with my mom to a thrift store. The other is a strange, neon-striped hybrid squirrel/koala/lemur that was likely obtained from a retention pond at a toxic waste dump. Neither of them receive frequent invitations to Audrey's popular tea parties or find themselves in situations of peril under the wheels of Jake's monster trucks.

Gabby asks, "So what do you think, Audrey?"

She stares at both of the animals, considering each of them like they are her own children. It's *Sophie's Choice* meets *Toy Story*. My wife offers another question to cut through the tension hanging in the air, speaking softly with great compassion.

"They were fun to play with a long time ago, but don't you think someone else may be able to give them a lot of love? Think of how happy some other little girl would be to get that teddy bear or that . . . um . . . other thing."

At this, my daughter's demeanor shifts. There is a visible change in the expression on her face as she considers her toys being loved by someone else. And loved well. Surprisingly, she takes both of the animals and tosses them into the giveaway pile, soon afterward turning back to her collection and selecting many more. By the end of the exercise, there are probably twenty-five stuffed animals she has chosen to part with, some of them previously treasured friends. There are even some Gabby and I want to take back because *we* are attached.

Remember how cute she was with Elmer the Elephant? Remember how much she loved Curious George?

All our gushing assumes these memories won't exist in the absence of the toy itself. How is it that we adults are the irrational ones? It's just silly. So we bury our nostalgia and allow Audrey her altruism. Our daughter is beaming, so we leave her to her work.

As I suspected, our "fun" is not yet over. Gabby invites me to come with her to the kitchen to help her purge our cabinets. We find a funnel cake maker in an unopened box. We're both hungry by this time, so she asks me if we should use it.

"Sure! The kids would have fun making 'em! I hope we have all the ingredients."

So she opens the package and says, "I think we're OK. There's a bag of funnel cake mix in the box!"

Upon closer examination, she discovers that the mix expired sometime early in George W. Bush's second administration.

Obviously, if we haven't used this specialty item in the past 10 years, we can put it on the donation pile.

Buh-bye.

Using this same mind-set, we quickly rid ourselves of a bunch of coffee cups, hypothetically musing that if somebody could figure out a way to power automobiles with used pens, stuffed animals, and commemorative coffee mugs, we could solve the energy crisis. There seems to be a never-ending supply.

As we are laughing about our observation, Gabby circles back to a cabinet filled with our "fancy dishes" and asks,

"What about our china?"

I gasp.

"You mean our wedding china?"

I'm horrified. As if giving away our prized wedding gifts somehow indicates she has given up on our marriage.

A long debate ensues. And not because I have a china fetish. There are a lot of happy memories tied to our fancy dinnerware. But I soon realize none of those memories actually involve eating off those plates. We've been waiting for a special occasion. Unfortunately, the Queen of England still hasn't RSVP'd. So the china goes unused. Just like fancy napkin rings and the "good towels" hanging in the bathroom.

Waiting for a guest who will never come.

I think about our garage junk. And the stuffed animals *I* wanted Audrey to keep. And the china. All of this evidence points to one diagnosis.

I think I am a hoarder.

Not the kind you see on reality TV shows, living on piles of clothing and old pizza boxes. I mean the kind of hoarder who takes more than he needs. And it all stems from the fact that I'm asking all the wrong questions.

When sifting through the clothes in my closet, I ask, "When might I wear this again?" No matter the item, I can always think of a situation. I play the "what if" game to my own detriment.

Maybe save it for a Halloween party! Or painting a room. Or a visit to the White House.

When looking at dishes in our cabinet or knick-knacks on a shelf, I ask, "Should I keep this?" No matter the item, I can always think of a reason.

It was very expensive. It was a gift. It might come in handy someday.

So it all stays in my house, tucked away in a junk drawer. Until the next time I stumble across them and try and remember why I still have them. Worried that giving things away somehow leaves me vulnerable.

I'm not alone in this. Consider the disciples in the Bible story of the loaves and fishes.

The story begins with Jesus setting out across the Sea of Galilee with his favored crew. When he gets to shore, they are shocked to see that five thousand people have come to see him. It's like Christ-a-Palooza: Healfest 32. The problem is, no one called the caterer. So the disciples are worried about crowd control. They have five thousand soon-to-be-"hangry" folks who know how to use a rod and a staff.

They tell Jesus,

> *"This is a deserted place, and the hour is now very late; send them away so that they may go into the surrounding country and villages and buy something for themselves to eat." But he answered them, "You give them something to eat." They said to him, "Are we to go and buy two hundred denarii worth of bread, and give it to them to eat?"*

They sound a bit defensive, don't they? Like a bunch of kids who don't want to share their juice boxes with the multitude.

> *And he said to them, "How many loaves have you? Go and see." When they had found out, they said, "Five, and two fish." Then he ordered them to get all the people to sit down in groups on the green grass. So they sat down in groups of hundreds and of fifties. Taking the five loaves and the two fish, he looked up to heaven, and blessed and broke the loaves, and gave them to his disciples to set before the people; and he divided the two fish among them all. And all ate and were filled. (Mark 6:35–42)*

Here's where things get interesting.

In the movie version of this story, when Jesus looks up to heaven to give thanks, he holds the basket above his perfectly coiffed, highlighted head. When he brings it back down, it is miraculously filled to the brim with food. And this is the image I've had in my head for decades: Jesus multiplying what he was given.

But I think our math is wrong. It's not a multiplication problem. In every account of the story, Jesus broke.

Distributed.

Divided.

And there was more than enough.

We tend to think miracles are like magic. Like Siegfried and Roy making a tiger appear where there was none before. Unfortunately, I wasn't at the seashore that day, so I can't be certain. But when I think of this story in the context of my reluctance to give, I wonder if the miracle may have been less an act of Jesus himself and more an act of God moving within those present. Finding satisfaction in the simple. Finally learning the definition of enough. Realizing that the "least of these" are often made whole through the generosity of those who have the "most of that."

Miraculous, I know.

My prayer today is that I change my questions. The old method of asking "How might I use this?" and "Should I keep this?" encouraged my creative mind to think of reasons to hang on. But hanging on is not the goal. It's all about giving in. Trusting. Sharing. Distributing. Dividing. It's about asking, "What harm will come if I give this away?" and "Who needs this more?"

The answer?

Not much.

Not me.

And in parting with those things I once held so tightly, may I finally find myself satisfied.

Chapter Twenty

Good-Bye Nana Claus

Let all that you do be done in love.
(1 Corinthians 16:14)

As time passes, we feel a steady change coming over us. While the pull is still there, stuff has far less of a hold on us than it did before we started. For example, our email has been trimmed of temptation. Whereas the previous version of our inboxes looked like an out-of-control, multicolored Bozo the clown wig, with crazy ads spilling over every which way, they are now reduced to more of a mullet, with your first impression being clean and functional and only a few ne'er-do-wells creeping in the back door for a hedonistic romp through materialism.

The same is true of other media. When we bring in the mail from the mailbox, our routine is now to dump all incoming catalogs and discount offers straight into the recycle bin. I have found that limiting my exposure to extra stuff has reduced my feelings of irrational envy, where I would silently covet the goods owned by the fake families found in advertisements. The ones with children selected for their rare ability to remain still and cooperative, and spouses that look like mannequins come to life, with six-pack abs and gleaming teeth.

We rarely ever bought things out of catalogs, but they would subconsciously imprint us with an image of something we wanted, so when we were out of the house and found ourselves with a few minutes of free time, we might just pop into a store and look for a cheap knock-off of something we had seen a month ago in an air-brushed ad. But now we are spending far less time in and around stores. Some places we used to visit once every week or two we now treat like a toxic ex-girlfriend. Don't call her. Don't text her. Don't chat with any of her close friends. On the rare occasion we *do* bump into this jilted lover by accident, we don't make eye contact or acknowledge she exists. We simply put on the blinders, enter the store, grab whatever necessity we came for, and quickly exit, hoping she's intensely jealous now that she sees how much better off we are without her.

This feeling of freedom is evident both physically and emotionally. The seven pounds I added during the spring have now melted away. I am personally learning to manage the cravings for consumption and find a proper outlet. It turns out the endorphin rush of a half-hour on a treadmill has more lasting benefits than the pleasure rush of eating a half-gallon of Rocky Road followed by a couple of Eggo waffles.

While we feel the changes in ourselves, we are wondering if our experiment is changing anyone else. Take my mom, for instance, otherwise known as "Nana" to our kids.

Nana is an incredible force in our family. If you need a reference point, she was created in a grandma lab somewhere by crossing the DNA of Mary Poppins, Jack Black, Julia Child, and Desmond Tutu. The woman has this intense, magical energy infused with culinary genius and a heart of gold. It's no wonder that children, myself included, can't wait to spend time with her.

Today she comes to the door, and the kids rush her like a couple of puppies, jumping and screaming and almost peeing on the floor from the sheer excitement of it all.

"It's Nana!" they shout.

When Mom walks through the door, they both give her a big hug. Then they pull away and immediately ask,"What did you bring us?!"

My mother is taken aback. The question shaves a bit of the sheen off the excitement. She responds by saying, "I brought Nana! What more did you expect?"

To which the children reply, "You mean you didn't bring us anything from Noah's Closet?"

Nana's heart of gold makes her a regular volunteer. When I was growing up, she was always serving others. She worked at a school for homeless kids, visited the homebound, and hosted Thanksgiving dinners for the less fortunate. Today, she donates her time to the local elementary school as well as a charity called The Ark, which operates a thrift store called Noah's Closet. The shop helps generate funding for the charity. As a special treat, she regularly picks up random items from this thrift store and brings them to the kids and every other member of our sixteen-person family. Clothes. Toys. Games. They love it, and so does she. It's like Christmas all year-round, and she is Nana Claus.

But this time, Nana is empty-handed.

"Nothing this time!" she says. "Sorry kids!"

It was like someone opened a gaping hole in a bucket full of joy. Audrey and Jake instantly deflate. Meanwhile, Gabby and I are mortified. Here we are, trying to teach ourselves how to be less driven by material wants and hoping our kids are soaking it up. Instead, they are treating their beloved grandmother like a bedazzled ATM.

I feel sick to my stomach.

Gabby jumps in, "Hey guys. Nana isn't here to bring you gifts. She's here to take you to the zoo." Her reprimand continues down the hall, as she talks to the kids about proper etiquette as they leave to put their shoes on for their special adventure, which now looks more like a trip to the Spanking Store based on the looks on their faces.

Embarrassed, I turn to my mom and say, "Sorry about that."

Apparently this isn't the first time it's happened. Mom launches into an explanation, "The past few times they have come over to visit, one of the first questions they ask has been, 'did you get us any presents?' I just got tired of it, so I stopped buying stuff."

This is significant. My mom is like some sort of professional bargain shopper. One of my most vivid memories of childhood is hiding in the clothing racks while Mom browsed the clearance items at a discount store. Her trips were never extravagant. Mom has always been one to "own what she has." But she does like to shop, so for her to say that she is sick of my kids and this "entitlement mentality" leaves quite an impression.

I am thrilled with this little development. The allure of stuff is now top-of-mind for all of us, and if my mom is talking about buying the kids less stuff, they may actually see Nana in her purest form. The woman we moved across the country to be near. The woman who has vowed since the birth of her first grandchild to be a driving force in every single grandkid's life. Investing time and energy to showing them how much she loves them, offering herself in abundance.

The truth is, the value of experience is far greater than the value of any tangible gift. In an interview with *The Atlantic* magazine a couple of years ago, Harvard happiness expert Dan Gilbert, said, "We favor objects because we think that experiences can be fun but leave us with nothing to show for them. But that turns out to be a good thing. Experiences have the nice property of going away. Cars need repairs, they rust in our driveway, and they ultimately disappoint us enough that we sell them and get new ones. Experiences are like good relatives that stay for a while and then leave. Objects are like relatives who move in and stay past their welcome."[1]

Gilbert is on to something here. Think of your own life. You have probably lived through dozens, if not a hundred major holidays, including Christmas, your birthday, Valentine's Day, and Easter. In our culture, these events are often punctuated with the giving of gifts. Some of them are large significant purchases, such as a bike or a diamond ring, and others less so, like the time you received a velvet painting of dogs playing poker at the company white-elephant gift exchange. You have likely had hundreds of opportunities throughout your time on Earth to receive a material gift from another person.

How many can you remember?

Seriously. Try to remember what you got for Christmas last year. Or two years ago?

Can you?

When I think of my own life, I am hard-pressed to remember 5 or 10 percent of those gifts. I know I *liked* many of them, but I just can't seem to *remember* them. Some gifts that I do recall have become disconnected from the giver. I simply can't remember who it was that gave me this material item I enjoy.

At first, my failure to recall the kindness of others leaves me feeling terribly sad, as if it is a reflection on my own ungrateful character or, worse yet, a measure of how little I care about the person who gave the gift. But when I take a step back, the sharp edges of my worry soften a bit when I begin to remember the givers. Family members. Friends. Coworkers.

The names of these people don't bring to mind any presents they gave to me. Instead, their names conjure an image in my mind. I'm not sure if you're like me, but the first image is usually one of their smiling faces, which quickly transforms into the context of some experience we shared together. And if I dig deeper, the experiences that come to mind are usually those where we shared some strong emotion together—excitement, frustration, joy, or anxiety. And for these moments I am truly grateful. The vacations where we got lost, ran out of money, or nearly died. The summer camp experiences filled with warmth and love. Or the crazy pranks that were horribly inappropriate, yet no one got hurt.

These are the moments that define us and make us who we are. And these moments are the things that we truly value. Because deep down we know that relationships are what matter most in our lives. And if someone cares enough about us, they give the most precious gift of all. It is like a gift of gold.

Time.

We talk of spending time as if it were money in our pocket. We anguish over wasting it and never seem to have enough. We meticulously organize it as a child might obsess over a collection of stuffed animals. And when we are lucky enough to have *free* time—truly free—in those rare moments, it is like reaching into the coin return slot on a vending machine and pulling out a hundred dollar bill.

I'm not trying to say material gifts are bad. We have all experienced the feelings of gratitude when we receive a gift that the giver has taken time to create for us, or something we truly need, or gifts that demonstrate how well the giver knows us and listens to us. There is tremendous value in that.

At the same time, we often give material gifts more power than they actually have. We expect gifts to bring us together. To give us joy. To satisfy us.

We want the gifts to be God for us.

But they're not God.

They are just gifts, with the power to help and also the power to drive a wedge between us. Distracting us. Or creating confusion as to what is important. And this is what Nana experienced. Initially, our kids were disappointed she didn't bring them a gift that day. But their disappointment soon turned to joy when they came home several hours later.

We asked, "So kids, how was the zoo?"

Their response was like a cacophony of happiness, with each one talking over the other. Words poured forth in a flood of excitement, the volume increasing with every tale of birds landing on their shoulders, monkeys flinging poop, flamingos fighting. So many stories that I lost count.

But they didn't.

They talked about the experience long afterward. Because that's what experiences do. They live long after the ticket stubs are gone and the commemorative cup breaks. Leaving only a smile and a warm memory. Gifts of love.

Lightweight and priceless.

Chapter Twenty-One

Our Discipline Problem

No discipline seems pleasant at the time, but painful. Later on, however, it produces a harvest of righteousness and peace for those who have been trained by it.

(Hebrews 12:11 NIV)

Business trips provide a nice diversion for me. I am so busy working that I don't have any time to think about buying stuff. Besides, my suitcase is usually packed to the gills, so I wouldn't have room to carry anything home with me anyway. This week, however, brings a more significant challenge.

I'm headed to Riyadh, Saudi Arabia.

Visiting a foreign country always puts me on edge, especially when I travel to a place with a vastly different culture from my own. I'm never sure if I'm going to accidentally break a law. To be on the safe side, I always do a brief web search to brush up on the local customs and try and uncover any surprises before I actually set foot in the country.

In researching Riyadh, I learn that it is one of the most conservative cities in Saudi Arabia. Outside the embassy walls, there are no movie theaters, bars, or dance clubs. There is no alcohol to be found. Women and men are not allowed to accompany one another in public, unless married. There is almost no crime. The customs admission form even includes a graphic of a skull and crossbones declaring drug traffickers will be subject to the death penalty.

I'll keep my allergy medicine in the hotel just in case.

Most everything that a typical westerner might call "fun" has been wiped from the community like a muddy footprint, save for one thing: shopping malls.

While retail represents 7.9 percent of the entire Gross Domestic Product in the United States, in Saudi Arabia, it's 17 percent.[1] You can't throw a kebab without hitting a Bath & Body Works. I'm stereotyping here, but Saudis visit the mall so much it's as if the entire country were made up of thirteen-year-old suburban girls aching for a Froyo fix. I thought the United States was a consumer society, but I wonder how such constant exposure to commercialism might impact the culture in Saudi Arabia, perhaps even leading to an imbalanced focus on acquiring stuff.

On my first night in Riyadh, I visit the mall. The place is filled with window shoppers. Women out for a girl's night. Families with kids in strollers. Guys hanging out and chatting. I notice some familiar stores such as Victoria's Secret, which seems quite out of place to my untrained eye. But you quickly realize that the long, black *abaya* worn in public by every adult woman is simply covering up clothing that fashionable ladies are sporting the world over, and making sure all of Victoria's Secrets remain . . . well . . . secrets.

Around six o' clock, I am getting hungry, so I head to McDonald's for a McArabic (an actual menu item) and a Diet Coke. As I finish my last French fry, I hear an unfamiliar sound echoing through the marble-floored mall. A jarring tune that doesn't fit any melody I've ever heard.

It is the Muslim call to prayer being broadcast over the loudspeaker.

Most men disappear. Women gather in close-knit groups. Metal gates drop from the ceiling in front of every store. Every. Single. One. The Gap, H&M, and Banana Republic are all closed to the public. With nothing else to do, I wander over to a bench and pull out my two-day-old *USA Today*. I make it through the first paragraph of an article when I get the unsettling sensation I am being watched. I turn around to see a rather large mall security guard standing behind me.

"You cannot sit here," he quietly commands.

I panic, as I often do when surprised. I drop my newspaper as I try to fold it. My mind drifts to the skull and crossbones as I wonder if reading a colorful newspaper is against Saudi law.

"Oh, I'm sorry."

"Go to Starbucks." The man is intimidating, speaking in broken English.

"Starbucks?"

"Let me show you."

He walks me to the elevator, presses the button, and escorts me inside. We spend an uncomfortable half-minute riding to the second floor, neither of us making a sound. When the doors open, he curtly gestures toward the Starbucks, which is also shuttered during prayer.

"Go there."

I do as I am told, walking sheepishly to the coffee shop and standing in front of the closed gate like a frightened puppy, afraid to even glance at my newspaper. *Is Starbucks just a holding pen for unruly Americans?* I wonder. Others are walking around and window shopping, but noticing security cameras in the ceiling, I remain still. I don't want to see the guard again.

I take part in a healthy dose of people watching for the next fifteen minutes, but there aren't many people to watch. All commercialism stops. Then, little by little, the stores open again. A slow trickle of patrons begins moving about. I take this as my cue to move from my statuesque spot and breathe a heavy sigh of relief when no alarms start to scream.

International incident averted.

The next day in my class, I am chatting with one of my participants, a woman by the name of Latifah, a housing manager for the local hospital. She approaches me during a break.

"How are you enjoying your trip?"

"Very much," I reply.

"It's very different from the U.S., no?" Her face is covered by a head scarf, but I can see the smile in her eyes.

"Yes, it is." I answer. "Can I ask you a question, Latifah?"

"You just did."

Good one. We both laugh. Her humor is breaking through my stereotype of Saudi women as passive, demure creatures without a voice or personality. I continue, "I was in the mall last night during the evening prayer. I sat down on a bench to read my newspaper, but a security guard quickly approached and ushered me off to Starbucks. Is it illegal to read during prayer time?"

She pauses, then laughs out loud.

"No, Mr. Scott," she responds, her eyes smiling at the worry on my face. "As a form of respect toward women, it is customary to leave them a place to sit. Especially during prayer time when women are not required to participate."

The only law I had broken was being a jerk. Like stealing a subway seat from somebody's grandmother. The security guard was just trying to salvage what little chivalrous honor I had left.

I then ask Latifah to tell me more about the prayer times. I had adjusted my classroom schedule to allow for prayer breaks, but had no real idea why. I was amazed how everything stopped during that time. Not just shopping, but business itself.

She explains that there are five prayer times each day and each one holds a separate significance. Each is designed to create a disciplined approach to life. A regular focus on the divine and what is truly important.

Before sunrise. *Fajr*. Remembering God.

At noon. *Dhuhr*. Asking for guidance in your day.

Late afternoon. *Asr*. In the midst of daily stress. Pausing to remember God's greater meaning in our lives.

Before dusk. *Maghrib*. Thankfulness for a day well-lived.

After dusk. *Isha*. Remembering God's presence, mercy, and forgiveness.

This is revolutionary to me. To say that I am a disorganized person is a grave understatement. Day planners and schedules give me the willies. Anytime I successfully create and execute a to-do list for the day, it's like I am discovering fire. Yet I am instantly overtaken by this concept of discipline. I think it seems less confining to me because of the meaning behind it. This regular practice of prayer brings intentionality to life that is strangely attractive.

When I get home from the trip, I reflect on the impulsiveness of our lives. We tend to ride along on the current of culture, occasionally grasping at our values, like they were branches hanging out over the water, sometimes steady, sometimes slipping through our fingers, leaving the water to drag us down river. And I'm not just talking about my own family. A recent *Daily Mail* survey estimates that parents spend an average of 36 minutes together with their children each weekday.[2] While I think we are likely over this average, I'm not certain that our time together could be classified as "meaningful."

In our house, every morning seems like a no-holds-barred, irritable rush-fest to get the kids to school and start the work day. No matter how hard we try, nothing seems to calm our nerves or entice the kids to put their shoes on in the time it takes a glacier to melt. We have adapted by setting alarms earlier, developing a checklist of chores, and doing some of the lunch prep the night before. Heck, we even committed to pre-dawn exercise to get the happy endorphins flowing each morning before the kids got up. All to no avail.

That's when we realize that we've tricked ourselves into thinking routine and discipline are the same thing. But that's not the case. Routine only becomes discipline when you add intentionality.

So one morning Gabby suggests that, since our year is all about connecting with others, we should make genuine togetherness the focus, instead of just shaving seconds off our morning prep time like we're auditioning for a NASCAR pit crew.

So, our intentionality begins as something simple. With the help of our youth pastor at church, Gabby finds an interactive morning devotional that is engaging for the kids. So each morning, rather than inhaling our breakfast while making lunches for the kids and shouting toward the kitchen table for them to quit bickering, we make lunches the night before and all sit down as a family. At the table together, we read the devotional out loud, do a tiny activity that goes along with the passage, and talk about how that day's concept ties in to what we might be doing at school or work that day.

The results are instantaneous. Our conversations move away from chore lists and nagging to actually talking about important things, and the kids really enjoy it. Don't get me wrong, brushing teeth and putting on shoes is still as painstakingly slow as a sloth running a 5K, but a daily focus and connection takes the edge off of our nagging.

Soon, we add another piece to our morning ritual, prompted by a suggestion from a friend. Rather than driving to school in a closed car and sitting in the kid drop-off line, sealed off from the world around us, we start walking to school with the kids. It's roughly 1.5 miles round-trip, which not only helps to get the blood pumping but also allows us to have meaningful conversations without radios and other stuff to distract us. It's a chance to talk about what the kids will be doing that day, what their friends are up to, and what they are excited about.

And this ritual helps us build community as well. We join in our walk with three other families in the neighborhood. In suburban "Generica," surrounded by the strip malls with Starbucks, Old Navy, Home Depot, and PetCo, it's easy to live your life behind shuttered doors and windows. These morning walks help us get to know our neighbors better. We're building friendships that we hope will deepen over time with both the adults and the kids. We can already see this "whole village" concept beginning to emerge, with kids moving from house-to-house and parent-to-parent depending on everyone's schedules. This "routine with intention" is such a success that we decide to build it into our evenings as well.

While the "Thorns and Roses" discussion has been in heavy rotation as a dinnertime staple for a few months, it's grown a bit stale. We're also finding that simply asking, "How was your day?" doesn't always elicit great conversation. So Gabby finds a fun list of "Dinnertime Questions" on the web and prints them out.[3] We cut each one out (there are more than a hundred of them) and drop them into a jar that we keep on the kitchen table.

"What is the most beautiful place you have ever seen?

"If you were an animal, what would you want to be and why?"

"Is honesty always the best policy, or are there times when lying is appropriate?"

Now, each night, every member of the family reaches into the jar to retrieve a question. And the conversations carry us through the whole meal, discussing fun, interesting subjects.

The final place for adding intention was the bedtime routine.

The hour preceding lights out has historically been a mad dash to see how fast we could get the kids to fall asleep. Bath time would usually devolve into a scene from a laundromat gone horribly wrong, with bubbles overflowing and splashing out into the hallway, and lots of people screaming from fatigue. And story time was a haphazard romp through the same old tried-and-true books that you had memorized page-by-page or character books picked up as a giveaway from some fast-food restaurant.

So we make a simple change. We introduce the kids to some chapter books. Books with depth and dialogue and cliffhangers. And, since our kids love movies, we also think it might be fun to select books that have started as literature but eventually became movies. That way, we can read the story and get hooked on the moral and the characters, and surprise the kids with the blockbuster Hollywood production later. Our first foray is C. S. Lewis's *The Lion, the Witch, and the Wardrobe*. Gabby selects it for its action-packed adventure and strong Christian allegory. I agree with her decision because it allows me to do lots of British accents.

The kids love it. Each night they beg us for "one more chapter, please!" And we discuss the characters and the story at different times throughout the day. When they finally watch the movie, it's as if their imaginations have come to life. Scary scenes aren't as scary anymore since they know that good will win in the end and love will prevail. And it helps our experiment that the movies were born and fleshed out of the author's imagination rather than a marketer's toolkit with McDonald's tie-ins and aisles of plush toys.

Don't get me wrong. It's not always sunshine and ponies in our house. We still have raised voices and hurt feelings and frantic rushes to get out the door. But the shift is significant. With all these intentional changes—the morning devotional, the walks to and from school, and the family story time—our routines now have us together for a couple of hours every weekday. But it's not just an increase in the quantity of time, but the quality as well. Our interactions simply have more meaning. It's not something we necessarily expected when we started the challenge, but it is helping us to build connections in our own family and focus on what is important to us. Getting closer to our mission and closer to one another in the process.

Chapter Twenty-Two

The Most Awkwardly Awesome Prom Ever

I thank my God every time I remember you, constantly praying with joy in every one of my prayers for all of you, because of your sharing in the gospel from the first day until now.
(Philippians 1:3–5)

Routines are nice, but so is variety. No matter how much we try to create a new normal around simplifying our lives and incorporating faithful discipline, curveballs always come our way. This time, it's the upcoming graduation celebration for our niece, Abby.

Gabby and I are in the car discussing what to do for her for the big day. Since we can't buy anything, I run through a list of options. No science experiments or homemade Mad Libs this time. It's a special, once-in-a-lifetime occasion, so we need to be creative. Could we make her some dorm bedding out of old T-shirts and two months' worth of dryer lint? Orchestrate the world's smallest flash mob? Maybe sculpt a likeness of her pet cat out of mashed potatoes?

Then a light bulb flashes above Gabby's head.

Our niece attended an online high school. You read that right. She went to high school on the Internet. Five hours per day doing lessons and homework. It's called Ohio Connections Academy.

I find it interesting to use the word *connections* to describe an academic experience where you never really meet anyone face-to-face, but the program is pretty progressive. If I had this option when I was her age, I would have made the most of this kind of "connection" by posting photos of GAP models as my profile pic and listing my hobbies as weight lifting, money counting, and kitten rescuing. Luckily, Abby and her classmates are much more mature than I was, so they simply got their work done and were productive members of society.

Gabby feels our niece's online high school experience, while functional, lacks one important teenage rite of passage. Namely, a large, uncomfortable, expensive function, complete with cringe-worthy, acne-riddled party pics to induce laughter and/or embarrassment twenty years later. You probably know it by its Latin name.

Prom.

So she suggests our gift to Abby should be a "Family Prom."

I know what you're thinking. The *last* thing a high school girl wants to do is get dressed up with her extended family, go out to a dinner with other adults and small children, and come back to a dimly lit room to dance the YMCA and Billy Idol's "Mony, Mony" with her parents.

And to you I say, you greatly underestimate the Dannemiller Family Prom Planning Committee (DFPPC).

I respond, "Cool! Let's do it!"

Gabby, questioning my grasp of hip lingo, makes it her first order of business to text Abby's boyfriend, Spencer, to tell him about the plan and find out if kids today still use the word *cool* to describe things besides temperature.

Gabby: *We are planning a prom for Abby, so start thinking about how you will ask her . . . BTW, You guys are a shoe-in for Prom King and Queen.*

Spencer (no doubt very surprised to be getting a text from his girlfriend's aunt): *Oh. OK. That's cool!*

Scott 1 – Gabby 0

Next up is the prom theme. The DFPPC (Gabby and I) have a difference of opinion on this one. I want something sentimental, reflecting the mood of my own senior prom. I offer up Rod

Stewart's "Forever Young." I can still feel the rhythm-less swaying and smell the overpowering aroma of Drakkar Noir anytime I hear that tune.

But Gabby wants something "cool."

So I suggest Phillip Phillips' "Home" as a possible idea. It's a catchy tune. Current. Peppy.

Gabby laughs and calls it "cheesy."

I counter by saying I don't think kids today use the word *cheesy* to describe anything other than curdled milk.

She counters by asserting, "Believe me, honey. They would call it "cheesy."

"Fine! Do you have a better idea?" I ask.

"I don't know. Maybe Michael Bublé or something?"

Raising my voice now, "Michael Bublé!? Abby would not think Michael Bublé was cool. She'll just ask 'Who in the hell is Michael Bubble? Sounds like a guy who sells shampoo!' "

Things continue to get more heated until we wake up and realize that we are a full-grown, forty-year-old married couple, driving down the highway, fighting over the theme to a fake senior prom.

Cooler heads prevail.

We text Abby to tell her we are throwing her a Family Prom and that she has to come. Nothing like giving a gift that you force on the receiver. We also tell her she has to pick a theme.

She texts back, "How about "Thrift Shop"?"

An obscure choice. I've heard of the song, which no doubt makes me "cool" by high school senior standards. But Gabby hasn't heard of it, so she Googles it on her phone, giving me the play-by-play as she searches for more information.

"It says it's by some guys named Macklemore and Ryan Lewis. It has an 'E' next to it. Does that mean it's for 'everyone?' "

She plays a snippet of the song on speakerphone. Thirty-eight seconds in, we learn that "E" does mean "everyone." As in, "*Everyone* in our car, preschoolers included, will now know *explicit* slang terms for copulation and genitalia."

Perhaps Abby is mocking our idea. Spencer must have tipped her off. But we call her bluff and accept the suggestion once we find a censored version of the song.

Now that the theme is settled, it's time to assign responsibilities. Gabby nominates herself president of the DFPPC. I second the nomination because I would like to stay married. Brother-in-law Owen and nephew Josh are put on transportation and sound amplification. Sister Kerri is assigned to dress acquisition and downloading non-explicit music. I take charge of the venue and emcee duties.

As a nod to the prom theme, and deference to our year without a purchase, we establish a rule that all attire has to be something you already own or something you purchase from an actual thrift shop. Obviously, Gabby and I are limited to the former.

Gabby was going to use an old bridesmaid's dress, but my mom heard of our fantastic prom theme and loaned Gabby a dress that she had bought from Noah's Closet some months before.

The village is in effect!

Gabby's sister Kerri, unable to resist the thrift store theme and the challenge of finding ridiculously good deals, outfits her entire family, smokin' hot dress included, for the cost of a Super-Sized McDonald's Value Meal #7.

I'm not kidding.

Meanwhile, I am in charge of the venue. Bowling alley? Skating rink? No. This has to be special. Even though Thrift Shop is the theme, this is a *real* fake prom. A graduating teenage girl gets only one shot at this, and it needs to be nice. As nice as you can get for free.

We already used some of my frequent traveler points to secure a hotel room in downtown Columbus for our family for graduation weekend. On a whim, I call the hotel to talk to someone in charge. I don't hold out much hope, but my mom taught me that it never hurts to ask for anything you want.

They transfer me to the hotel's sales director to inquire about space. As the phone rings on her extension, I wonder if it's technically called "sales" if the customer asks for something and doesn't plan to pay for it. Unfortunately, no one answers the phone, so I don't get an immediate answer.

I leave a message instead.

"Hi. We're going to be staying at your hotel this weekend and I have an odd request. Our niece is graduating from an online high school and didn't get to have a prom. So, we're throwing her a Family Prom. Little five-year-old cousins are taking each other as dates. The whole nine yards. Anyway, the problem is, we need a venue. Maybe a ballroom? A conference room? Just seven big people and four children for a couple of hours. If there is anything you can do, I'd love to chat with you."

I hang up the phone, fully expecting that I'll never receive a response. Imagine my surprise when the phone rings exactly fifteen minutes later. I answer, anticipating a big, fat no. Or, at the very least, a chokeable, non-thrifty price tag.

"Hi Scott. This is Lindsay, the sales director at the hotel. I received your voice mail and must admit . . ."

My anxiety grows, as if I had asked Lindsay to be my date to the prom and was now waiting to find out if she would accept my invitation or crush my dreams, as many girls throughout high school did, sending me into a downward spiral of despair filled with ice cream bingeing and over-coiffing my hair with Aqua Net.

". . . your idea is the coolest thing I have ever heard. I want to make this the best prom ever, and I can't wait to plan it for you."

Score! Caught up in a wave of excitement, I respond without thinking, "Great! Then you can be the president of our prom planning committee! Our theme is Thrift Shop."

She reacts as if she won a dream date with a wealthy GAP model who works out, has piles of money, and rescues kittens. I don't have the heart to tell her that the DFPPC already has a president, so she will technically be sharing the power with Gabby, but I don't think it matters. Lindsay is so excited that she doesn't bat an eyelash when I remind her we can't spend any money.

"That is so awesome! I am totally calling my girlfriends to discuss decorations."

Judging from Gabby's original level of excitement, and now Lindsay's potential coup d'état of the DFPPC, I believe every grown woman secretly wishes she could plan her own prom.

Maybe because it's kind of like planning a wedding, only without the open bar and the pressure of lifelong commitment.

In the days that follow, Lindsay and I exchange a barrage of enthusiastic emails. Luck is on our side. There are no events for the evening in question. Absolutely none. So she gives us the largest and best conference room they have, complete with giant, two-story pillars and huge glass windows. She also provides free valet parking and offers to look for decorations on her off hours, paying for them out of her own pocket or repurposing office supplies. She's like a prom angel, taking care of every last detail.

Meanwhile, the DFPPC drama builds in our house. It's like a reality TV show without the cameras. Gabby needles me.

"You know you have to get me a corsage, right?"

"But honey, I'm not allowed to buy anything, remember?"

"Then you had better figure out how to grow some flowers really fast or make one from scratch."

I contemplate ripping a rosebud out of someone's garden, but figure that will only bring about some bad prom mojo. So I search the web for "How to make fake flowers" and stumble on a Martha Stewart crafting website.

If it's good enough for Martha, then it's good enough for my wife.

I click the link and am instantly amazed by the beautiful array of flowers I can create using my own two hands. Tulips. Peonies. Gerber daisies. They are absolutely stunning. Martha writes, "Crepe-paper flowers capture the essence of flowers without all the botanical details. Their whimsy makes them not only a pleasure to behold, but also an enjoyable project to undertake."[1]

Damn skippy!

I look over the directions. It takes seventeen steps to make the stamen alone. And a lot more to make the actual flower part. The materials required light, medium, and heavy crepe paper in varying shades, eighteen-gauge fabric-wrapped floral wire, something called "floral tape," and other doodads. I glance at the raw materials at my disposal:

- ½ roll of wrinkled crepe paper left over from somebody's birthday party (red).
- 34 old pipe cleaners that Audrey twisted into bracelets and collars for her stuffed animals (assorted colors)
- ¼ roll of masking tape (yellow)
- A healthy fear of the DFPPC (Co-)President's wrath if she doesn't have a corsage for prom

These items, paired with my gumption, prove worthy. I pare Martha's dozens of steps down to three: Cut, fold, tape.

Forty-five minutes and several failed attempts into the project, I have something that resembles a green tapeworm assaulting a strawberry Fruit Roll-Up. Yet, after considerable effort for another thirty minutes, I am able to transform it into something more acceptable. Even though it's not perfect, my wife still smiles when I present it to her at dinner, proving that it truly is the thought that counts. Or maybe it just proves she enjoys the house chardonnay.

Either way, I win.

But Family Prom is not about me and my date. The night is about spending quality time with family we love and showing Abby what a special girl she is.

And I believe we succeeded.

We got dressed up. We chatted over giant plates of Italian food. We squished eleven family members into a big conversion van and rode together to the prom. We laughed. Popped balloons. We danced to prom standards, such as "Shout," "YMCA," and "The Chicken Dance." My seven-year-old son taught me the Harlem Shake. We broke our backs doing the limbo. We did the Hokey Pokey.

And Abby and Spencer were crowned Prom Queen and King in a landslide vote. As it should be.

It was a fabulous night to commemorate a fabulous girl's first eighteen years on the planet. She starts college in the fall. It's an exciting time for her. Breaking out on her own for the first time. That likely means less time at home. Fewer conversations.

Absences at the most mundane daily events of life. Her little brother's soccer games. Her little sister's spontaneous dance recitals. She will be missed.

And at the same time, we can all feel blessed to have placed a big bow around all the memories she's given over the years. And making new memories in the process. Bringing us all closer together. More than any gift we could have wrapped in a box.

Chapter Twenty-Three

The Perfect Birthday—Just Add Aqua Velva

If I speak in the tongues of men or of angels, but do not have love, I am only a resounding gong or a clanging cymbal. If I have the gift of prophecy and can fathom all mysteries and all knowledge, and if I have a faith that can move mountains, but do not have love, I am nothing. If I give all I possess to the poor and give over my body to hardship that I may boast, but do not have love, I gain nothing.

(1 Corinthians 13:1–3 NIV)

I love looking through old photo albums. We have some fantastic specimens from the mid-'70s. Giant puffy volumes covered in padded fabric that may have been harvested from a couch in Burt Reynolds's bachelor pad. They smell like an old librarian's purse seasoned with a splash of Aqua Velva.

Vintage.

But there's something missing from the albums. Namely, photos of my childhood birthday parties.

My first thought is to blame birth order. My sister came first. There are so many baby pictures of her, you can put them in a stack, hold them tightly, flick through them with your thumb, and relive the first three years of her life as if it were a home movie.

Next came my brother. He was the first boy. Enough said.

I was the baby. Tucked away deep inside the album is a picture of me in a onesie and one of my high school graduation. Nothing in between. With three kids, my parents were just too exhausted to advance the film on their old Vivitar camera.

Maybe I'm exaggerating. But not much. The real reason there aren't any photos of my grade school birthday parties is because I had only one. That's right. Just one official party where I sent real invitations. I was five years old. Even though it was long ago, my memories of this party are vivid. I wore my favorite outfit—a tan jumpsuit my mom made for me with a pattern she bought from Montgomery Ward. It was covered in little cars. I had a yellow cake with chocolate icing. I blew out all the candles. We played red rover, and I busted through the line. I don't remember a single gift from that party, but I do remember that I got to hold Amy Clifton's hand during said red-rover game.

Note to self: wear more jumpsuits.

But I never had another birthday party. Sure, I invited a friend or two over and we went swimming or saw a movie or blew a bucket of tokens at an arcade, but nothing official. It's not as if my parents banned parties as "the devil's handiwork" or anything. In fact, my mom encouraged them. Every year she would ask, and every year I would decline.

You want to know a secret?

I didn't want to have another birthday party because I was afraid two things might happen. I was afraid *no one* would show up, and I was afraid *everyone* would show up. If no one showed up, that would tell me my friends weren't *really* my friends. And that's not something I wanted to know.

And if everyone showed up? Well, all eyes would be on me, and that's just too much pressure. I know it's surprising to think that a guy who makes a living speaking in front of groups of people would shy away from attention, but it's true.

Fast forward 35 years.

In preparation for my fortieth birthday, I tell Gabby I don't want anything special. No parties. I just want to relax with my family and have some cake and ice cream. With our challenge in full swing, I know that she would have to work wonders to throw a major fiesta. Just in case, I keep a close watch on our supply of toilet paper and Ziploc baggies just to make sure she's not pilfering from the stash to make streamers and homemade balloons.

The morning of my birthday comes early. Call it neurosis, paranoia, or simply a healthy lifestyle, but I want to give myself the gift of accomplishment by running farther than I ever have before. So I wake up at 6:00 a.m., strap on my running shoes, and give Father Time a one-finger wave as I walk out the door. Gabby, face down in her pillow, musters a muffled "Happy Birthday" before I set out.

Perfect.

My Dannemarathon lasts just over an hour. When I arrive home, I'm greeted by the smell of Gabby's famous chocolate-chip pancakes and two very loud, overly excited children. According to my calculations, these two small people are burning the caloric equivalent of a surprise party of forty full-grown adults. And it's *exactly* what I want for this special day.

I peer over toward my seat at the table and spot a CD case. On the front of the case is a beautiful photo of Gabby and the kids, each holding a guitar. I ask where she had the picture done, and she told me our friend Mari, a professional photographer, was happy to donate her services to the cause.

Inside the case are three CDs and a thick booklet. As I leaf through the pages, I see a list of songs submitted by friends, each with a story of why the song reminded them of me. There are over fifty tunes from a variety of genres. There's "Never Gonna' Give You Up" by Rick Astley, submitted by my brother because "Scott and Rick Astley have never been seen in the same place at the same time." "Play That Funky Music White Boy" was submitted twice.

I'm not sure whether to be flattered or offended.

Every single song tells a story, and I am anxious to listen, as I know the memories it'll bring. When I put the CDs in the player, the first track on the playlist isn't a song at all. Apparently, Gabby coordinated with family members who own a local music store to commandeer their studio for an evening and record my kids' voices for posterity. First up is a priceless interview with Jake. Gabby asks him all sorts of questions about me, and he answers in his tiny, toothless voice. I am so grateful she captured this moment in time.

Track two brings me to my knees. It's Audrey's song to me. Every night she asks me to sing her to sleep with "Somewhere Over The Rainbow." As a gift to me, Gabby had her sing along to a version of the song recorded by a children's choir from Newtown, Connecticut. Instant waterworks.

It doesn't get much better than this.

The next day, we fill the car with gas and enough highly processed snack foods to send a dozen pro wrestlers into a diabetic coma. We're headed to Florida to meet up with my family for a week's vacation. We know that no souvenirs will be purchased, but we're excited just the same. My brother and sister have been taking their families to the gulf coast every year for the better part of a decade, but we've joined them only once. This year, we vow to make the trip. Since Gabby's birthday is three days after mine, this is our gift to each other.

I pop one of my new CDs into the car stereo and relax. A few hundred miles of highway in front of us means I have ample time to chat with my wife. I kick off the gab-fest.

"So, what do you see yourself doing once Audrey starts kindergarten?" I ask her. "It'll be the first time we've had both kids in school."

I wait for a meaningful response. Instead, I hear,

"Huh?"

"Audrey. Starting Kindergarten. Are you excited?"

I glance over at Gabby and catch her with her nose in her phone, texting. She answers without looking up.

"Oh. Yeah. Sorry. Just trying to see where your sister is."

I'm irritated. "Why does it matter? We're not in any big rush. We'll all get there today."

"Yeah. I know."

But the texting continues for the whole drive. We're mid conversation, and Gabby is taking breaks to send more messages. She can see me fuming but ignores it.

"Don't you just want to listen to your CD?" she asks.

I didn't realize I was such a crappy conversationalist.

The drive lasts eight hours. Somewhat perturbed, I am ready to sit on the couch and have a cold drink. I pull up to the house where we'll be staying for the week and breathe a sigh of relief.

And that's when I see her.

A woman.

The spitting image of an old friend from Austin whom I haven't seen in years. She's standing next to my dad on the porch of a beach vacation rental. I think to myself, *That woman looks like Carla.*

Then I look closer.

Wait . . . it is *Carla! What a coincidence that she happens to be in Florida at the same beach house at the same time as us?!*

I turn toward Gabby to say, "Can you believe it?!" when I notice she has a huge smile on her face and tears in her eyes. I look back at the porch and see a flood of people come out of the house. More old friends. Gabby's dear family. Other kids. Thirty people. All making a surprise trip to Florida to celebrate a week-long birthday party.

For me.

Gabby has been planning it for eighteen months. How everyone kept the secret, I'll never know. I chalk it up to a magical combination of her amazing planning skills and my lack of attention to detail. (Really, it's severe. Gabby has a tattoo on her ankle, but to this day I couldn't tell you, to save my life, whether it is on the right or left leg.)

Whatever the case, it takes several days for the surprise to sink in. The week is a beautiful blur of time with people I love. Sharing meals. Riding bikes. Swimming. Playing in the sand with nieces, nephews, and other kids. An honest-to-goodness, heart-to-heart talk with my old pal David. Sitting on the porch drinking beer, telling stories for hours on end with family and friends, old and new. It's the best gift I could have received.

And the best part?

It is my very own, official birthday party with real invitations. No trinkets. No baubles. No gift-wrapped stuff. Just a flood of family and friends who show me by their very presence just how much I mean to them and how much we mean to one another, and it fills me to overflowing with gratitude for life.

Chapter Twenty-Four

What Do You Get the Woman Who Has Everything?

Be devoted to one another in love. Honor one another above yourselves.

(Romans 12:10 NIV)

My mom is an absolutely beautiful woman, inside and out. She is a mere five-foot-two, but she is filled to the brim with spunkiness. Just over 40 years ago she was a much larger version of herself, all on account of yours truly. You see, she gained so much weight carrying me the doctor was afraid it might make for a troublesome delivery. He would constantly caution her against consuming too much unhealthy food. My mother would always listen closely to his advice, then leave his office and proceed directly to the A&W drive-in for a burger, fries, and a large chocolate milkshake.

I was born at 3:53 p.m. on June 8, 1973. Dad wasn't around. He was busy moving the car to avoid getting a parking ticket when his time expired at 4:00 p.m. When I finally came bursting forth into this world, I weighed a whopping 9 pounds and 4 ounces. Upon seeing my chubby, angelic face for the first time, my mother's loving response was,

"See doc, I *told* you I wasn't a lard ass!"

She had me at "lard ass."

I have loved this woman my entire life. While Dad taught me the value of a job well done and the gift of storytelling, Mom taught me all about the twin joys of spontaneity and compassion. I will never be able to repay her for all she has given me.

But once a year, I try. Mom's birthday.

I am wracking my brain, trying to decide what experience gift I might get the woman who gave me life. Small kitchen appliances or home décor are off the table, since these would require me to visit an actual store or do something less than acceptable, such as gift wrap our own used frying pans, whose non-stick coating is already flaking off into our eggs and giving us untold diseases.

On the homemade gift front, we *do* have a stash of those makeshift science experiment kits—Mentos and 2-liter bottles of Diet Coke—that we've been giving as birthday gifts to the kids' friends. But Mom has been there and done that. I could also create some original artwork or handicraft for her, but my skills have scarcely improved since the last time I fashioned her a macaroni necklace back in the third grade. And today, I'm afraid Mom would rather cook such an item than wear it. In fact, I suspect that's what happened with the original.

Then the perfect gift idea comes to me. I think, "How about a nice lunch date with Mom?"

To be a suitable experience gift, we would have to go to one of her favorite places. That means no Buffalo Wild Wings or any other establishment featuring large screens showing sports. She's never been much of a sports nut unless her own grandkids are playing, and hot sauce tends to splatter and stain her sassy wardrobe. We would also have to avoid any establishment featuring waitresses wearing outfits that were too revealing, otherwise Mom might get into a deep conversation with them about poor life choices and delay our order.

So I invite Mom to the Cottage Café.

The Cottage Café is not exactly my style. Sure, I may not be the most manly guy on the planet. My love of wilderness survival reality TV shows and mastery in the art of flatulence is far outweighed by my ability to joyously demonstrate "jazz hands" and my intimate knowledge of color palettes.

I'm an "autumn," for those who know what that means.

But the Cottage Café may be the girliest restaurant on the face of the earth. The place makes me look like a professional wrestler. It's covered in lace doilies and filled with scented candles and household knick-knacks. At the door, they do a quick blood screen. Those measuring high in testosterone are given a fanny pack shaped like a uterus. All the animals on the menu are given a complete facial and pedicure before becoming a key ingredient in tiny sandwichlettes. Those caught talking about football are strapped to a chair Clockwork-Orange-style and forced to watch the Lifetime channel.

I'm telling you. It's *that* girly. But the food is amazing, and Mom loves it.

On the day of our date, I meet her in the parking lot. Mom gives me a hug, and we walk together into the restaurant. We give our name to the hostess and wait for a table. The place is packed. I glance around and notice two other guys in the restaurant, but I am the only male under the age of sixty-five. I suspect the other fellas are former electricians slowly losing their hearing. When their wives said "Cottage Café," they heard "Wattage Delay" and came running. Now they are draped in gingham napkins with confused looks spread across their faces, eating pimento cheese crackers and wondering why no one's asking them to fix the wiring.

But the Cottage Café's pimento cheese will do that to a guy. They bring you a plate of it as a complimentary appetizer. It's so good it'll make you forget anything you were worried about before.

Kinda' like Mom.

Once we are seated, time stops. You see, it's been a while since I have talked to my mom. Sure, we get to spend time together now and again, but we're usually surrounded by lots of other people. Or kids. Or meals to prepare. So four hours at a family party becomes only five minutes of actual contact time. The rest is spent mopping spills, filling plates, cutting food, and cleaning up.

But this is different.

Mom and I have an honest-to-goodness *talk*. No distractions. No agendas. Uninterrupted conversation as beautiful and sublime as uninterrupted sleep. The depth of it leaves you feeling so refreshed that you feel you can tackle all the world's problems with a smile on your face.

We eat crackers and reminisce about my childhood. I pick from her salad while we discuss the issues of the day. We contemplate dessert as Mom shares with me her thoughts on her future with my dad. Where they might live. Where they might go.

And two hours pass. Two. Hours. The longest lunch ever in the history of mothers and sons. I fail to notice the tables turn multiple times as we savor our time together. People coming and going while we sit still.

To say that I orchestrated this beautiful connection would be a lie. I thought I was just buying my mom a nice lunch. But now I see it's so much more. People change as years pass. We've all had the experience of reuniting with old friends from high school or college, or perhaps even visiting with friends who were passing through town again after moving away. In many cases, you never skip a beat. Conversations flow like water as you recount all your shared experiences and tell the old stories that make everyone laugh. It's good for the soul to feel how connected you once were.

At the same time, we know that we're not the same people. When we dig deeper into conversation, we learn how our friends have grown and learned and adapted. How they have been shaped by their life experiences. If we don't listen well, we can get frustrated that things just aren't the way they used to be and lament the loss of the past. But if we do listen well, we can learn from where they have been and enjoy the surprises.

That's how it is on my lunch date with Mom. In some ways, it's as if we're getting reacquainted. She has an opportunity to get to know the man who grew from the little boy who cluttered her house for nearly twenty years. The little strawberry blonde kid whose hair changed to brown and now shows gray around the temples. Gray caused by stresses that have come and gone for the mother. Stresses she has packed away as wisdom.

And I come to know the genuine, flesh-and-blood woman who lives underneath the SuperMom cape she wore during my youth. I learn she has worries just like the rest of us. I even learn things about my own childhood that I never knew. Things that shaped who I am.

And that's when it hits me. When it comes to truly honoring another person, there is so much we miss when we demonstrate our gratitude with gifts alone. For one of the deepest human desires is to be truly known—known to the marrow. Known as God knows us. The one who formed us, shaped us, and accepts us for who we are. While the choice of gift can demonstrate how much we know a person, it falls short of acceptance. Because this genuine connection requires more than face time. It requires openness.

And that is what we have to offer. As I sit across the table from my own mother, I realize that I have spent my life knowing her, yet I am still capable of learning more about her. There's a message in there for all of us, I think. No matter how well we know a person, there is always more to discover. And so much more to learn. Not just about God's plans for all of us, but also how he has knit us together. Thread by beautiful thread.

Chapter Twenty-Five

Gala People?

We ought always to thank God for you, brothers and sisters, and rightly so, because your faith is growing more and more, and the love all of you have for one another is increasing.
(2 Thessalonians 1:3 NIV)

Late last year, prior to our commitment to abolish unnecessary purchases, a friend invited us to a fundraising gala to benefit a local charity. It seemed like a fun event, all except for one minor problem:

We are not "gala people."

Gala people wear fancy clothes. Gala people know which fork to use. Gala people start foundations and have their names on university buildings and hospitals.

Gabby and I tell loud, somewhat inappropriate stories. We snort when we laugh. We use our pinky fingernail to pick food out of our teeth. At the table.

No. We are not gala people.

But there we were, browsing the tables laden with offerings for the silent auction. Artwork. Box seats to NFL football games. Gift baskets overflowing with wines and restaurant gift cards. Money raised from all this stuff would go to provide support services for kids in foster care or those who have aged out of the program.

"Should we bid on something?" Gabby asked.

"I don't know. It *is* for a good cause."

"That's true."

I then pulled out the trump card, whispering aloud, "This *could* be our tithe. We still haven't written our latest giving check. Maybe we could just tithe to the auction?"

"Does that count?" Gabby asked skeptically.

In addition to diagnosing car problems and performing triage in medical emergencies, my wife is the de facto moral compass in our relationship. And her compass was telling her that tithing at the charity auction is like putting money in the church offering plate and then asking the pastor to make you a meatball sub with the communion loaf.

"Sure! It's giving!" I say this last statement with emphasis to make it sound as if I am confident, even though inside I wonder if I am punching a one-way ticket to the devil's playground. I start placing bids before Gabby can ask any more questions.

I told you. We're not gala people.

Caught up in the frenzy of purchasing gifts financed by Our Lord and Savior, we keep adding our name to the bid lists. We up the ante by a dollar or two each time we are outbid on something. Competing bidders immediately come and raise the stakes. The whole affair is drenched in euphoria. Excitement at the thought of winning. And by winning, I mean in the same way eighty-year-old billionaires "win" trophy wives half their age. By the end of the evening we have "won" a dinner for two at an Italian restaurant and weekend lodging at a Tennessee lake house for a small army.

And Jesus wept. A little.

In our defense, we planned on sharing the lake house with our Nashville family as an "experience." It's not every day you cram eighteen people into one house for three days in a no-holds-barred test of will to see who will emerge unscathed. They make reality shows about stuff like that. Only on reality television, the house mates don't ever have to see one another again. In the Dannemiller version of the show, there are some long-term ramifications to the togetherness. Stealing the "big bedroom" at the lake house could come back to haunt you one day when you are in desperate need of a blood-relative match for a kidney.

Gabby and I would be lying if we said we weren't anxious about the whole thing. For one, even though it's technically an experience gift and the donation went to a good cause that supports abandoned and troubled youth, a big lake house is definitely an extravagance in our year without a purchase. Second, my family loves to be in nature, as long as it is air conditioned and bug-free. And the lake has things like algae. And spider webs. And hair-crushing humidity. But most of my personal anxiety is due to an unexpected turn of events. At a family gathering a few months before the trip, my sixteen-year-old niece Mia taps me on the shoulder to ask a question.

"Hey Uncle Scott. I was wondering if you would baptize me and Julianna when we all go to the lake this summer."

Baptize?! I had to get five stiches in my chin from my jaw dropping to the kitchen floor. Most teenagers speak to adults only in a special language of angst-ridden grunts and clicks. And here are my twin nieces, mature beyond their years, speaking to me about something of deep, personal significance.

I wonder aloud what would prompt such a request. My sister elaborates that the girls want to commit their lives to something greater than themselves and thought it would be special if they could share the event with Gabby and me, since we have done mission service in the past and continue to wear our faith on our sleeves, albeit in an odd way with our choice of annual challenges.

I am honored beyond comprehension. But the last time I checked, I am not a pastor. I have no formal training in baptism. My only qualifications are a summer of swim lessons when I was five years old and having a slight OCD tendency toward personal cleanliness that requires two or three showers per day.

In response to Mia's request, my brain tells me to launch into an explanation of how I am not certified for this sort of thing. I mean, there are whole books in my Bible that still have that new book smell (ever spend a lot of time reading Amos? Anyone?). But my impulsive heart says,

"Sure."

God definitely has a sense of humor.

When I get home, I immediately conduct some research. I look up passages in the Bible of ordinary people baptizing others and find quite a few. James and John were just fisherman, but they baptized people all over the place. Paul was a tentmaker who persecuted Christ's followers, yet he "laid hands" on hundreds. None of these folks had seminary degrees or had been ordained in a church. So, I technically have a leg up on all of them, since I actually spent a year as a missionary and received an ordination through the First International Church of the Web. For $25 and a 250-word statement of faith, they send you a really nice certificate and a laminated card to place in your dash that reads "Clergy." It's supposed to give you preferred parking spots at the hospital, but I'm saving it for just the right time. Perhaps an emergency appendectomy.

But even with these extra credentials, I want to make sure things are on the up and up. So I consult a higher authority.

Google.

I go to my computer and type "Am I allowed to baptize somebody" into the search box. A long list of links appears. Some are official church websites. Others are blogs from pastors. Essentially, they all say the same thing, which is, "Jesus says it's OK."

> *Now the eleven disciples went to Galilee, to the mountain to which Jesus had directed them. When they saw him, they worshiped him; but some doubted. And Jesus came and said to them, "All authority in heaven and on earth has been given to me. Go therefore and make disciples of all nations, baptizing them in the name of the Father and of the Son and of the Holy Spirit, and teaching them to obey everything that I have commanded you. And remember, I am with you always, to the end of the age."* (Matthew 28:16–20)

Knowing that I have been given the green light by the Savior of the World himself, I am feeling better about things. With Gabby's help, I start to build a baptism service using a format that seems "church-ish." I stress over the details. I want to make sure all the prayers are just right. I want to make sure I use some official sounding language. I want to sprinkle the forehead at just the right time. Then I come back to what Jesus said.

It's not about the water.

No. The water is the easy part. Like taking a shower. The hard part is what comes after the baptism. The "teaching them to obey everything I have commanded you" part. That's where the real work is. The baptism is a symbol. But commitment is the goal.

The trip to the lake is amazing, filled with hours of fun that have absolutely nothing to do with buying stuff. We go fishing. We swim off the dock and dry ourselves in the sun. We bounce around the lake on inner tubes. We celebrate the twins' birthday with chocolate fondue. We share laughs and stories the entire weekend, and even care for a few cuts and scrapes.

And then comes the baptism.

On Sunday morning, our entire family is gathered on the top deck of a two-story boat dock. Eighteen in all. We come together to celebrate the lives of two sixteen-year-old girls, Mia and Julianna. All they have meant to our family and all the promise of their futures. Mia, with a personality to match her fiery red hair, filled with relentless determination, drive, and discipline. And her twin sister, Julianna, with a heart so big it can hardly fit inside her chest, overflowing with compassion and confidence.

All my plans for pomp and circumstance get thrown out the window. Instead, I determine that this all works best if I just get out of the way.

For several minutes, people share thoughts about each of the girls. Not surface stories of embarrassing moments or trophies won. They are tearful, meaningful stories of shared history. Of admiration. Of unconditional love. A large family, stopping for a moment to thank God for the lives of two young women and, in turn, giving thanks for the beauty of family. A family who loves abundantly. A family bound together by commitment. Teaching one another, each and every day.

Then, with hands outstretched, this same family prays over the water as two amazing girls take the plunge. Both with courage and confidence. One choosing to jump from the second story, dropping twenty feet into the world's largest baptismal font. The other, deciding to hang from a ladder on the edge of the dock and fall backward into the Father, Son, and Holy Spirit.

No. It's not about the water. It's about stripping away the day-to-day and reminding ourselves of the things that really matter in this life. It's about celebrating grace and our shared commitment to one another.

When we first started this challenge, we wanted to reconnect with and strengthen our family mission statement. The one where we vow to live with integrity and grow in faith together. But we never would have imagined that a donation at a fundraising gala could turn into an opportunity for our extended family to come together to support two young women as they commit their lives to God. It is such a wonderful surprise. The Big Guy taking a self-serving act of charity, combining it with a Google search, and turning it into something beautiful.

I know I said before that we don't consider ourselves to be gala people. It sounds way too fancy. But now I'm not so sure. Technically (that is, Merriam-Webster says) a gala isn't defined by the price of the dinner or the vintage of wine served. No, Merriam Webster simply defines *gala* as "a festive celebration; especially: . . . marking a special occasion."[1]

So maybe we are gala people after all.

Part Four

Serving God's People

Growing in faith is essential, but what next?

Chapter Twenty-Six

Ontario with Ellis

He has told you, O mortal, what is good;
and what does the LORD require of you
but to do justice, and to love kindness,
and to walk humbly with your God?
(Micah 6:8)

A trance comes over me as I stare at the ticket machine. I'm on another business trip, dressed in a sport coat, trying to figure out how to take the train from the busy Chicago airport to my hotel downtown. Normally I rent a car or take a cab, but the year without a purchase has encouraged me to try something less extravagant. So here I am with a purple suitcase propped up at my side and people buzzing around me. Drool is starting to pool at the corner of my mouth, but I continue staring in hopes that the dispenser might take pity on my ignorance and spit out the required fare.

That's when she elbows me in the side.

"Hey! I'm talking to you!"

I'm not paying attention. Maybe I am too caught up in the act of buying a ticket to even notice her. But when I turn my head and catch a glimpse of her, another possibility comes to mind. I see a woman in her mid-fifties. She's wearing several layers of clothing. Far too many for the temperature outside. Her hair is tucked beneath a rumpled corduroy hat, but it's no match for several wayward strands that have escaped and shot out in several directions. We look like polar opposites, the business guy and the disheveled woman.

"Sorry?" I say.

"I was trying to get your attention," she pleads.

My subconscious steels itself for the inevitable request to come. That voice is in my head again, reminding me to be cautious. The voice of James Earl Jones, Moses, and Mom, whispering, "*Pay attention.*"

She continues, "You lost? You look like you need some help."

This is not the question I was expecting. I wonder what I can say to look less vulnerable and quickly extract myself from a somewhat uncomfortable situation.

"I'm fine. Just buying a ride downtown." I break eye contact and nod toward the machine. "Trying to pick the right fare."

I guess I was not dismissive enough, because she is still standing beside me.

"That's what I thought," she continues, gesturing on certain words to add emphasis. "I saw your *bag* . . . with the *sign* . . . and the way you're *dressed* . . . and you *staring* . . . and it all looked a little . . . I don't know . . . *confusing*!"

Confusing? Me?

"Here." She holds out her hand with a flimsy plastic card pinched between her fingers. "Take this day pass. I'm done with it. It'll get you downtown."

Huh?

The card is in my hand before I can stop her. I examine the front and the back. It is a genuine, bona-fide ticket to ride. And it'll save me six bucks. I look up to acknowledge the gift, but she is already walking away toward the terminal. I call out, "Thanks!" but she doesn't look at me. She just holds her right arm above her head and waves good-bye.

Now I really *am* confused. I expected this woman to ask for a handout, and instead she offers me a free ride on the train. She didn't have to do it. She could simply have thrown her ticket in the trash as hundreds of others would do that evening. But she didn't.

She gave it to *me*.

I'm obsessed with this thought for the entire ride downtown. I'm embarrassed for having misjudged the woman and overwhelmed by her simple act of kindness. Before I know it, the conductor's voice calls out, "Next stop is Grand!" interrupting my daydream and reminding me I need to get off the train.

I'm not entirely sure where I'm going, so I open my backpack and do a cursory check of my hotel itinerary. It's a place I've stayed before, but it's been a couple of years. I trust myself to find it quickly given that the landscape in downtown Chicago doesn't change much. I glance at the address and then stuff the paper back in my bag.

I exit the train and climb the steps out of the subway. When I finally reach street level, I'm not sure if I came up on the east side or the west side of the block, so I look around for signage that will tell me which way to go. I stand motionless for ten seconds when a friendly man in a long, black, wool overcoat approaches me.

"Can I help you out? Where you going? You look lost."

I must be wearing a permanent look of confusion on my face. And fear. The voice calls out again, *"Pay attention."*

"Don't be scared. We're not New Yorkers!" he adds.

Now that's funny.

"I'm headed to the Fairfield Inn on Erie," I say. "Just trying to figure out which way to go on State to get there."

"Erie?" His face crinkles. "I think you mean Ontario. There's no Fairfield Inn on Erie. I've lived here for nearly thirty years, so I know. My name's Ellis. What's yours?"

"I'm Scott."

"Well, Scott, I'm headed that direction, so just follow me."

James Earl Jones's monologue in my head quickly changes to the voice of my own mother warning of "Stranger Danger." But Ellis didn't offer free candy or ask me to help find his lost puppy, and it *feels* as if he's walking the right direction, so I tag along behind. We walk a half dozen steps when he stops.

"Here. Lemme get that for you." Ellis reaches down and grabs the handle of my purple suitcase. It all happens too quickly for me to react. "It'll be easier for me," he adds.

Now the stranger has my belongings.

And he's walking fast.

James, Moses, and Mom form a chorus in my head, "*We told you to pay attention!*"

I consider wrestling the handle away from him, but decide against it. I'm not really known for my clear-headed response in a crisis. My tiny purple suitcase doesn't look as if it is owned by a businessperson. If I grabbed for it now, there's a high probability the police would descend on the scene, witness a lanky guy with a sport coat and a weak grip screaming like a third-grade girl, frantically trying to pry a child's suitcase from the hands of a very frightened man. Common sense suggests I'd be the one on the receiving end of the Taser.

I decide to stay right on his heels in lieu of causing any undue drama. Besides, looking at Ellis's physique, I feel fairly confident I could outrun him. As I close the gap, he notices my close proximity and uses it as an opportunity to engage in a bit of idle patter. He asks where I'm from. He talks about local landmarks. He riffs on the value of a positive attitude. It's a scattershot of words and anecdotes. Then he randomly shouts out, "Hoo wee! Mighty fine woman!"

"Which one?" I ask, glancing around for a supermodel.

"Doesn't matter, Scott. I like 'em all. I just gotta say it out loud every once in a while so they know I appreciate 'em."

Ellis is a quirky, fast-talking man. And seems genuinely helpful.

But I'm still skeptical.

We walk a few more blocks and finally reach the corner of Michigan Avenue. Things are beginning to look familiar to me. Ellis stops at the crosswalk to make his way across the boulevard, so I seize the opportunity.

"Hey, Ellis. I remember how to get there from here." I reach for my bag. "I think I'll take the scenic route up Michigan and then cut across when I get to Erie."

"You sure? I'm happy to take you there. Gonna walk right by the place."

"I'm sure."

"Alright. Here you go." He tilts the handle of the suitcase toward me. "Enjoy the evening. Just do me a favor and look down Ontario as you cross. I think your hotel is there."

Happy to have my purple bag back, I offer my hand. "Will do, Ellis. I appreciate the help."

During our conversation, the red, lighted hand that was stopping traffic in Ellis's crosswalk has moved to mine. The green stick figure beckons him across Michigan, so he shakes hands quickly, offers a genuine "Nice to meet you," and steps into the street.

I'm alone again, and the apprehension is gone. I breathe a little deeper as I walk down Michigan Avenue, marveling at an entire Magnificent Mile of prime real estate dedicated to purchasing stuff we don't need. I notice all the tourists window shopping or coming in and out of the stores with bags filled with goodies, and I'm reminded that many people consider shopping a hobby. It's a way to pass the time. To entertain. And it's a hobby I used to enjoy.

But not anymore.

Now, I drag my purple suitcase past Eddie Bauer and see the fancy duffel bags and luggage displayed on the racks at the back of the store, and I'm not sure whether to feel excited or sad that I no longer feel compelled to upgrade. The thought clatters in my head as I reach the next intersection and see the street sign.

Ontario.

I *could* just open my backpack to check the hotel's address, but I'm up for continuing the adventure that started back at the airport, so I walk down Ontario a couple of blocks to see if Ellis is the real deal. I spot a Garrett's Popcorn shop that trips a memory, but I can't decide if this is truly familiar or if it's déjà vu from the Garrett's store back at the airport. That's when I hear it.

"Hey, Scott! Scott!"

The sound of my name is echoing off the buildings, so I can't tell which direction to look. Then I see a figure standing on the next corner, waving his arms like mad above his head.

"See, Scott! I told you so! Ontario!"

It's Ellis. He took a different path than I did, but ended up walking past the hotel, just as he said he would. He proudly shouts into the air, pronouncing each syllable as if he's in a spelling bee.

"ON-TAIR-EEE-OH!"

Up ahead I see the flags hanging from the building with the familiar Fairfield Inn logo. I look back at Ellis without breaking stride, and he points toward the hotel and shrugs his shoulders as if to say, "And you doubted me?"

He stays put as I approach.

"You were right!" I confess. "I appreciate it."

"No problem! Just glad you got here. Have a good one, Scott." He turns to walk away, and I finally notice his feet. His ankles are protruding from the bottom hem of his trench coat. The cuffs of his pants are ragged and worn. One of his brown loafers is falling apart, the sole ripping off the leather upper, leaving a big hole on the right side. The voices cry out, *"Now you're paying attention!"*

"Hey, Ellis!" I call out. He wheels around on his heels to face me, and I ask, "What can I do for you? You know, to say thanks."

"Me?" he asks, pointing to his chest and raising his eyebrows. It appears he is as surprised by my question as I am. He thinks for a beat.

"I could use a cup of coffee?"

It's a declaration that sounds like a question. "No problem," I say. "They usually have a fresh pot in the lobby."

We walk through the hotel doors, and Ellis's head is on a swivel. He is looking around at the modern decor. The same decor I see nearly every week and take for granted. He is less talkative now. We proceed side by side to the coffee station that sits near the elevators.

"Fresh out!" shouts the hotel attendant when he notices us staring at the empty table. "But we'll have more in about a half an hour."

Ellis dismisses the inconvenience. "That's OK." He turns to leave.

It's after seven o'clock, and I haven't eaten. I remember seeing a sandwich shop next door. I hear the voice of my mother in my head, but this time, it's not the voice telling me not to run with scissors or play with matches. This is the voice reading me the words she inscribed in a Bible she gave me for my fifteenth birthday.

> *Scotty,*
>
> *The true secret of success and happiness can be found on these pages. Matthew 25—"The sheep and the goats"—is God's message to us on reaching the kingdom by serving him through the needy.*
>
> *This book is more valuable than a college degree. Pray to the Holy Spirit to help you understand and gain wisdom from these words. Pray always for guidance and listen. You will always make a difference in someone's life.*
>
> *God Bless You, Mom*

My mom may be a chronic shopper, but she also knows what's truly important. This challenge is supposed to be about becoming more connected to those around me. I feel that we've succeeded when it comes to close family and friends. But now I see the opportunity I've been missing.

"Hey, Ellis. I'm really hungry. I was going to grab a sandwich next door. You wanna join me? I'm sure they have coffee."

He doesn't hesitate to accept the offer. We walk into Subway, where we stand in line, marinating in the cologne of fresh-baked bread and deli meat. Surrounded by less extravagant decor, Ellis becomes animated again, chatting it up with the sandwich artists behind the counter.

I interrupt to ask if they have coffee. No dice. Just sodas.

I turn to Ellis, "How about I buy you dinner instead."

He pauses for a beat, then accepts. "OK, Scott. That'll be fine. I haven't eaten all day."

"Nothing?"

A crack appears in his enthusiastic facade, and he looks at me with heavy eyes. Eyes that confess his lack of a meal is not due to his simply being too busy. Or on a diet.

"Not. A. Thing."

His enthusiasm returns as he orders a foot-long sub, piling on ingredients like it's a salad-bar buffet. As the sandwich artist finishes the masterpiece, Ellis says under his breath, "I'm gonna' crush this sandwich!"

I pay at the cashier, and we take our plastic dinner baggies. I grab a bottle of water while Ellis fills his mammoth-sized fountain drink that Subway calls a "regular." A testament to our "more-is-better" society.

When he places the lid on his cup, he looks toward the door, then notices that I have taken a seat in a booth.

"Oh! You're eating here?" he asks.

He looks confused. Like an out-of-towner trying to buy a train ticket.

"I am," I say. "You're welcome to join me if you like. Unless you have somewhere else you need to be."

Ellis sits down across from me without removing his coat. We talk nonstop while we finish our sandwiches. We chat about childhood. Where we grew up. What kind of movies we like. And all the while I can't help but think of the people walking by outside and peering in the window. Noticing two men eating sandwiches. Connecting. One in a wool overcoat. One in a sport coat. Unable to see our shoes. Blind to our differences.

Just as it should be.

Chapter Twenty-Seven

My Better Half

Only be careful, and watch yourselves closely so that you do not forget the things your eyes have seen or let them fade from your heart as long as you live. Teach them to your children and to their children after them.

(*Deuteronomy 4:9 NIV*)

This Chicago experience stays with me for days, like the all-you-can-eat fried seafood buffet at Captain D's. It's satisfying but leaves me feeling a bit unsettled. I'm not sure what to make of the whole ordeal.

The voice in my head had been telling me to pay attention. And deep down, I believe the recent turn of events was orchestrated by the voice as well. It's not every day you find yourself on the receiving end of generosity from people who aren't in a position to offer it. It's got to mean something.

"*Come on, Scott. Pay attention.*"

Over the past several months, our daily focus has been on a couple of areas. The first is *owning what we have*. We have learned to live with gratitude and appreciation, using everything at our disposal and redefining our needs. Every time I see my suitcase or my socks, I am reminded of how we are already abundantly supplied.

Our second area of focus has been on *growing in faith together*. Admittedly, the *together* part has been more intentional than the *faith* part. We are spending more quality time with those we love. It's not always time spent in service to God, but we can easily look back on events such as the lake baptism and our daily devotionals and see that we truly have gown closer to the divine, even if by accident.

But what about the third leg of our mission statement, *serving others*?

Not so much.

It's easy to get distracted from serving others. It's enough just to handle the day-to-day needs of your own family, much less anything "extra." In fact, those daily chores often feel like an act of service. Though Saint Peter may disagree when I finally reach the Pearly Gates, I can make a pretty strong argument that shoving food into a toddler's face hole and cleaning up what comes out the egress a couple of hours later is not exactly a pleasurable, selfish experience.

I push this thought to the back of my mind when I pick Jake up from school. Before we go home, we need to visit Home Depot to replace light bulbs (no, we are not operating on candle power in the Dannemiller house) and make a stop at the post office to mail a package. I go into multitasking mode, using the excursion as an excuse to spend some quality time with my son while getting some things checked off my to-do list. My mom used to do the same thing with me, only her hardware store was the clearance rack at TJ Maxx. We had so much of this kind of "togetherness" that I knew she wore a size 4 petite before I had learned to tie a shoe (which mom would like in a low heel, size 6, if you could check in the back).

I pull up in front of the school, and Jake independently straps his seven-year-old body into the car seat with no help needed from Dad. I marvel at the simple sign of growth, but silently lament the fact that we are one step closer to the days when I will be a social anchor around his neck, embarrassing him by singing Whitney Houston songs at the top of my lungs in front of his friends and wearing black dress socks with sandals.

But innocence remains. At our first stop, we jump out of the car and he grabs my hand as we walk into the post office. I smile as we make small talk. I ask him about his day, and he responds by grilling me about Kevin Durant's shoe size and Wilt Chamberlain's inseam length. It doesn't matter that he doesn't really answer my question. "Dudes" come in small packages these days, and my kid is a walking book of sports statistics. It's what makes him who he is.

Our conversation is interrupted by a voice coming from below.

"Hey buddy, you got a second?"

I look down and see a man sitting on the curb. His eyes are tired, like half-drawn mini blinds. A woman sits beside him with her head in her hands. I get that familiar feeling. The same feeling I felt with Ellis back in Chicago. A body split in two. One half wanting to hear the man's story, and the other wishing I had chosen the other entrance and avoided this interaction altogether.

The sliding doors open, but I don't slide through. One half of me wants to, but my better half is attached to a compassionate second-grader who knows the meaning of the word "ignored."

I turn toward the couple, "Sure. What's up?"

The woman starts to speak and then coughs into her lap, deferring to the man. He explains, "My wife and I sell papers." He grasps the lanyard around his neck, displaying a badge that says he works for *The Contributor*, Nashville's homeless newspaper. "We've been really sick, so this morning we went to the clinic. The doctor says we both have pneumonia."

The wife coughs on cue.

"By the time we got back, there were no more papers for us to sell, and we don't have enough money for rent. Can you help us out?"

I glance down and realize I've let go of Jake's hand and taken two more steps toward the door. But Jake isn't moving. He's enthralled, and he's doing precisely what I tell him to do dozens of times per week.

Look someone in the eye when they are talking to you, son.

I could simply say, "Sorry! I don't have any cash on me." But Jake turns toward me and his eyes meet mine, just as the man finishes his request.

Quality time.

Looking into my son's eyes, I realize any kid that remembers Derek Jeter's batting average with runners in scoring position also remembers exactly how much money I took out on our recent trip to the ATM. There's no getting around it. While I still feel torn in two, I would much rather my better half explain to Jake that we should help people no matter the circumstance, rather than have the other half explain the meaning of the word *cynical.*

So my better half reaches into my wallet and pulls out the only bill there, while the other half wishes cash machines spit out bills in much smaller denominations.

I say, "God Bless" as I hand the man a twenty. He takes it in his right hand and quickly shoves it into his coat pocket. The wife looks up and nods in acknowledgment while he thanks us profusely, going on and on about how much this helps and how we're so generous. I quickly blurt out, "No problem. Really. No problem at all." The man is gracious beyond words, yet I am unable to fully accept his gratitude knowing the turmoil I felt inside.

Once we're back in the car, we're silent. This is rare with our kids. I have to look back to make sure Jake is still breathing. He just smiles and looks out the window. I know he must be thinking about the couple. Another half mile down the road, his voice cuts through.

"What's pneumonia?"

"What's rent?"

Always the fact finder, his questions are about details. I answer him with the best *Webster's* dictionary response I can, happy to be having a good conversation with him. Eventually I guide him to the point of our exchange, which was all about helping people. Even if we weren't sure exactly what they were going to do with the money.

Later that night, we sit down to dinner. The kids are being loud (as usual), and I am getting unnecessarily agitated by the fact that they are not stuffing their faces fast enough (as usual). That's when Gabby reminds us of our ritual that calms everyone down.

Thorns and Roses.

We make our way around the table, moving from youngest to oldest. Audrey shares how her thorn was that her best friend Ellie wasn't at school, and her rose was that she got to have art class. She tries to change the subject and ask us about whether dragons are real or not, when Jake chimes in.

"My turn!"

Per the rules, we agree to table the dragon discussion until after the game. Audrey is reluctant at first but then concedes to her brother.

I ask, "OK, buddy, what do you want to start with?"

"A thorn."

"So what's your thorn for today?"

All eager at first, now that he has the floor his voice gets quiet and we have to wait for him to finally get the courage to respond with, "We didn't get to go out at recess because it was raining."

"And what's your rose?"

He's still a bit sheepish when he shares, "We got to help people today. They needed money to pay for their house and we gave it to them."

Gabby asks for details, and he shares them. It's a proud moment. One of those times where you pat yourself on the back for doing something right as a parent. A moment to overshadow all the times you overreacted to toys on the floor or dry toothpaste spit crusting in the sink. I hoped it would be one of those supremely beautiful moments when we all ponder the plight of the poor and resolve to give more on a daily basis.

But that doesn't happen. Instead, halfway through the story of the people at the post office, Audrey asks why Jake's story is more important than her own questions about whether dragons are real or not. Sure, she acknowledges the importance of the rose in Jake's day, but there's no need to belabor the point for crying out loud.

But that's not why I'm disappointed.

I'm disappointed in myself. I had this incredible experience in Chicago and helped Ellis get a meal, but it was a reciprocal exchange. And the post office? It wasn't a purely selfless act. While it is true that we have redefined what our needs are over the past several months, and even spent less money, I still hesitate to give of myself. It's not automatic. So I ask: What's that all about? What will it take to truly change? To become more selfless?

How can I turn my better half into a better whole?

Chapter Twenty-Eight

Brainiacs Revisited

Each of you should give what you have decided in your heart to give, not reluctantly or under compulsion, for God loves a cheerful giver.

(2 Corinthians 9:7 NIV)

What can I say? I'm stingy. A tight-wad. Ebenezer Scrooge in cargo pants.

Sure, I may reach deep into my pockets for some strangers, but it takes a crowbar to my hands to finally pry the treasure loose. It's as if the more stuff I accumulate, the more I tend to hoard it, and this gets in the way of actually helping my fellow man. How horrible is that? It's not something I want to put on my résumé, that's for sure. But the good news is, I'm not alone. There is a mountain of research showing that it is human nature to be selfish with our stuff. Think Darwin. We're hardwired to look out for numero uno. Survival of the fittest. And the scientific support of selfishness teaches me that there *is* something I am consistently willing to share with no strings attached.

Blame.

I will gladly hand over the responsibility for my shortcomings to someone else entirely. I call it "effective delegation." So, having scientific backing for my selfishness is very reassuring.

See? It's not my fault that God made us all selfish. Darwin said so.

But there's a major problem with this theory that humans are inherently selfish, and it is this: some people give of their time and treasure even when they don't get anything in return. So what does science say about them?

Answer: not much.

Up until a few decades ago, these truly altruistic givers were considered a rare anomaly. Like albino monkeys. Or people who can eat a spinach salad without big chunks of it getting stuck in their teeth. These freaks of nature were swept aside. But that was before the advent of technology such as functional MRI machines that can show what's going on in your brain when you are actively doing things, like shopping or giving to charity, for example. And this has inspired a new set of researchers who are hell-bent on identifying the heavenly roots of generosity. While this is surprising to me, given that the people who would benefit most from an increase in altruism are those least likely to have the cash needed to fund a huge research project, scholars are doing it anyway.

In 2009, the University of Notre Dame started its Science of Generosity Initiative, which explores economics, psychology, sociology, and neuroscience to find out why we give. I figured their collection of research on the subject might be able to tell me why I'm so tight-fisted and perhaps even suggest how I could overcome these shortcomings.

I sifted through the web looking for clues. There were lots of interesting studies they referenced, such as one about senior citizens and how those who volunteer more actually live longer.[1] Another study shows that wealthy people tend to give less.[2] A paper shows that children as young as eighteen months old will help an adult stranger, even when no immediate benefit is offered.[3]

And then I ran across something familiar: our old friend the *nucleus accumbens*. We last talked about the *nucleus accumbens* in chapter 12 when we explored the physiological reason behind our love of shopping. In case you've forgotten, this is the area of the brain that is flooded with the pleasure hormone dopamine anytime our cravings or expectations are satisfied, such as when we get a great deal on that new Snuggie we've been lusting over on late-night TV. It's essentially a reward center tucked inside your melon, and it drives a lot of our buying decisions.

Interestingly enough, a couple of studies showed that this same area lights up when we give to charity. But how is that? We're not getting any material goods in return for our giving; we have less than we had before making the donation. The subjects of the studies were being paid for their help (some as much as $100), but their donations came directly from their own proceeds—in some cases, involuntarily.[4] But the *nucleus accumbens* still lit up. Why?

It appears that people actually *do* get something from giving, even though it can't be measured. For some, it's an ego boost. We simply feel like better human beings when we help those less fortunate. For others, the pleasure comes from being able to visualize the good that our generosity accomplishes, as evidenced by a study where people gave more when they saw actual photos of people they were helping, rather than just silhouettes.[5] Or maybe it's just feeling connected to others that creates these good feelings. This is supported by research showing that subjects who were given a nasal spray of oxytocin (the hormone released when we bond with others) were 80 percent more likely to donate than those who were given a saline spray.[6] All this is to say that researchers still aren't sure what the primary motivator is, but their findings are taking a sledgehammer to the theory that humans are inherently self-serving.

And this same sledgehammer hits me square on the forehead.

I now realize I need to change my weird relationship with stuff. I see *my* stuff as *mine*. And we're not just talking about tangible items. This applies to *my* time as well. I *own* it. I am *entitled* to it. The trouble is, this attitude only amplifies the sense of loss I feel when I give it away. It's taking the *owning what we have* part of our mission statement to the extreme, and it leads to my operating from a mentality of scarcity rather than abundance. "Give 'til it hurts" isn't working for me. It should be "Give 'til it helps."

One of the big questions at the start of this challenge was wondering if avoiding purchases would actually help us fulfill the *serving others* portion of our mission statement. And now it's staring me in the face. It's not the purchases that are getting in the way. Nope. It's my attitude toward *my* time and *my* treasure. And that's where I need to shift.

Gabby and I discuss this at length. We are true partners when it comes to charitable giving. She is the one who manages our family finances, schedules social events and volunteer efforts, and donates money like she's passing out breath mints. Meanwhile, my job is to grumble and run to the bathroom anytime she pulls out a pen and a checkbook.

I have a nervous belly.

After a bit of back-and-forth, Gabby and I agree we've been fairly haphazard in our giving. In a lot of cases, we give to causes where we have direct contact and receive tangible rewards, such as donating to our kid's school so that it can get a new computer lab. Or donating to friends who are running a marathon to benefit cancer. Or donating to our church, where we spend a good deal of time. It's not all of our giving, but quite a bit could be categorized as self-serving.

We need a strategy.

Gabby suggests we focus. "Why don't we pick a cause and stick with it?" she declares. "We can develop a relationship with them. Be more consistent. Maybe even volunteer on a regular basis."

"But what about our friends? What do we do when they ask for a donation?" I ask, throwing cold water on her plan.

"We would still do all of that. This would just be . . . additional."

Additional?

I think I have to go to the bathroom.

After thirty minutes and a sleeve of Tums, I am finally on the bandwagon. The tough part is choosing an area of focus. The task feels overwhelming. The world has more than enough need, so selecting one cause feels inadequate. If we choose to help the homeless, does that mean we're turning our backs on domestic-violence victims? Or what about prison ministry? Environmental clean up? Animal rights? Mental health?

Yes. We should do all of that and more.

But we can't.

Here is where the voice of James Earl Jones would come in handy. Dear God, where are you calling us now? And answer promptly, please.

We're quite impatient.

Chapter Twenty-Nine

Filling

For we are God's handiwork, created in Christ Jesus to do good works, which God prepared in advance for us to do.
(Ephesians 2:10 NIV)

If this year is about anything, it's all about getting back to the basics. We're not taking things to the extreme, but we are trying our best to strip away the fluff. So, as we prayed for direction to finally focus on serving others, the cause became evident.

Hunger. The most basic need of all.

I've never been hungry in my life. Never missed a meal because the cupboards are empty. But I'll still say, "I'm starving" if it's been over five hours since I last ate.

Can someone say, "Exaggeration"?

And this is the trouble with abundance. If we are around it too long, it starts to seem normal somehow, as if that is how it has always been and that is how it will always be. So we lose our perspective. We stop noticing. If abundance is average, then overwhelming excess becomes our new definition of plenty.

Time to recalibrate.

In looking for a cause to connect us, we decide on a charity called the Society of St. Andrew (SoSA). We have known about them for some time and have been involved on the periphery. Their whole mission is to reclaim some of the 133 billion pounds of food that is wasted in the United States every year—roughly 1,300 calories per person, per day—and then distribute it to those who need it most.[1] Food pantries. Soup kitchens. Hungry individuals. They do this primarily by coordinating with growers to glean their crops, salvaging fruits and vegetables that would normally rot in the fields because it simply doesn't meet the size and shape specifications of the distributors and grocers.

Yes. We Americans are very picky about our stuff. Produce included.

As soon as we make this choice, it feels like a switch has flipped. We instantly feel more connected and part of something bigger than ourselves. Sure, maybe it's prideful. Or selfish. Or an abomination to the Scriptures that tell us that we should not boast of the good we do. But I honestly believe God is making good use of our ugliest traits—traits such as selfish pride—and using them for the good of the kingdom.

So we meet the fine folks at SoSA. They are a very small organization that does big things. With just two people on staff at the local office, it's easy for us to build a personal connection with them, including Lynette, the local director. And we happily support them financially, knowing that 96 percent of the money we donate will go directly to helping feed hungry people. But money is just part of the equation. We know we need to get physically involved and pry loose the stranglehold we have on *our* time.

Lynette tells us of an upcoming opportunity. A local church will be hosting a Green Bean Drop, so we agree to volunteer.

When we arrive at the church, we see a big section of the parking lot is roped off, and in the center is a giant pile of green beans in crazy shapes and sizes. Green beans that were destined for a giant rotting hole at the landfill.

The beauty of this work is the kids can get involved too. We spend several hours sifting rocks out of the beans and putting them in recycled plastic grocery bags. Meanwhile, representatives from local food pantries and soup kitchens come by to collect them. There are also plenty of hungry individuals dropping in to take home a bag or two for their own families. It's a beautiful buzz of activity. Our kids shake the hands of the recipients and offer bags of fresh abundance. Both giver and receiver see Christ in the eyes of the other.

Our brains light up.

And so do our hearts.

So we get more involved.

A few weeks later we go to a warehouse near downtown Nashville where a semitrailer has just dropped thousands of pounds of sweet potatoes. Some are shaped like cucumbers. Or broken Slinkys. Others are the size of a toddler. In a grocery store, my judgmental nature would think they were the result of farming near a toxic waste dump. But SoSA sees the beauty in the mess and transforms it into something life-giving.

Kind of like God.

There is literally a ton of work to be done to sack the potatoes and help distribute them to food pantries and soup kitchens all over the metro area. No individual recipients this time. And the kids are a bit distracted. They are the only children around, so they start picking out choice spuds and creating a little Dannemiller potato head family on the ground, giving them special voices and personalities like it was some sort of stop-action movie. Jake is screaming, "Look, Dad! This one looks like you, with a long skinny head!" Or they're riding four-wheeled dollies down the ramp of the loading dock. It seems putting potatoes onto a truck doesn't create the same connection for them as handing green beans directly to the people who will be eating them.

Frankly, I'm feeling the same way. This time it feels more like work.

I'm reminded of the research participants who were more likely to give when they saw a photo of the person they were helping. The less connected we are to those around us, the more selfish we become. This thought is all at once humbling and enlightening. On the way home, I look in the rearview mirror and interrupt the kids, who are in the middle of a fight over the arm rest.

"So guys, what did you think about today?"

Audrey is the first to answer, "It was fun at first, and I liked making the potato family, but then it got boring. All we were doing was putting a bunch of weird-shaped potatoes into a bag."

"What about you, Jake?"

My son nods in agreement. Kids arc kids. You can't fault them for wanting life to be fun. And there are only so many potato sacking games you can play before your children figure out helping others isn't always a thrill a minute.

Gabby sees where this is going and takes over.

"Do you know who those people were who picked up the potatoes?"

"No," they answer in unison.

Gabby explains how they weren't going to eat several hundred pounds of potatoes all by themselves, but rather give them away to people they know who need them. This leads to a discussion of soup kitchens and food pantries and what they do. The kids have a small frame of reference from a couple of times we have served at homeless shelters in the past.

Then she talks about where the potatoes came from, how they were going to be wasted, and how our small act of sacking helped ensure that something God made wasn't going to rot but instead was going to help make casseroles to feed hungry people. Maybe even casseroles topped with marshmallows.

They are silent for a moment. I interpret this to mean that they were deep in thought. Considering the plight of their fellow man. Ruminating on how they had done some good for the kingdom of God. Then Audrey breaks the silence.

"I don't think I like sweet potatoes, even if they have marshmallows on them."

And this is the big takeaway from the event. Food critique. Gabby and I agree to revise our tactics and our expectations.

In the weeks that follow, we learn about the ministry of our local food bank, Second Harvest. It turns out that they have a fantastic opportunity for people of all ages to serve. Each week, they fill backpacks with food and distribute them to local schools. The schools send them home with kids who won't have enough to eat over the weekend. Thousands of backpacks.

It's staggering.

We go on a Wednesday night, eager for a "do-over," and are met by Marian, a representative of the food bank. She is bright and cheerful and tolerant. She kindly offers a snack of peanut butter sandwiches, which our kids gladly accept. While I silently ponder the bad karma that will come if my kids don't finish every last bite of the food they have been generously offered by a food pantry, Marian orients us to our task, explaining how we will be filling gallon Ziploc bags with a variety of food items; and those bags will be given to the schools, who will place them in the backpacks to send home with the kids. She has a sample backpack for display, and it looks just like any you might see slung over the shoulders of a kid at JFK Elementary School in Anytown, USA. She also explains that the food in the packs may be the only thing the kids have to eat all weekend.

My kids don't finish their sandwiches.

In an effort to avoid the lightning bolt that is sure to come straight from heaven, Gabby fashions a to-go container out of napkins and brings the PB&Js with us to the packing room. There are roughly twenty people volunteering this night, children included, and we are the only newbies. The others already know the drill, so they quickly set up alongside a makeshift assembly line of tables covered with fruit cups, cereal, packets of mac and cheese, juice boxes, canned Beanie Weenies, and chocolate milk. Behind the tables are stacks of boxes with replacement supplies. It's a well-oiled machine.

Our kids are mesmerized by the tasty treats in front of them. It's all the food they love to eat. If meal planning was left to them, they would subsist on a steady diet of macaroni and juice, with a stray chicken finger thrown in every leap year. Even though we forbid them to eat any of the food, the giant pile of goodies ignites their enthusiasm. They quickly go to work filling the plastic baggies as instructed. Audrey is soon recruited off the line for box crushing, which is akin to popping bubble wrap, only bigger and stompier. Meanwhile, Jake's competitive nature kicks in and he starts revamping the packing process to maximize our speed, as if it's a training program for a NASCAR pit crew.

As a group, we fill 1,500 bags, and they are neatly packed into boxes to be sent to the schools. When it's over, Gabby and I look at that huge pallet of boxes and feel a mix of satisfaction and sadness. Our act of service has been very small, but when that energy is coupled with the hands of others, we can accomplish a considerable amount of good. Like we're all in the same boat rowing in unison toward a better world.

At the same time, each of those bags represents a tiny, hungry face.

When we get to the car, Gabby hands the kids their leftover sandwiches. Judging from their level of interest, we might as well have passed them each a copy of last week's *Wall Street Journal*. Audrey dreams aloud, "I wish I had some of that mac and cheese right now instead of this sandwich."

I want to scream.

But I don't.

Instead, I ask a question.

"What do you think about all those bags you packed tonight?"

Jake answers, "It was good. I liked how fast we were able to do it."

Audrey adds, "I liked the fruit cup."

Gabby switches directions, "Did you know those bags are for kids who don't get enough to eat? They put those bags in backpacks just like yours and send them home with them so they'll have enough to eat over the weekend."

Audrey is still thinking of the fruit cup. "I wish I got one of those backpacks," she says.

An idea springs to mind.

"Hey guys, imagine if you *did* get one of those backpacks and you got to take it home on Friday. What would you eat for dinner that first night?"

We scroll through the list of items that was in each bag: two packets of mac and cheese, cereal, a juice box, a fruit cup, a serving of chocolate milk, and a can of Beanie Weenies.

Audrey answers without hesitation, "I'd have mac and cheese, the juice box, and the cereal."

"What about for breakfast the next morning?"

"Chocolate milk and the fruit!"

Audrey is on a roll.

"And what about Saturday for lunch?" I ask.

Jake jumps in, filled with excitement at the prospect of turning eating into a game. "Mac and cheese and fruit!"

Gabby is quick to respond.

"Nope, you already ate your fruit. You gotta pick something else, or just stick with your mac and cheese."

Jake gets conservative, "Let's just do mac and cheese then." He pauses for a moment, then adds, "and a water."

Audrey nods in agreement. The line of questioning continues, "And what about dinner Saturday night?"

"What's left?" Jake asks, straining to remember.

"I think you only have some Beanie Weenies."

Audrey sounds worried. "Wait. We don't have any more fruit? Or juice? Or chocolate milk? I thought we had another juice."

Gabby is keeping tabs as well. "No, you already had all of that on Friday night and Saturday morning."

"So Beanie Weenies and water for dinner." Jake's voice is declarative. So it is written. And so shall it be done.

"What about breakfast on Sunday?" I ask.

"We don't have anything left, Dad!" He sounds incredulous. "Weren't you paying attention?"

"You're right. We don't have anything left. It's Sunday morning, and we may not get anything else to eat until we show up to school on Monday. One whole day with nothing but water."

One. Whole. Day.

The game isn't fun anymore. It's silent in the back seat. And silent in the front. Because in some ways, Jake is right. I hadn't lost track of our list of food, but I haven't been paying attention to the need that exists just beyond the pile of plenty that is immediately in front of me.

My son slices through the silence with a tentative question.

"Do any kids at *my* school get backpacks like that?"

Gabby answers this time. "I don't know, Jake. Probably so. We'd never know. Those backpacks look just like yours. And they're attached to kids who look just like you."

It's a quiet ride home. Rare. And raw. The connection has been made. I look in the rearview mirror, and both Audrey and Jake are eating their leftover sandwiches. Crumbs falling from their cheeks.

It's late, and tomorrow is a school day. We pull into the garage and hustle the kids to the bathtub. We clean them in five minutes flat. They are in their pajamas faster than Clark Kent in a bedtime phone booth. Things slow down when we get them into bed. A kiss goodnight. A quick prayer. A touch to the forehead.

"Daddy?" she stops me as I am about to close the door to her room.

"Yes, Audrey?"

Her voice is soft and sweet.

"We should do the backpacks again."

"Yes, we should, Audrey. Yes, we should."

And we are filled to overflowing.

Chapter Thirty

A Homemade Halloween

We do not dare to classify or compare ourselves with some of those who commend themselves. But when they measure themselves by one another, and compare themselves with one another, they do not show good sense.

(2 Corinthians 10:12)

I have been rejuvenated by seeing how this challenge has led us into a more intentional mode of service. While I would love to say this service-mindedness is a lasting thing, I can already see trouble on the horizon. The truth is, we're having a hard time staying focused. We've become distracted by the gauntlet of fall holidays that encourage navel-gazing and excess. There's Halloween with its excess candy, Thanksgiving with its excess food, and Christmas with its excess stuff.

It's not pretty.

At first glance, Halloween doesn't present an immediate threat to our vow of simplicity. It's OK to buy candy according to our rules, and since our neighborhood is literally infested with kids, we tend to buy a truckload of sweets for the occasion. Sure, we would rather purchase healthier snacks, but when my hand reaches for the pretzels and peanuts I'm reminded of that Halloween in third grade when my mom decided to pass out little baggies of dried potato sticks instead of the typical Sweet Tarts or Smarties. I woke up the next morning to find a bunch of angry trick-or-treaters had dumped the little chiplets all over our driveway, tossed the baggies into our front yard, and egged my grandfather's car.

Sugar withdrawal is real, and there is no cure.

So I buy Tootsie Rolls and Nerds, plus a bag of mini Reese's cups that may "accidentally" get lost in the back of the cupboard. When I go to hide my stash in the pantry, I find a bunch of candy that someone else had tucked behind a bag of granola.

"What's this?" I ask.

"Oh, man!" Gabby laments. "You weren't supposed to find that!" She takes hold of the bag as if it were her purse, and I was rummaging through it. She backs away to find another hiding spot.

"Wait. You were hiding it from *me*?! Why?"

Her only response is a dead-on impersonation of a giant, gluttonous man eating himself sick.

Point taken.

With the candy now safely ensconced in a concrete bunker fifty feet underground, we turn our attention toward the kids. When it comes to costume selection, they are waffling in the weeks leading up to the big day.

At first, Audrey wanted to go as a chicken. I was impressed by the originality of her choice and thrilled because her best friend went as a chicken the year prior and we could easily shoehorn the girl into a hand-me-over costume. But just as we were about to make a call to her friend's mom to reserve the chicken suit, Audrey's affections were somehow drawn to another animal—the bat.

I wonder how we can salvage this. Although the chicken and the bat are both winged creatures, that's where the resemblance stops. One good look at the free chicken costume and I realize that the answer is not a can of black spray paint and a fistful of imagination. At best she would come out looking like Foghorn Leghorn covered in soot after a tragic gunpowder accident, but never a bat.

And Jake? In keeping with the aviary theme, our sports-loving son wants to be an eagle.

I clarify, "You mean like one of the Philadelphia Eagles, right?"

He is looking at me like I've just asked him to eat a cupcake with spinach icing.

"No, Dad! Like the bird. A bald eagle."

I can't fathom why a second-grader would be so overcome with patriotic spirit that he would wish to actually *become* our national bird.

"Why do you want to be a bald eagle?"

"Because Collin says they can fly really fast and kill a full-grown man with their claws."

Of course.

As with most American families, we don't happen to have a bat outfit and a bald eagle costume just hanging in the closet. If our kids are going to have the costumes they want, we are going to have to do things the way they did it in prehistoric times and make them.

I go online and search for "homemade bat costumes." As soon as I hit ENTER, my screen is filled with images of people dressed in black. I look at each one for clues on how we might construct such a thing. Some of the outfits, particularly the adult female bat costumes, aren't really bat costumes at all, but merely bat-ish suggestions of such. Based on the high skin-to-fabric ratio, I think the women in the pictures are actually nannies of the child models who ran off screaming when they realized their bat costumes had shrunk to the size of hamster-wear, so the good-hearted gals are just trying to salvage the photo shoot as best they can. God bless 'em.

Looking past the scantily clad bat set, my eyes are drawn to some of the more elaborate kid costumes. Some have giant wings that extend three feet out, draping from the wrist. Others have complex headgear that looks as though it may have some embedded sonar technology. It's quite the visual feast. Looking over my shoulder, Gabby says, "Why don't you check Pinterest?"

"Pinterest? That's a mom thing, right? I don't think I have an account."

"OK. Let me pull it up." Gabby moves toward her computer and starts clicking away.

For those of you unfamiliar with Pinterest, allow me to explain. If Mary Poppins and Pottery Barn got married and had a baby website, this would be it. Pinterest is to crafting what Steve Jobs is to gadgets. Inspiring? Yes. But there is no equal in terms of its ability to make you feel that you have not lived up to your full potential as a human being. Still, it's impossible to look at Pinterest and not feel that you are simply one hot-glue gun away from having the perfect life.

Gabby types "homemade eagle costume" into the Pinterest search bar. Up pops no less than two dozen pictures of eagle costumes, each one more exquisite than the last. When I look at the birds, I can easily see why my kid wants to be an eagle. These outfits look so amazing they could be props at the next presidential inauguration.

Gabby clicks on one of the more tantalizing links, which takes her to a page of instructions on how to make an eagle that is full of awesome. The first step is: "Cut out feathers. You will need about 100 small 2" x 4" brown feathers, 70 large 3" x 6" and 80–100 small 2" x 4" white feathers." They fail to mention you will also need a dozen pair of scissors, a sharpening stone, enough felt to wrap the Superdome, and the steely resolve of Aron Ralston, that mountain climber who cut off his own hand with a dull knife to avoid dying while trapped beneath a giant boulder.

Next page?

We scan the pictures and their accompanying instructions for the next half hour. None of the costumes appear to be simple, and many use raw materials that would require a purchase. Deep down, we know that even if we *did* have everything we needed, our handiwork would pale in comparison to the pictures on the screen. And that's when it hits us: This website is the devil.

The site itself was created as a place where people could share ideas, inspire creativity, and organize information. Unfortunately, it has become an unrealistic measuring stick by which to judge your worth as a person. The *Today* show surveyed over 7,000 online fans to ask about their reactions to Pinterest, and nearly half of respondents report suffering from "Pinterest Stress"—the feeling that they just aren't crafty or creative enough.[1]

Other studies found a similar pattern with Facebook users. Research by Ethan Kross, a social psychologist at the University of

Michigan, found that the more time people spent on the popular social media site, the more depressed and lonely they felt.[2] Similar studies suggest that this is due to a phenomenon called "social comparison," the tendency to compare our own lives with those of others and believe that we are worse off than they are. These feelings are particularly powerful on Facebook, where people tend to show an overly favorable image of themselves.[3] Prompted by images of familial perfection, our lives look rather dull. We begin comparing the "highlight reels" of others to our own cutting-room floor. The pictures on the website show happy, well-dressed kids, smiling ear-to-ear as they bite into their birthday cake shaped like the Millennium Falcon. Next to the cake are homemade granola bars formed into tiny Chewbaccas and raw vegetables that have been sliced and diced to look like Storm Trooper helmets and space creatures. Then, we look up from our computers and see a seven-year-old boy running through the living room with underwear on his head. His little sister is right behind him, sporting a "panty cap" herself. She stops to jab a free hand, half-covered in spaghetti sauce, into the couch cushion to retrieve a muddy piece of gravel she pulled out of the garden for her rock collection. The toilet is running, and I start to yell, because dry leaves, carried on the cold fall breeze, are pouring into the house by way of the front door, which was left wide open.

Forgive us if we don't grab a camera to document the moment.

The contrast of a perfect website to the chaos of real life is jarring. But it's not Pinterest's fault. It's not Facebook's fault. It's us. The *Today* poll also showed that three-fourths of all women surveyed felt that they put far more pressure and judgment on themselves than anyone else did. And it led to an average level of stress that rated 8.5 out of 10.

Don't get me wrong. Our intentions are noble. We all want to do the right thing—to provide a safe, happy environment for our families. So we read the articles, scan the reviews, and sign up for newsletters. We look to simplify. Get back to basics. Shun the false idol of materialism.

So we go homemade. Nothing store-bought. Organic is best. And it feels so right. It's like getting back to our roots and getting by on our own imagination and initiative, just like our ancestors did. Who needs to buy granola bars when you can bake your own? Who needs pre-printed birthday invitations when do-it-yourself kits abound? Who needs mass-produced costumes when there are countless examples of homemade options on the web? And this is what we find ourselves saying at one o' clock in the morning, rocking back and forth in the corner, tucked in the fetal position like a crazy person while a homemade baby food concoction of pureed carrots and strained peas bubbles over on the stove.

Because that's what good parents do.

And this is the slippery slope we need to avoid. Because even though we may not be shopping, this kind of self-induced stress, while noble, sucks the grace out of life. In an attempt to live more authentically, we run the risk of replacing one obsession with another and losing our authentic selves in the process.

Gabby and I turn off the computer and gather some basic materials. We have some fabric, a couple pairs of sweatpants, black T-shirts, scraps of felt, buttons, a ball cap, a headband, a hot glue gun, and a used piñata shaped like a toucan. It feels a little like finding a bunch of leftovers in your fridge and trying to make a meal out of it. It reminds us of that old quote attributed to Michelangelo, where he said of one of his famous sculptures, "I saw the angel in the marble, and I carved until I set him free."

But we don't need an angel. We just need a bat and a bird.

Gabby constructs some bat wings out of felt and uses a safety pin to attach it to the shirt. I cut the giant beak off the piñata and use some elastic to strap it to the hat. We borrow some dove wings from the church Christmas play costume closet. We sew buttons and hot glue some pointy bat ears onto a kitty cat headband. The kids lend a hand to any tasks that have a minimal chance of inducing widespread frustration. The whole process takes roughly an hour.

When Halloween arrives, the kids put on their costumes, and they love them. It's certainly not because they look like a picture in a magazine but more likely because they had a hand in making them. As a nod to the pure awesomeness of the outfit, Audrey asks if hers can actually fly. And with some imagination, we tell her it can. Friends and family come over for the party to feast on hot dogs before taking to the streets to shake down all our neighbors for Snickers bars. When darkness falls, a dozen kids gather on the front porch, fueled by an excitement that can be matched only by the sugar rush to come. Before they head out like a wild band of pint-sized pirates, a few parents line them up to snap some pictures. It's chaotic. Half of the kids aren't looking. Others are poking at the costumes of the others.

But we will post the Halloween pictures online anyway. Because even though we know the photos will never end up in a magazine and no one will be clamoring for the instructions on how to create our eagle and bat outfits, we are certain that every time we look at the pictures in years to come, we hope to notice one thing above all.

Smiles. An endless stream of smiles.

Chapter Thirty-One

Christmas Tree Carnage

"For I know the plans I have for you," declares the LORD, *"plans to prosper you and not to harm you, plans to give you hope and a future."*

(Jeremiah 29:11 NIV)

No sooner have the kids come in from trick-or-treating than we begin to focus on what the rest of the year might bring. We feel a bit like a horse after a long ride that can smell the barn from about a mile away. The end of our challenge is in sight, with the giant hurdle of Christmas in front of us. We just hope the end of our year smells better than a paddock full of manure.

Thanksgiving is a wonderful experience. We spend the day with thirty family members sharing stories, laughter, and copious amounts of pie. The day leaves both our hearts and our bellies feeling full, though gorging myself on a trough of casserole side dishes makes me wonder why we've decided that shopping is off limits, but the sin of gluttony is perfectly acceptable. This food purchase loophole is nothing if not convenient for me, allowing excess as long as my waistband can contain it. Eating becomes my relief valve from the materialistic binge that normally follows Thanksgiving: Black Friday.

Black Friday is the busiest shopping day of the year. The term was coined by police in Philadelphia back in 1961, who named the day based on the horrendous traffic jams caused by shoppers enjoying a day off after stuffing their faces just twenty-four hours prior. It wasn't until the early '80s that Philadelphia businesses, upset by the negative connotation, redefined the term by telling the story that most retailers operate "in the red" for the first eleven months of the year due to a lack of profitability. So Black Friday is called "black" because it marks the time when businesses finally begin to operate "in the black."

Well played, capitalism.

As the television blasts nonstop advertisements for doorbuster sales, we are unfazed. Our ten months of training have finally paid off. It's relatively easy to stay away from the stampeding hoards who trample women and children in pursuit of a killer deal on a smartphone. Instead, we turn our attention toward family fun. Filled with leftover pumpkin pie and self-righteousness, I climb into the attic to retrieve our ghosts of Christmas past. We have three Rubbermaid tubs filled with decorations and several boxes of lights and other assorted Christmas accoutrements. By the time we finish adorning the house, the Griswold outdoor light display is out in full force, and it looks like a bunch of elves were doing keg stands with eggnog and puking up tinsel all over our living room.

Just the way we like it.

But there is one critical item I am unable to retrieve from the attic. I hesitate to mention it here, as I don't want this book to become overly political, but circumstance warrants that I state my position clearly.

We are "real tree" people.

Putting up an artificial Christmas tree is akin to giving St. Nicholas a wedgie. No. Make that an atomic wedgie. In fact, the only Christmas sin worse than an artificial Christmas tree would be replacing "Silent Night" with "Grandma Got Run Over by a Reindeer" as the closing hymn at the candlelight Christmas Eve service. If God had intended us to celebrate our Savior's birth with a plastic icon in our living rooms, he would have sent Jesus Christ to Earth as a department store mannequin.

Trust me. It's in the Bible.

But God laughs when we get all high and mighty. And somewhere, our Creator is having a good chuckle, because even though we may be avoiding the Black Friday sales, we also forgot to factor the real tree into our Year without a Purchase.

Each year, we normally stroll through the wooded majesty of the local Home Depot forest to select the perfect specimen for our home. It's a family tradition dating back centuries to the Dannemillers of old who also lacked basic skills in hunting, sawing, and shoe tying. But this year, we could not simply plunk down $29.99 for Christmas convenience. Gabby and I agree that such a purchase would certainly be a violation of the rules.

Ignoring our neighborhood covenant restrictions, I walk out our back gate and take a short stroll through the thorny woods behind our house. I spot many potential Christmas branches and Christmas bushes. Several cedar trees show promise. One in particular is about sixteen feet tall. Since we have a twelve-foot ceiling in the living room, I figure I could just chop it off at the four-foot mark and haul it home. Then I come to my senses. First, the only greenery is on the top three– to four-foot segment of the tree. The rest is barren. If I chopped it down, we would have a very tall "Christmas Stick" with a Texas cheerleader hairdo. Second, this tree is not on our property, and, if caught, I would certainly get a fine and a NastyGram from the neighborhood association president.

But third, and most important, the land behind our house is an overgrown old cemetery, complete with a handful of slate headstones remaining intact. Not that I'm superstitious, but this tree was most likely planted in honor of someone buried there. And if I were to chop it down and take it home, our holiday home would be plagued by the same sort of zombie magic that visited the Brady Bunch on their Hawaiian vacation when they removed the tiki idol from the ancient gravesite.

That's when a friend suggests we might be able to use the "experience" loophole. We could go to a tree farm, support a local farmer, and cut down our own tree. As soon as she mentions it, I have visions of an idyllic family outing. We could all get bundled in our warm coats, trudge up and down the rolling hills of a Tennessee farm in the brisk winter air, select the perfect tree, cut it down together, and drag it back to the farmer's barn, where his wife would have hot cocoa waiting. Then we would all snuggle up next to a glowing yule log and talk about our favorite Christmas memories.

And thus begins our adventure of overblown expectations.

The day after Thanksgiving, temperatures outside are hovering in the low 40s, yet our son insists on wearing less clothing than the average Hooters' waitress. It shouldn't surprise me, but it still drives me completely insane.

We load the car with the kids and their two cousins, Jack and Ava, and the arm wrestling and poking begins immediately. I'm not sure if it's the purchase withdrawal talking or something deeper, but my answer to this problem is to begin dishing out unrealistic threats.

"If you can't behave, we just won't have a Christmas tree. Santa will just have to put presents outside under the tree in our front yard. And what if it rains? Too bad. They'll all get wet. And it will be a result of your poor choices."

My strategy works as well as you might imagine.

We finally make it to the tree farm, where we are greeted by a cheerful guy wearing an orange apron, which reminds me of the same ones they wear at Home Depot, easing my transition. He is incredibly friendly, saying, "Welcome back!"

This happens to me a lot. People often think they know me, even though we have never met. I chalk it up to the fact that I bear a striking resemblance to "The Safe One" in every boy band on planet Earth. Or Steve, the host of the popular children's program *Blue's Clues*. But I don't correct our host for fear of hurting his feelings.

The man is extremely helpful, giving us a tour of the lot, showing us where we can find the "cut your own" trees, giving me a quick sawing lesson, and offering us hot chocolate. Rather than diving into the treats right away, Gabby and I hold them for ransom, as would any good parent.

"If you behave while we are finding our tree, then we'll have hot chocolate and candy canes afterward."

The kids take off running like greased pigs released from a branding pen, grabbing and shaking every tree in the "cut your own" forest. Even the fragile Charlie Brown-sized ones.

Our guide explains that the trees come in several varieties.

First is the Norway Spruce. It's a beautiful tree with firm branches for holding heavy ornaments. But when Audrey sticks her hand in, it comes out looking like she shook hands with a cheese grater. I believe the needles of the Norway are commonly used for sewing buffalo hide and applying prison tattoos.

Too pokey.

Next is the White Pine. This is a very fragrant tree with supple greenery. Unfortunately, it's freakishly long needles give it the appearance of Don King's hairdo.

Too bushy.

Finally, we sample the Leyland Cypress. Though it doesn't have needles, it has a perfect conical shape and a deep green color. At least that's what we tell ourselves when we get tired of the kids acting like crazy people.

It's just right.

We walk the rows of trees looking for the perfect cypress. But Jake will have none of it. I hear him call out from two rows over.

"I want the chubby tree!"

"Which one?" I shout, walking toward his voice.

"The chubby one! Right over here!"

I finally find him standing by what is perhaps the most oddly-shaped Christmas tree in the history of trees. It looks as if it has been fed a steady diet of simple carbs and unfiltered Camel cigarettes, stunting its growth.

"Buddy. That's tiny," I prod. "Besides, it's one of the pokey trees. Come look at this one over here."

He stands defiantly and asserts his seven-year-old power. "But I want *this* tree."

I look at the price tag. $30. Time for a little reasoning. I decide to point out the inferior aspects of the tree. "But son, look how short it is."

"I know. I like it!"

I dig deep into the vault of dad-isms. "We have a Christmas-tree rule. The tree has to be taller than mom and dad."

"Huh?"

"Yep. That's the rule. Just made it up, but it's the rule."

It does no good. Jake keeps complaining while we scout more options in the cypress row. Audrey helps us find just the right one. I fall to the ground and start sawing the tree. Jake whimpers in the background. My lack of lumberjack training is apparent, leading to a painfully long process. My sweatshirt is muddy. My shoulders are burning. My nose is running. Jake's sadness is growing with every back-and-forth of the blade. He is attached to the chubby tree. Like it had saved his life in Vietnam or something. By the time our cypress finally falls, he is crying, and I am fresh out of compassion.

This is definitely an "experience."

We drag the tree, our kids, and their cousins back up to the barn. Our cheery hosts point us toward the hot chocolate. Audrey pulls the handle on the dispenser.

All out.

More weeping, which we try to soothe with candy canes. Jake comments, "That's a tiny, stupid candy cane. We have bigger ones at home."

I snatch the tiny cane from his hand and offer, "Well, you can wait 'til we get home then!" Gabby checks my high school transcript and confirms that I failed Maturity 101.

Meanwhile, smoke from the yule log is blowing directly at us, giving me a mild asthma attack. The kids start sneezing and coughing dramatically.

The fresh pot of hot chocolate arrives, and the kids fill their cups to the brim and insert the stir sticks. Although we have given them a fair warning, Jake immediately sips through the straw and burns his mouth. No tears this time. Just anger.

"It's too hot to drink," he screams. If he could fight a Styrofoam cup, he would.

Meanwhile, Audrey runs up to me in tears. She filled her cup and went over to the fire. When she tried to sit down on the stump adjacent to the fire, she lost her grip and spilled cocoa all over her pants. Maybe it's all in my head, but I believe the resulting stain resembles the antichrist.

I feel her leg, which is still pretty warm. The cocoa is hot enough to cause tears, but not hot enough for a lawsuit.

I pat her on the back. "It'll be fine, honey."

"No it won't! My pants are ruined, and I don't have any more cocoa!"

Gabby sees me struggling like a fallen wrestler in a WWF tag team cage match and comes to my rescue. She takes Audrey to the car to look for a spare pair of pants. I turn to see Jake spill cocoa all over his white shirt. Another angry outburst follows.

Audrey returns wearing a pair of mismatched sweatpants. I hand her a cup of cocoa that I have been trying to cool by blowing on it while she was changing. For some reason, she grabs a plastic stir stick and, instead of putting it into the cup, she jams it into her mouth instead, piercing the roof of her mouth.

Tears.

"What happened, Audrey?"

"Part of my mouth came loose and is hanging down!"

Great.

Trying to be as patient as possible, I say, "Well, honey. That sometimes happens when you jam sticks into your mouth."

Trust me, the words sounded better in my head than they did when they hit the air in front of my face. Even so, an unspeakable rage is still bubbling inside me, fueled by impatience. It is so strong that I can see the remaining trees beginning to wilt. Somewhere an elf is having an aneurysm. This is not turning out as I had planned. This was supposed to be a wonderful family experience.

"Let's go!" I say, through gritted teeth.

Jake chimes in, "But I'm not done with my hot chocolate."

"Well, drink up, because we're leaving."

I turn to see Gabby holding her camera toward me.

"Here. Settle down, Dannemiller, and take a picture with me and my girls."

She has somehow consoled Audrey, who is now playing with her cousin Ava. I begrudgingly grab the camera and start snapping pics. Ava and Audrey start climbing all over Gabby, giggling and having a grand old time.

I want to say, "What the hell do you think is so funny?! Stop having fun! This trip has been a royal pain in the ass, and you should behave accordingly!"

But, thank the Baby Jesus, I don't say it. Instead, I just keep snapping. Capturing genuine smiles. Joy. Happiness.

I look at those photos later. They make life look perfect, if you look past the mismatched pants, stained shirts, and tear-streaked cheeks. Kinda like the images we see on Facebook and Pinterest. And this can be beneficial, because these pictures will be around for decades, reminding us of good times we had as a family. As I stare at the smiles shining back at me, the negative aspects of the outing slowly get pushed aside.

But why should we be in such a rush to forget the tough times? As clean and sanitized as perfection can be, it's also very boring. The truth is, when we ask ourselves which story is more likely to get told and retold—becoming a lasting family memory that brings laughter for future generations—the one that begins with, "Remember when we went to the tree farm and cut down the perfect tree?" is not the one that remains. The story that is rich in truth and beauty is the one that goes, "Remember when we went to the tree farm, and Jake cried because we wouldn't buy a midget Christmas tree, and Daddy got a rotator cuff injury, and Audrey spilled cocoa all over her pants and got that scar on the roof of her mouth from the stir stick?"

That's the one that lasts.

So perhaps the best gift we can give ourselves is to let go of perfection. No one cares if the dinner plates all match, or if the cider isn't warm enough, or if a strand of lights burns out. Those accidents happen. It's what we *do* with those accidents that make them extraordinary. The spirit we bring.

Last time I checked, the Bethlehem innkeeper's stable was not decorated by Restoration Hardware. Nope. It was chaotic, smelly, and messy. But we're still telling the story two thousand years later, joy-filled and grateful.

Chapter Thirty-Two

The Santa Clause

Take delight in the Lord,
and he will give you the
desires of your heart.
(Psalm 37:4 NIV)

The cypress tree is up, and the house is lit. As much as we want to reinforce the idea that Christmas is really about hope and joy coming to dwell with us on Earth, our kids think it's an all-you-can-eat toy buffet. I'm a little saddened by this, but at the same time, I can't fault Jake and Audrey. I was the same way when I was a kid. I would start making my Christmas list for the next year on December 26.

In a promotional video for Advent Conspiracy, a church movement that seeks to focus on the true meaning of the holiday, it is reported that Americans spend $450 billion on Christmas gifts every year.[1] That's billion. With a *B*. To put that in perspective, according to the United Nations Statistics Division, that is more than the gross domestic product of all but twenty-six of the world's nearly two hundred countries. It's hard to fathom. Thinking of it another way, Americans spend enough money each year at Christmas to purchase every single product and service produced by the sovereign nation of Austria in an entire year (estimated at just over $415 billion), which leaves us an extra $35 billion to liquidate Jordan ($33.8 billion in GDP) while we're at it.[2]

I do love their almonds.

It's no question that we are a bit gift-crazy in this country. It's a result of living in the most prosperous nation on the planet. And honestly, spending $450 billion is not a bad thing, as long as there is value in what you purchase. But my problem is that, like most Americans, I can hardly remember the Christmas gifts I received twelve months ago, much less during my childhood. I can count on one hand the number of presents that come to mind spontaneously when I think of Christmases past. There was the year my brother and I got one of those remote-controlled car tracks that smelled like electrical fire. And I remember the year we got new fishing poles, and Dad borrowed his boss's camper so that we could go to Lake Texoma and catch what felt like an entire lake full of fish. Then there was the time I asked for a puppy and got a stuffed animal instead, and the year after that, when Dad brought home a scraggly mutt from the pound, who I named Buckwheat.

I miss that dog.

I also miss the apple pie my mom used to make. I miss my siblings and I all waking up in our pajamas and running into my parents' bedroom at 5:00 a.m. I miss my grandpa coming to visit and bringing his dog Scamp, even though he bit me. Grandpa did too, actually. I only wish the dog had dentures as soft as Grandpa's.

But you know what? I don't miss any of the other presents.

As Christmas draws closer, the most consistent question our friends have been asking is, "Will your kids get *anything* on the big day?" Honestly, it is a struggle. When I think of Jake and Audrey waking up on Christmas morning, I try and remind myself that none of those gifts really matter. It's easy to say in my own head but harder to live in reality when your child excitedly makes out a Christmas list filled with things you know would make her squeal with delight. As we scan the lists that our kids have created, we hope to see lots of gifts that fit within our rules, such as "a charitable donation to Multiple Sclerosis" or "just make my favorite chocolate-chip pancakes and I'll be content." Instead, Jake's list is filled with techno gadgets and a few random toys he found in a Toys"R"Us catalog that somehow snuck past our mail security system using its fake ID. Audrey saw the same advertisements and cut out pictures of every stuffed animal and taped it to the paper.

Gabby and I peruse the lists and begin to suffer from our self-induced anxiety.

You may call it cheating. You may even call it blasphemy, but we decide to break the rules and buy a few gifts for our kids. Honestly, it was part of the plan all along. We called it "The Santa Clause." Cancelling Christmas, while possible in theory, just wasn't in the cards for us. We don't have the willpower. And now that we have almost a whole year behind us, we have learned that stuff isn't inherently bad, but it's the meaning we give to the stuff and the stress we shoulder in pursuit of it. But the question remains: Where is the middle ground for us to be *in* the Christmas world but not *of* it?

On one hand, if we don't give our children any gifts, we may inadvertently teach them to hate Christmas. On the other hand, if we over indulge them, we run the risk of cancelling out all the learning that has taken place over the past eleven months. In response to this conundrum, we decide to carry forward a gift-giving program we implemented the previous year. It's a tactic Gabby's sister Amy told us about: "Wise Men Gifts." Essentially, you limit your kids to three Christmas presents. The logic behind the concept is that if three gifts were good enough for the Savior of the world, then it's certainly good enough for our little snot factories. When we did it last year, it turned out to be a successful way of demonstrating the connection between the commercial holiday and the Christian tradition. And since we started the tradition early in their lives, they know no different.

Though gold, frankincense, and myrrh aren't on Jake and Audrey's lists, they do have some items that seem pretty benign. The robot dog and iPod are definite no's on Jake's list. But the basketball, basketball hoop, and football board game are workable. If we stretch the definition of "experience gifts," these are all thing that we can enjoy together as a family. We can play basketball in the driveway, then retire to the kitchen table to make fake tackling noises with our mouths as the tiny plastic men fight over the pigskin. Sounds like a pretty nice little Christmas. None of the gifts are too expensive, and they also encourage interaction and can be used by more than one person.

Audrey is a bit more challenging. Her list is just a hodgepodge of stuffed animals. I don't see how any of this qualifies as an experience, unless I rip a hole in the bottom of each animal, tear out the stuffing, shove my hand in, and start doing an improvised puppet show. I look to Gabby for some help, but she's having the same trouble that I am. While Audrey has "thinned the herd" of stuffed animals to ensure that the fragile ecosystem inside our house is able to flourish, we're still overpopulated. I give my wife a knowing look and say, "If we bring another stuffed animal into this house, the city will have to change its zoning laws."

"We can't do it." There is silence for a moment. Then her face softens and she adds, "Unless we use the 'One In, One Out' method."

"One In, One Out" is a tactic Gabby heard about as a way to maintain a minimum level of stuff once the year is over. Her first thought was applying it to clothing. After purging our closets of excess stuff, in the coming years she plans to donate an item every time she purchases another. Buy a shirt, give a shirt. The same rule could be applied to stuffed animals, right?

So we cave and agree that St. Nicholas will bring Audrey a plush dolphin toy. And we add a Spirograph to the list as an "experience gift." Our daughter loves art, and this old-school '70s drawing kit is an activity we can enjoy together. Just like Jake's football game.

When we get to the toy store, we feel out of place. It's been a long time since we have shopped for entirely unnecessary stuff. Stepping into Toys"R"Us feels like visiting another planet. One that's populated by little plastic figurines priced well below retail. We have the kids' lists in hand, so we do our best to avoid distractions.

But it's hard.

The previous Christmas was a challenge for us. Gabby and I both grew up in homes where the holidays were a time of abundance. There were more than three gifts beneath the tree. And, as with many people who had a positive upbringing, we want our kids to have the same experience that we did. Our own childhood becomes the definition of a "good childhood." We know it's a complete fallacy, but it is one buried deep inside us.

The previous year we succeeded in buying only three gifts, and the kids had a wonderful Christmas. Sure, Jake came home from school rattling off a list of the numbers of gifts his friends received, but both he and Audrey said they loved the holidays. And based on their level of excitement for this year's celebration, our three-gift limit didn't scar them.

But walking through the toy store, Gabby and I look down at the lists. A basketball? A stuffed animal? A board game? A toy from the '70s? These all seem so simple when talking robots and giant castles are staring you in the face. Sadly, this feeling multiplies when we get to the stuffed-animal section of the store and see that the dolphin Audrey wants is only $5.99. As if the cost of the gift is a measure of her life's worth. Logically, we know it's ridiculous. Emotionally, it feels as if we are somehow devaluing our own child.

After some back-and-forth debate, we come to terms with our decision. Focusing on the number and price of things is what made us feel disconnected in the first place. This is the mindset that overcomplicates things. This year is about finding abundance in the midst of simplicity.

So we keep it simple.

We finish shopping in thirty minutes. A mere half-hour. We feel a sense of peace at the checkout. We have our three gifts for Jake. And for Audrey, we have the Spirograph and the stuffed animal. Just two gifts for her.

We got the gold.

We got the frankincense.

What about the myrrh?

Chapter Thirty-Three

The Belly of the Beast

There was a man sent from God, whose name was John. He came as a witness to testify to the light, so that all might believe through him. He himself was not the light, but he came to testify to the light. The true light, which enlightens everyone, was coming into the world. He was in the world, and the world came into being through him; yet the world did not know him.
(John 1:6–10)

I'm standing motionless outside the mall. I stare up at the sign. A giant star adorns the marquee, begging me to come inside.

"American Girl."

For the uninitiated, American Girl dolls are not just any doll. They are über-wholesome, unbearably cute, and culturally diverse. Think Barbie with a back story and realistic measurements. This is the doll Barbie wishes she could be if she could just get her act together, stop throwing beach parties, and get serious about life.

Two weeks prior to Christmas, Audrey came home and added one of these American Girl dolls to her list. This was a whale of a plot twist. She has never before, in her short history on the planet, ever cared about such things. If given the choice between, say, playing with a Barbie or getting a flu shot, I'd put my money on the immunization. We were so shocked by this new development that you would have thought she had told us we weren't her real parents and that she now wished to be raised by wolves. Wolves who regularly spend $100 on dolls of historical significance.

There are only a dozen stores in the country that sell these dolls, and my business trip has brought me within five miles of one in the suburbs of Washington DC. I walk through the door, unsure of what to expect. Once inside, I feel like a Viagra pill trapped inside a woman's body. I haven't a clue which way to go.

I look around. Different sections of the store have floor-to-ceiling shelves stocked with dolls. There is a section for Julie. Another for Addy. Rows and rows of dolls standing upright in their identical boxes. No gaps between each clone. No empty racks. Hundreds of faces, all of them peering out through a thin plastic window that has been sealed tightly to the front of each carton. Whenever one doll disappears, another one comes to take its place. A chill runs up my spine. I've seen sci-fi movies like this, and none of them end well for the new guy whose name didn't make the opening credits.

A look of fear and confusion must be plastered across my face, because I am greeted within ten seconds by a very enthusiastic salesman.

Yes. A full-grown man.

"Hi! Welcome to American Girl! I'm Jerry. How can I help you?"

I wait in silence for a moment, half-expecting Jerry to cautiously do a 180-degree sweep with his eyes and whisper, "*Get out now. Before it's too late.*"

But he doesn't.

Either Jerry has already been brainwashed or he just genuinely wants to help. I stick to my script.

"Saige. I'm looking for Saige."

One of the reasons we justified this extravagance is because Audrey's best friend has an American Girl doll named Saige. Every time they play together, Saige makes an appearance. They dress the doll. They feed her. They teach her how to add and subtract. It's as if she is a member of the family. And for the past several weeks, Audrey has been talking nonstop about Saige, and if they had two of them, they could really get imaginative. And so

I'm seeking out Saige's twin. It's a sorry excuse for breaking the rules and a total stretch to say this is an experience gift, but our defenses are weakened by the evil man in the red suit.

Jerry appreciates my knowledge of their product line and beckons me to the front corner of the store. I follow him to a wall of Saiges that appear ready for world domination. Sure, they are all smiling, but their beady eyes are staring into my soul.

"Who are you shopping for?" Jerry asks.

"My daughter."

"How old is she?"

"Six."

"Is this her first American Girl?"

"Yes."

I am the least excited person in the store. Bordering on hostile. My short, callous responses to Jerry's questions seem out of place in this pink room punctuated by shimmering stars and shiny faces. While Jerry seems like a nice enough guy, I don't want to give him too much ammunition. A fellow parent warned us of the American Girl experience and how a simple trip to purchase a doll can quickly devolve into a process that takes longer than a Chinese adoption. This place has a little doll furniture shop and a doll hair salon. It has a restaurant where you can have lunch with your new American Girl. You can even have one of these things custom-made to look like your child, which leaves me feeling amazed and diuretic all at the same time. It's pure craziness.

Meanwhile, Jerry politely ignores my curt replies and plods ahead.

"Saige is our 'Girl of the Year,'" he beams. "She is very popular."

It's unclear whether Jerry means *popular* as in, "we sell a lot of these dolls," or if he means *popular* as in, "Saige has a lot of friends, was elected vice-president of the student council, and sometimes ignores that nerdy kid in her algebra class who will one day turn out to be a male supermodel/Nobel Prize-winning physicist." It's hard to tell, since this store operates on a different spatial plane, locked somewhere between fantasy and reality.

Speaking of reality, I am immediately brought back to it when I look at the doll's price tag. Saige costs $110, which includes a book and the clothes on her back. My eyes wander to the other accessories available. The doll's special hairbrush is $8. Her extra clothes cost anywhere from $24 to $36, depending on the outfit. The sparkle dress is particularly well-constructed and fashionable. I look down at my own shirt, which I bought for $14 at Target three years ago, and immediately feel inferior. I can even buy a bunch of sketches and paintings that Saige has done, which provide the perfect decor should I choose to buy her a bed and other home furnishings, also available for purchase.

This is the point at which I am overwhelmed. My emotional brain is telling me that my daughter may not have a happy childhood unless I buy her a mountain of Saige stuff. My rational brain is telling me that this whole thing is madness. It's a swirl of confusion, and I need help. I look at Jerry.

"Could you give me a couple of minutes?"

He's seen this before. He gives me a knowing smile and says, "Take all the time you need."

I break away to make a phone call. I want my mommy.

"Hello?"

"Hey, Mom. It's me."

"Hi, Scotty! Where are you?" Mom knows to ask this question since I travel a lot.

"I'm in Washington DC, standing in the middle of an American Girl store."

"Oh really?!"

Her *really* is loaded with meaning. With one word, she in conveying how happy she is that her son has become a dad who shops for dolls. She is also announcing astonishment that I'm about to make an actual purchase. And finally, she is expressing a twinge of surprise that I have been sucked in to the vortex of American Girl.

"Yes. Really. I am standing here, surrounded by a million dollars' worth of dolls. I feel like I'm being suckered. I'm about to spend $100 on a doll that Audrey will play with for about five minutes." I am looking for sympathy. A voice of reason.

"Well?" She hesitates. "You never know, Scotty. Audrey is a little girl, and little girls love dolls. I still have my Terri Lee doll."

I look over at Jerry to make sure he hasn't hacked my cell phone and is now impersonating my mom's voice. I wouldn't put it past the high-tech folks at American Girl to pull off such a feat. Alas, Jerry is helping another person who has pulled out a photograph of her granddaughter to find an appropriate biological match.

Mom goes on to tell me a long story about Terri Lee, a doll she got when she was a kid. She talks about the hours she spent playing with her friends, making up games for Terri Lee. She talks about dressing the doll in different outfits. Having tea parties with Terri Lee. In fact, she still has Terri Lee and all her clothes nearly sixty years later. This doll has seen her wardrobe go in-and-out-of style three times in that span.

As Mom continues her story, I notice some of her best memories aren't of the doll herself, but what the doll *meant* to her. The hours playing with her friends. And the fact that she didn't buy the outfits from the store. Instead, her mom made the outfits by hand. My grandmother was not the warmest of women, but my mom vividly remembers her painstakingly sewing a faux fur collar on Terri Lee's leopard print jacket. It was a sign of love, and one that still lives on with that doll and her clothes.

After my chat with Mom, I call Gabby to confirm the purchase. As much as it feels like failure, Saige is coming home with us for Christmas. We rationalize that Audrey will spend hours playing with her own best friend. Gabby will even work with Audrey to sew some fun outfits for this doll, keeping that chain of love going. There's no need to buy anything special. We'll get Saige with the factory equipment. And maybe, just maybe this is one purchase that will mean a lot. Creating lasting memories that matter.

Later that night, I am by myself back at the hotel, feeling silly for all the worry I put into a single purchase.

It's just one thing, right? And what can it hurt? It's just a doll for goodness' sake.

I hit the light switch on the wall, and the room goes dark, save for a bright spot in the corner. I walk over to the work desk that is now lit by a single, recessed halogen bulb in the ceiling. As I reach over to turn it out, I see Saige, lying on the desk in her cardboard cradle, bathed in a golden pool of light. It looks like the scene of Jesus' birth in every Christmas pageant you've ever seen. As if the Bethlehem Star itself is shining down on her. Only instead of being surrounded by wise men and animals, Saige is flanked by a couple of bottles of water and leftover Chinese takeout containers. It's strangely fitting, given that I am holding out hope that she is the Savior of Christmas. And that's a lot of pressure to put on a doll.

Before my hand can flip the switch, I look down at Saige, with all her lifelike features, and I can swear I hear her saying, "Thanks for buying me, but I'm afraid you're missing the point."

Chapter Thirty-Four

Christmas Present

He said to him, "'You shall love the Lord your God with all your heart, and with all your soul, and with all your mind.' This is the greatest and first commandment. And a second is like it: 'You shall love your neighbor as yourself.'"
(Matthew 22:37–39)

The Santa gifts are wrapped and stashed in the attic. There are three for each kid, along with some candy to cram into their stockings. The Fat Man also took a page from the Easter Bunny's playbook and got them each a five-dollar gift card. Jake's is for Taco Bell and Audrey's is for Arby's. Even though these food purchases are allowable under our rules, we were second-guessing both the candy and the cards, thinking we might be indirectly giving our children Type-2 diabetes for Christmas.

We also set aside one "experience gift" for the whole family. This is another tradition we started the year prior. While Santa brings three gifts, Mom and Dad bring only one, and it's always a short family road trip to a fun place we've never visited before. So this year, we type a letter telling the kids that Mom and Dad are taking them to the Smoky Mountains before they go back to school in January. And perhaps we can hit the Taco Bell and Arby's drive-thrus on the way.

My purchase anxiety is muted by the sounds of jingle bells dancing in the air. It also helps that this year's collection of gifts is far less than it has been in past years. We can feel content knowing this challenge has had a profound impact on us. In terms of an average American Christmas, it's quite conservative, but in terms of what the rest of the world enjoys on a daily basis, even the fast food gift cards could be seen as an extravagance.

It's all relative.

Even so, I can't stop obsessing about the gifts in the attic. Little Saige's "Made in China" heart is beating inside her plastic body like the Tell-Tale Heart in the Edgar Allen Poe book, keeping me awake at night. My conscience won't let me rest. Sadly, I'm not sure why it bothers me so much. Is it because I realize it will take more than a simple vow to shed my materialistic nature? Or is it a pride thing? That I am too embarrassed to admit to my friends and family that we couldn't make it twelve months without buying "stuff"?

Gabby has a way of noticing when I am "awful-izing" in my head like this. Perhaps I make some sort of inaudible squealing sound only wives can hear. Whatever the case, tonight as we're settling down into bed, she stops me to ask what's the matter.

I launch into a long sermonette on how I feel that we've failed. I talk about how we don't need anything besides the roof over our heads and the food in our refrigerator, and how we've now gone overboard. I rant about Saige. And the other gifts. And flunking Christmas.

Meanwhile, she just stares at me, listening intently. When my torrent of words finally stops, her eyes lock on mine. It's like she's looking straight into my heart. We are two halves of the same person. She feels what I feel. Her lips part, and I wait for her to say something profound. Something to ease the struggle in my soul. Then her voice breaks through the pregnant silence.

"You're weird."

If I had bought my wife an actual gift for Christmas, I would have returned it.

I argue my position. "What do you mean, weird? Don't you feel it, too? It's like we've been sucked back into the vortex."

"I don't see it that way," she counters.

Before I can stop her, she continues talking and making perfect sense. I hate when she does that. Ever the voice of reason, my wife reminds me that our challenge was supposed to help us overcome the power of stuff. To focus on what is truly important in our lives. And now I am doing just the opposite.

Obsessing over stuff. The toys. The gift cards. The candy.

She reasons that it's two sides of the same coin. There is nothing inherently wrong with material gifts. They become a problem only when we give them far more meaning than they deserve. And here I am, giving Saige far more meaning than even the people in the American Girl store bestow on her, and letting all that nonsense get in the way of the spirit of giving.

These thoughts run through my head as I stare at the ceiling. Then I hear Gabby roll over and turn off the light on her night stand.

"Go to bed," she sighs. "We'll figure it out tomorrow."

The room goes dark.

But I'm still looking for something.

The next day, I see her sitting in front of her computer. She is perched on the very edge of her chair, almost as if she is hovering in midair, leaving the remaining 98 percent of the seat for her imaginary friend. This is always a sign that she is engaged in something important.

"Whatcha working on?" I ask, fully expecting that she is knee-deep in some work-related task. But her answer surprises me.

"The Jesus gift."

"Jesus gift? What's that?"

She reminds me about the Jesus-gift tradition we started last year. She read about it in a book some time ago and immediately fell in love with it. The concept is simple, yet profound. On Christmas morning, you wrap a box and place it under the tree as a present for Jesus. After Christmas, you leave it out as a reminder that lasts the entire year. Ours has spent the past twelve months on an end table, serving as a makeshift coaster wrapped in gold paper with silver stars.

At this point, you might be asking yourself, what do you put inside this box? What do you get the Savior of the world for his birthday? A new pair of sandals? Some power tools for his next carpentry project? A Snuggie for those cold nights in the manger?

Nope.

Instead, you put a list of all the ways you served others during the year. This includes your gifts to charity, tithes to the church, and time spent volunteering—basically anything you did to step out of your self-serving spirit and serve God instead. Reminded of this, my first instinct is to panic, since I can't remember any altruistic acts offhand. Instead, I flash back to the beginning of the year when I was eating all the ice cream in the house, including the portions that were earmarked for my own flesh-and-blood. That's not exactly what Jesus would want to see in his box. Stealing sweets from kids.

Before I can repent, Gabby distracts me.

"Look at this."

She is busily typing a document on her computer. It's a list of different things we did as a family. As I read through each item, I am reminded of the fullness of our year. Bagging green beans. Sacking sweet potatoes. Filling backpacks. Sorting canned goods. Donating furniture. Delivering gifts. Decorating the Angel Tree. Giving blood—and nearly passing out on the gurney. Granted, we won't be winning any philanthropic medals, but it is more than we had done in the past, and they were beautiful moments to share as a family.

Then Gabby points to a stack of papers on the desk. They are piled one on top of the other, slightly askew, forming a short, jagged tower.

"These are the notes and letters we received from charities we supported this year. I held on to them all so that we could keep track."

I leaf through each one. As I read the notes, I am transported back in time to all the conversations Gabby and I had throughout the year. Debating whether or not to support *this* charity, or *that* cause, or *these* people. Each time, we quickly said, "Sure! We're not buying anything this year. Might as well!" I wasn't keeping track, but she was.

Gabby opens another document on her computer. This one is a spreadsheet of the various charities we have supported over the past few months. She scrolls through the list. There are entries for church tithes. Gifts to the food bank and Society of St. Andrew. Other miscellaneous causes. Since Gabby is the one who pays our bills, I rarely, if ever, see this list. We just have short conversations whenever we hear about a need, and if we agree, she is the one who ultimately makes sure that we give a little something to the cause. I look at the word *Total,* printed in bold letters at the bottom of the sheet.

"That's not right," I say. I hone in on the number highlighted in yellow. It looks like a big mistake.

"What do you mean 'that's not right'?" Gabby bristles at me, miffed that I am challenging her competence.

"It's too high," I say. "We didn't give that much."

She recalculates the column. The total comes out the same. We normally tithe our biblical best, but this is nearly twice as much as we've ever given. I'm stunned silent for a moment. And then I start to get nervous. Did we let the euphoria overtake us? Have we been irresponsible? I know this year was not about money, but we should have saved more, right?

All this worry is motivated by fear. Just like the worry we felt earlier in the year. We were afraid our kids might feel deprived. We were afraid of what our friends would think. We were afraid that we might be judged for our decisions. And now I'm awfulizing about our future, afraid we've gone too far. Reckless. Then like a time machine, Gabby snaps me back to the present. The here and now.

"Scott, if I hadn't shown you this spreadsheet, would you have even noticed the money was gone? Did you even feel it?"

Wow.

No.

I didn't feel it. We ate food. We stayed warm. We had fun.

Before I can react, she turns the tables and calculates what all of that giving meant to other people. Focusing on the gain instead of the loss. All the meals served. All the warm beds offered. People comforted. Wounds healed. All these things she speaks aloud as she types them out as line items on the page. When she is finished, she prints the list on paper, retrieves it from the printer, and one by one, she cuts out long narrow strips of each entry and places them all in the Jesus box.

Our gift.

"This is what I'm talking about. Giving our daughter a doll is not going to ruin Christmas if we focus on *this* stuff."

And that's when I start to feel it.

On paper, we have given more this year than we ever have before, courtesy of my wife's stealthy generosity. It's a pittance compared to what some give, but it's far more than we could have fathomed if you had asked us back on January 1. It's a by-product of focusing less on stuff and more on connecting with others. And in doing so, our lives haven't changed in the ways we might have imagined. We are not deprived or destitute. We still have more than we need. But now it's clear that we have capacity to change lives for the better.

And I want to feel it even more.

I don't want to feel holier-than-thou. I don't want to feel like a do-gooder. I want to feel the fear that you feel when you give more than seems reasonable and have to place your trust in God that it makes perfect sense.

"What if we gave something big?" I ask. "Something that can truly make a difference, if even for just one person."

"Like what?"

"I don't know. Like a car. What if we bought a car for someone who needed one for work? Someone who can't get a job without it."

Gabby is a little too eager. She doesn't stop me. Just like when I originally floated the idea to spend a year as missionaries, she doesn't question the idea in the slightest. Unlike me, she sees it all as gain and immediately starts planning. I know when this happens, I should just go along for the ride.

She quickly corresponds with the new friends we've made at a local charity. It takes them no time at all to identify several candidates. This is both sad and exciting at the same time. The stories are similar. They are all single mothers with young children. Women who have overcome difficult situations and are just trying to find some stability for their families.

One woman in particular, Kathy, is caught in the never-ending, spin-and-rinse cycle of poverty. She has worked a low-paying job while going to school, where she completed a training program in nursing. With two small kids, she is barely getting by. Now, she doesn't have enough money to feed her kids, keep the roof over her head, *and* pay her student loans. She could get a job as a nurse, which pays better, but the entry-level jobs are all a haphazard blend of shift work at odd hours. The busses don't run when she needs to work. She has no family or reliable friends nearby.

She is stuck.

But a car?

A car could change all that.

I'm reminded of that woman in the Bible who gave the two small coins. Jesus says of her,

> *"Truly I tell you, this poor widow has put in more than all those who are contributing to the treasury. For all of them have contributed out of their abundance; but she out of her poverty has put in everything she had, all she had to live on." (Mark 12:43–44)*

She was praised for giving all she had. And us? We're not like that at all. We still have far more than we need and easily could have tightened our rules and sacrificed more this year. The woman in that story gave from her poverty. We are simply giving from abundance. An abundance that we kept for ourselves instead of sharing it. But now we can see how shunning a few simple purchases is allowing us to do something that can truly make a difference.

We drive downtown and meet Deb, the development director for the Martha O' Brien Center, a local charity that empowers children, youth, and adults in poverty to transform their lives through work, education, employment, and fellowship. She is full of life and optimism, telling us that our donation will not only buy a car for Kathy but will help the other families with some medical bills and additional expenses. As much as we would like to be more fully involved in the transaction and meet Kathy face-to-face, we know that's not the point now. This is an opportunity for the social workers and friends of the women to share some good news, and perhaps a hug or two. Building connections.

Our selfishness is satisfied later when Deb shares her story of taking Kathy on her car shopping spree to buy her car. Apparently, it was a virtual lovefest. Kathy gushed the entire time, feeling blessed. Deb got to enjoy being around the electric event, and the dealer was even caught up in the euphoria, providing some free service on the car. Kathy called it a "miracle," making it possible for her to find meaningful work and opening the door for her kids to participate in things such as soccer and T-ball, which used to be impossible due to transportation difficulties.

Who knew humans could do that? Make miracles.

When Deb relays the story, I feel a strange mix of pride and guilt. My pride comes from an overblown sense of self. Taking credit for God's blessings. And the guilt is a by-product of this realization. But I later settle into the feeling, wondering if this is the real reason God gave us a sense of pride in the first place, taking something selfish and using it for good, no matter how small the act.

Christmas morning is a buzz of activity around our house. Our kids are as thrilled as the grand-prize winners on a game show. Nana and Papa spent the night, so Jake and Audrey wake them up just as Santa's sleigh is pulling out of sight. They tear into their stockings and have a breakfast of chocolate and Starburst. Then they attack their gifts. They savor the unwrapping the way I savor a half-gallon of ice cream. The whole ordeal is over in the span of ten minutes, which is quite nice, since it leaves more time for playing.

Audrey immediately adopts Saige as a member of the family. They do Spirograph together on the kitchen table with Gabby and my mom. Meanwhile, it's twenty degrees outside, but my dad and I spend the next two hours assembling a basketball goal for Jake in the driveway while he looks on, amazed at my ineptitude.

Eventually, it stands tall, and he shoots a few baskets before his hands approach frostbite. Soon, we are all back inside, enjoying the warmth.

Time for the Jesus box.

We gather beside the tree in the living room. The kids lift open the lid and reach inside to pull out the slips of paper. Jake reads each one aloud. We all listen and remember the fun we had together as a family during the year, connecting and serving.

Jake finally gets to the last note in the stack. It's a multiple-choice question.

Today, to honor Jesus' birth, would you like to A) sing carols at a senior center, B) hand out snacks and hugs to people at the hospital who are visiting loved ones who can't be at home, or C) put thank-you notes and random amounts of money into envelopes and hand them out to people who have to work on Christmas and can't be with their families?

The kids decide without hesitation. They want to hand out envelopes.

So we fill twenty envelopes with money and decorate them with a simple Christmas greeting. When we get into the car, the kids are excited and nervous. We spend some time brainstorming a list of places that are likely open on Christmas, where people are working instead of spending time with their families. The kids are a big help. "The gas station!" Audrey yells. Jake adds "Restaurants!" to the mix.

So we set out in search of people. Trying our best to remember that the day is all about giving. We stop by a nursing home and find several caregivers working long shifts. The kids eagerly offer "Merry Christmas" greetings and envelopes. The same happens at a local pharmacy where a clerk is working alone. With each stop, the kids are getting bolder.

When we finally find a gas station, I hear Jake ask from the back seat, "Dad, can we do this one by ourselves?"

"I don't see why not."

So he and Audrey slip out of their seats, grab a couple of envelopes, and exit the car alone. It takes both of them to open the heavy door of the convenience store. Once inside, we can see them approach the counter and strike up a conversation with the clerk on duty.

"What do you think they're saying?" I ask.

"Who knows?" Gabby quips. "But they're having fun. And learning what Christmas is really about."

"I think you're right," I offer.

I see the kids move toward the back of the store to find another man who is busily stocking shelves in the cooler. As my gaze drifts in that direction, I catch a glimpse of something in the rearview mirror.

It's Saige.

Audrey brought her along for the ride. That much-debated doll. She is seated upright in between two car seats, as a member of the family. Her eyes are fixed straight ahead with a knowing expression. It's as if she is watching them, too. A permanent smile painted on her face.

Kind of how I imagine God.

Part Five

The Results

Did we learn anything? Anything at all?

Chapter Thirty-Five

Year in Review

Do not conform to the pattern of this world, but be transformed by the renewing of your mind. Then you will be able to test and approve what God's will is—his good, pleasing and perfect will.

(*Romans 12:2 NIV*)

The New Year is upon us. Sitting in the playroom, we stare intently at a gently worn paper wall calendar. You know the kind. They usually have pictures of kittens or mountain scenes or half-naked firefighters with well-placed hoses in the foreground. Ours is a Catholic saints calendar bought by a friend at a church fund-raiser. She gave it to us out of pity as our experiment began twelve months ago, and today it's time to turn the final page, thank Jesus, Mary, and Joseph! (who, incidentally, are all beautifully depicted in color for the month of December).

This has been a challenging year, but not nearly as hard as it could have been. For starters, our rules didn't require us to grow our own food or reuse toilet paper. We were free to buy the basics, and *our* definition of basics is far more than any family truly needs. Even without shopping, we lived luxuriously compared to the vast majority of families on the planet. We slept in a lovely three-bedroom, two-bath house in the suburbs. We had more than enough food to eat. We had plenty of clothes to cover our bodies. Bottom line: we already have more than we deserve.

It also helps that we had a less-than-perfect track record. There were the Christmas gifts. We also bought a new vacuum cleaner when our old one died, which probably wasn't a necessity for the survival of our family but likely was required to save our marriage. Then there were Jake's shoes. And let's not forget the $3 swim mask and flippers we bought for Audrey when she passed her swim test. It was purely a guilt-driven purchase, since we had bought some for our son the year before when he passed *his* test and feared the perceived inequality would send Audrey to a psychiatrist years later complaining that Mom and Dad always loved her brother best.

All told, our year without a purchase turned into the year of four purchases. In black and white terms, most would call it a failure.

But I still think we won.

There were a number of questions haunting us at the start of the year. As you may recall, we wondered:

Will it create more tension in our house, or bring us closer together?

Will our friends support us, or think we are nut-balls crazy?

Will we learn anything from the experience, or will it be a waste of time?

Will our kids jump on the bandwagon, or will they fight it?

Initially, we felt some tension. The change in lifestyle caused some anxiety, which led to shorter tempers. But after the first few weeks, our home became more harmonious. There was less stress, less rushing around, and less worrying. We had to become more resourceful, but rather than feeling like extra work, it felt satisfying and rewarding to live with intention.

And our friends? If they thought we were nut-balls crazy, they kept it to themselves, which we truly appreciate. So from our standpoint, they supported us 100 percent. Our village came alive and became more connected. Not only did people come out of the woodwork to offer things they thought we needed (which was humbling), but we also connected with more people in the process (which was fulfilling). Perhaps the biggest surprise was how many of our friends said they also found themselves purchasing less and enjoying more experiences. Apparently, our view of simplicity was quite contagious—kinda like spreading a cold by sneezing in the ball pit at Chuck-E-Cheese.

Only *this* disease is beneficial.

And there was plenty of learning. It's hard to condense it all, but reflecting back on the year, we can see three big things we gained from the experience.

First, we have more *energy* for things that matter. Prior to this year, we never realized how much physical and mental effort we expended in the direct pursuit of things we thought would make us happier. Sometimes, this effort was tangible, such as the extra work I might pick up so that we could afford this thing or that thing, or the hours we would spend shopping. This was time that could have been spent with family or friends, but we chose to sacrifice it to materialistic pursuits.

In other cases, the effort was less visible, such as the mental energy we would spend thinking of what life might be like if we had that "special something." At times, we even called this "dreaming" or "wishing." What we failed to realize was that all of these dreams and aspirations would float in and out of our heads as worthless worries, distracting us from appreciating and owning the things we already have. Now, we recognize we don't have an infinite well of energy, and by investing what precious little mental resources we have into loving our present blessings and sharing them with others, we realize joyful returns that are exponentially greater than anything we could have purchased from a store.

Second, we have more *money* for things that matter. Over the past twelve months we have donated nearly twice as much as we have in years past and still saved a bit for our family nest egg. It is a result we hadn't expected. We have always known we are the hands and feet of God, but we never realized how we had bound those hands with fashionable gloves and shackled those feet with designer shoes.

While dollars are a way to measure the success of our challenge, the more important thing to us is the sense of satisfaction and connectedness we feel through being able to do something beyond the scope of our own household. We found an abundance we never knew we had, and we feel abundantly blessed to share it. And the joy we feel in giving lasts so much longer than the temporary euphoria of bringing home a beautiful bargain.

Third, we have a deeper *understanding* of things that matter. When you strip away the clutter of life, your purpose becomes much clearer. Through this experience, we had to examine the "why" behind our purchases. This brought us face-to-face with some harsh realities. Once we moved beyond the excuses and arguments with ourselves, we had to acknowledge we sometimes purchased things to gain the approval or, worse yet, *envy* of others.

In some warped way, we believed buying stuff would make our lives better. It's not that stuff is inherently bad. What makes it bad is the value we place on it. We want all these shiny objects to give us joy and satisfaction. But those expectations aren't realistic, even though the advertisers might tell us otherwise. Think about it: We are asking an object without flesh or a heart or a soul to stir something meaningful inside us. That's a job that no single thing can accomplish. Things aren't built for that.

But people are.

We are the ones to make meaning and stir satisfaction. And we do this through the Spirit of God that has been planted inside each human being. Excess stuff just gets in the way of releasing that Spirit and letting it show us how interconnected we are. And that is what's important.

While these three things are now evident to Gabby and me, we wonder if our year had any effect on our children. You'll remember that we never told our kids what we were doing. This was partly to keep us entertained and partly to see if they would even notice this way we were living *in* the world but not *of* the world.

Sadly, our challenge did *not* keep them from asking for stuff. While limited exposure to advertisements keep the requests down, they still seem just as attracted to stuff as their adult counterparts. Let's face it; the lure of things is powerful. Over the past few months, when Jake or Audrey would point to an item in the store or on the street or on TV, we stuck to our talking points:

- "That's too expensive."
- "You don't *need* another stuffed animal."
- "Target doesn't allow you to buy toys. It's just a toy museum. Only for looking."

Our responses never made the kids happy, but through the year, we did start to notice a change in the way they asked for things. Rather than saying "Can I have this?" or "I want that!" they started making more appreciative comments, such as, "See that stuffed hippo, Daddy? I think he's cute!" This didn't happen every time, mind you, but it is certainly a shift *we* observed.

But did *they* observe anything different about the year?

We plan a brief family meeting during lunch to survey our research subjects. When we started last January, we wondered whether our kids would feel neglected. Or deprived. Heck, we wondered whether they would even notice at all. We question them while nibbling on turkey sandwiches.

"So, guys. Did you notice anything different about last year?"

Audrey chimes in first. "It was 2013, and now it's 2014."

My wife acknowledges her accuracy but probes for more. "Good answer. How about you, Jake?"

Like a contestant on *Jeopardy*, he phrases his answer in the form of a question. "We didn't watch the BCS Championship game?"

Obviously, not buying stuff left a huge impression on them.

I probe deeper. "That's true, but did you notice anything different about our family last year and what we chose to do? Like, for special occasions?"

Their eyes scan the air in search of an answer. It's not looking good. Finally Jake offers, "We decided to take a trip on everybody's birthday."

"Right! We visited friends or spent time with them doing fun things. Did you like that?"

Heads nod.

"Did you notice that we did not buy any "things" the whole year?" I ask.

They stare silently. Confused. Finally Jake breaks in,

"No . . . I mean . . . wait!" My fact-oriented seven-year-old launches into a list. "You bought *things*! You bought milk. And ice cream. And soap and stuff . . ."

I affirm his attention to detail, but try to steer him in another direction. "You're right. We *did* buy things we need. Like food and milk and stuff we could use up. But . . ."

Jake interrupts, saying something we would never have dreamed he might say just twelve short months ago.

"Oh, you mean, like, we didn't buy anything *worthless*."

Worthless.

Wow.

Gabby and I look at each other and fall silent. After a beat, she takes over.

"That's right, Jake. So what do you think of that? Worthless stuff. Were you sad that you didn't get any *things* from us last year?"

Audrey steals his answer, and for once, Jake doesn't seem to mind.

"Well, I think it's good." As she speaks, her gestures add ten years to her age. "You know how when I get a new stuffed animal, I change my mind about all the other ones, and I don't play with them anymore? So that's kind of a thing that's worthless that won't really last a long time."

We are floored.

They *did* notice.

Just not in the way we might have expected.

We thought they might notice and complain. Instead, they noticed the heart of the experiment. It's as if they internalized our aspirations to make them an actual force in their tiny, little lives. It's exciting to think that a change in behavior over the course of a year might actually leave a lasting impression on our family.

We continue talking with the kids, and our euphoria softens a bit. The chatter bobs and weaves, and eventually they both start talking about things they want for their next birthdays. They *are* still kids, after all. On the surface, it's as if all the learning of the last twelve months disappears. But listening closely, the spirit remains.

There is a different tone to their desires. It is less "I really, really, really want that hockey game for my next birthday! I can't live without it!" and more "That hockey game seems really cool. That might be a fun thing to have." It's a subtle change. But a *huge* one. And one we hope lasts a lifetime.

This has been a beautiful experience. It is not that we were unhappy before we started the challenge; but divorced from buying stuff, we can honestly say that life has a lightness it did not have before. A freedom from the clutches of materialism. Our unconscious motives for buying things have now been brought to our attention. There is no more hidden agenda. Now that the veil has been lifted, we approach purchases differently. Those that truly make life easier and less stressful are worthwhile. Others are simply fluff. Distractions. Worthless.

Worth.

Less.

We now feel more connected to our family mission statement than we did before. We are living life in alignment with our values. Owning and appreciating what we have instead of fixating on the things we want. Growing in faith together by focusing on our worth as it is defined by God's standards rather than the world's. And serving God's people to foster the genuine connection that exists between us all.

For all of us who feel disconnected, I'll leave you with this—

All too often our pursuits are predicated on the idea that the more we have, the more we're worth. Whether we seek to amass goals, accomplishments, or shiny piles of precious stuff, it's all an attempt to find satisfaction by gaining acceptance according to the standards of society. To find success and fulfillment.

But here's the secret.

We're all searching for something we've never lost. It's been with us all along. It's the love of God buried deep inside our souls. We've somehow missed it. That feeling of disconnectedness is not the result of being disconnected from friends and family. No, that's not it at all.

We've disconnected from that voice inside.

And if we can just remove all the fancy decoration, strip away the showy signs of status, and pause our pursuits long enough, we can hear that voice whispering,

"I love you."

"I made you."

"You, my child, are enough."

And in hearing this, we'll once again enter that thin place where God is just a breath away. Finally realizing . . .

We have so much more than we'll ever need.

Epilogue

I'm all alone on the couch. The kids are tucked in for the night, the echoes of their bedtime protests still ringing through the living room. I sprawl across the cushions and take up every last inch of upholstery. Gabby's sister Kerri is in town for a visit, and they are out for the night—a "staycation" I got her for Christmas. There is no need to sit like a gentleman since no one is here to notice. With this kind of freedom, adopting the posture of a disgusting, mouth-breathing slob is perfectly acceptable.

It's mid-February and twenty-five degrees outside, but that doesn't stop me from using my belly as a table while diving into a half-eaten carton of Rocky Road. I flip the channels in search of a college basketball game, pausing on a commercial for PODS, the portable storage container company. Even though we finished our year without a purchase experiment nearly two months ago, I'm still amazed when I see evidence of the power of stuff in our world.

Since the challenge officially concluded, we bought a toaster oven on Craigslist for fifty bucks to replace the one that broke last year. It was like reuniting with a long-lost friend. A friend who can toast four slices of bread in a flash. I also went to Costco and splurged on a new six-pack of underwear. Mine were getting to be too holey. And not in a Jesus kind of way. Gabby suggests that they may have been that way since last January, but my lack of attention to detail keeps me from remembering such things.

I see a soft, fluffy blanket draped over the arm of the couch and position it over my legs, using part of it as a table cloth. I find a game on ESPN and turn up the volume loud enough to hear but not loud enough for Jake to notice and come out of his room and ask for an update on the score.

A late evening nap may be in my near future.

Bing, bong!

My phone interrupts my peace. From where I sit, I can't see who is texting me, so I'm a little perturbed that I might actually have to move from this delightful horizontal position. I worry that it might be Gabby reminding me of something I forgot to do or, worse yet, telling me that she and her sister are stranded somewhere needing to be rescued. I go to the kitchen counter to grab my phone.

The text is from a number I don't know. It reads: "Bank Alert. Suspicious Activity" along with a toll-free number. A shudder goes through me. I once had a credit card stolen on a business trip, and it was a nightmare to rectify the problem.

I dial the bank number and wait.

"This is Brandon with the fraud department. Who am I speaking with?"

I verify they are my bank, and Brandon verifies my information. He explains the situation.

"Yes, we wanted to let you know about abnormal activity on your account."

"OK. What is it?"

"Our records show a number of transactions this evening that are inconsistent with your normal purchase patterns."

Brandon continues talking, but I am stuck on the phrase.

Normal purchase patterns?

Then it hits me.

I interrupt Brandon mid-sentence.

"Um . . . Brandon. It's a long story . . . but I'm guessing this has something to do with the fact that my wife and I spent last year not buying anything, and her sister, a professional shopper, is now in town for their first 'girl's weekend' of 2014."

Brandon answers with a hesitant tone. "OK? So . . ."

"Lemme guess," I continue. "The charges are something from the Opry Mills Outlet Mall in Nashville?"

Brandon sounds surprised. "As a matter of fact, yes. Two different stores, actually. A children's clothing store and a lingerie store."

I guess I'm not the only one who needed new underwear. "All the charges are legit, Brandon."

He chuckles a bit before saying, "OK. Thank you, sir. That was all we needed."

"No, Brandon, thank you for checking up on us."

I push the little red button to end the call.

Inconsistent with normal purchase patterns.

I saunter back to the couch and shove a celebratory spoonful of ice cream into my mouth. It's an unbelievable sign, really. The world has turned upside down. Our credit card company—the great enabler of consumerism—has now become our watchdog, worried that we actually spent some money. I'll call that success.

And never has it tasted so sweet.

Appendix A

Practical Tips: Eight Ways to "Own What You Have"

1. Fix What's Broken

By making a rule to fix what breaks, you take better care of what you *do* have (so it won't break) and develop an appreciation for the things you have repaired. If something breaks and you don't know how to fix it, search YouTube for a tutorial. You would be amazed at the resources available.

2. Limit Exposure to Commercials

Turn off the TV. But if you must consume media, choose an advertising-free service such as Netflix or use a Digital Video Recording (DVR) device through your cable subscriber. And if your kids see advertisements, have a conversation with them about what advertising is so that they can begin to see through the hype.

3. Limit Exposure to Catalogs

Contact catalog companies to remove yourself from the mailing lists. If this seems too daunting, just throw them into the recycle bin as soon as you receive them. Remember: exposure = expectation.

4. Limit Exposure to Coupons

Research shows that coupon usage and coupon exposure leads to an increase in spending. When searching for discounts, make your grocery list first, *then* search the web for coupons for the items you were planning to buy anyway.

5. Conduct an Appreciation Audit

Try a month-long challenge. Each day, list five things for which you are grateful and the reasons you are grateful for them. Your life satisfaction should improve significantly.

6. Practice the "One In, One Out" Method

To simplify your surroundings, vow to donate one or more items for every new item you bring into your house.

7. Do a "Not Much, Not Me" Purge

When cleaning out unnecessary items, *stop* asking, "When might I use this again?" Instead, *start* asking, "What would happen if didn't have this item?" and "Who could use this more?" If your answers are "Not Much and Not Me," then donate the item.

8. Love It or Leave It

Too often we buy things just because they are on sale. Before buying something, ask "Do I truly love it?" If the answer is no, don't buy it. Just because something is a good deal doesn't mean it's a good idea.

Appendix B

Practical Tips: Eight Ways to "Grow in Faith Together"

1. Develop a Family Mission Statement

If you don't know where you're going, any road will take you there. Develop your own family mission statement to guide all your major decisions. Check out Family-iD at www.family-id.com for tips and techniques.

2. Start a Family Devotional

Center your life on what is important. Find a simple, short devotional you can read as a family each day at mealtime. Search the web or your church for a free resource.

3. Play Thorns and Roses

Families have to find a time to connect, and sometimes a simple framework can help make this happen. Whether it's breakfast, dinner, or a simple car ride, start a tradition to share your Thorns and Roses each day.

4. Use Family Dinner Questions

Put a bunch of random, open-ended questions in a jar and place them on the family table. To spur mealtime conversation, have each person draw a question for everyone to answer. A free, printable list can be found at www.howdoesshe.com/family-dinner-printables/.

5. Give Experience Gifts

Instead of tangible presents, start giving experiences as gifts for birthdays and Christmas. These experiences are meant to be not solo pursuits but shared memories. And, if you want some fun ideas for kids, search the web or check out these free science experiments from Toronto 4 Kids at www.toronto4kids.com/May-2013/15-At-Home-Science-Experiments/.

6. "Fill 40 Bags in 40 Days" Challenge

Use Lent as a tool for simplifying your life. The "40 Bags in 40 Days" challenge invites you to de-clutter your entire home by filling one bag each day during Lent. It's a great metaphor to symbolize the Lenten sacrifice and get back to what's important. Donating the excess items is also a wonderful gift to the community. Get more information at http://www.whitehouseblackshutters.com/40-bags-in-40-days-2014/.

7. Read *The Power of Enough* or *Firstfruits Living* by Lynn A. Miller

These books planted the seed for our challenge and are a great study for any adult Sunday school class.

8. Institute "Wise Men Gifts"

Limit your Christmas gift purchases. Institute "Wise Men Gifts" (three gifts for each child) to help build a connection to Jesus and the offerings of the three wise men.

Appendix C

Practical Tips: Eight Ways to "Serve God's People"

1. Find Your Passion

Once you have defined your family mission statement, your passions may become more obvious. We often gain the greatest personal benefit from knowing we are making a difference. Focus your energy toward a limited number of charities to help foster deeper relationships and make a greater impact.

2. Be a Gleaner

The Society of St. Andrew (SoSA) gleans crops in a dozen states in the eastern and southern United States to recover food that would be wasted and use it to feed the hungry. Support them financially or join them for a gleaning project (www.endhunger.org).

3. Serve Your Local Food Bank

Local food banks have service projects for all ages. Sort cans, stock shelves, move boxes, and touch lives. Find a local food bank at http://feedingamerica.org/foodbank-results.aspx.

4. Sponsor a Child

Several organizations pair a child in poverty with someone in the developed world. The focus is on building connection. Lives are transformed on both sides of the relationship. Learn more about how to sponsor a child through Compassion International, http://www.compassion.com/, or World Vision, http://www.worldvision.org/.

5. Take a Mission Trip Focused on "Being"

Step outside your comfort zone and serve on a short-term mission trip. While at your service site, focus on human *being* (being present with those you meet and letting them teach you about Christ's love) rather than human *doing* (working without connecting).

6. Focus on Relationship

Take some time to get to know someone living on the margins, like having dinner with Ellis (chapter 26). Before serving at the soup kitchen, simply share a meal and conversation with the people in need. Deliver a regular route for Meals on Wheels and develop friendships with those you serve. Teach an ESL (English as a Second Language) class and learn the stories of the undocumented workers in our midst.

7. Wrap a "Jesus Gift"

Keep a record of charitable donations and service projects you participate in during the year and print them each on a separate scrap of paper. Place the scraps in the box and have the family read them aloud on Christmas morning. Keep the box in view all year to remind you of the importance of serving throughout all twelve months of the calendar.

8. Christmas Day Service Project

Spend time giving of yourself on Christmas Day to refocus on what the celebration is all about. It can be something easy that doesn't require scheduling. Give small gifts to people who have to work the holiday. Visit a nursing home and chat with residents who don't have family nearby. Drive through your community and hand out blankets to anyone in need who you might meet—anything that shows "God with us."

Notes

Introduction to the Worst Book Ever

1. For the 95 percent on $10 a day, see Martin Ravallion, Shaohua Chen, and Prem Sangraula, *Dollar a Day Revisited*, World Bank, May 2008. They note that 95 percent of developing country populations lived on less than $10 a day. Using 2005 population numbers, this is equivalent to just under 79.7 percent of the *world* population and does *not* include populations living on less than $10 a day from industrialized nations.

Chapter 3: How to Screw Up a Good Thing

1. Lynn A. Miller, *Firstfruits Living: Giving God Our Best* (Harrisonburg, VA: Herald Press, 1991).

Chapter 4: The Rules

1. Ben Gose, "Wealthiest Don't Rate High on Giving Measure," *The Chronicle of Philanthropy* (August 19, 2012), http://philanthropy.com/article/America-s-Geographic-Giving/133591/, accessed September 24, 2012.
2. Ken Stern, "Why the Rich Don't Give to Charity," *The Atlantic* (April 2013), http://www.theatlantic.com/magazine/archive/2013/04/why-the-rich-dont-give/309254, accessed September 21, 2014.

Chapter 5: The Monster under the Bed

1. Viviana A. Zelizer, "The Gender of Money," *The Wall Street Journal* (January 27, 2011), http://blogs.wsj.com/ideas-market/2011/01/27/the-gender-of-money/, accessed September 7, 2014.

Chapter 6: Our Little Science Experiment

1. Check out the good folks at Oxfam at http://www.oxfam.org/. And maybe even buy a goat for someone you love.
2. "Top Kids Party Trends of 2012," http://www.gigmasters.com/articles/top-kids-party-trends-of-2012, accessed September 29, 2014.

Chapter 7: Darn!

1. "Municipal Solid Waste," The United States Environmental Protection Agency, http://www.epa.gov/epawaste/nonhaz/municipal/index.htm, accessed August 22, 2014.
2. "Statistics That Will Make You Want to Recycle Your Cell Phone," http://www.scjohnson.com/en/green-choices/Reduce-and-Recycle/Articles/Article-Details.aspx?date=12-02-15&title=Statistics-That-Will-Make-You-Want-To-Recycle-Your-Cell-Phone, accessed September 22, 2014.
3. Zachary Shahan, "How Many Clothes Do You Throw Away Each Year," *PlanetSave* (April 1, 2011), http://planetsave.com/2011/04/01/how-many-clothes-do-you-throw-away-each-year/, accessed August 15, 2014.
4. "News Release: USDA and EPA Launch U.S. Food Waste Challenge," United States Department of Agriculture, http://www.usda.gov/wps/portal/usda/usdahome?contentidonly=true&contentid=2013/06/0112.xml, accessed September 26, 2014.

Chapter 8: The Price Is Right?

1. "New Research Explores Attitudes and Behaviors of Digital Coupon Users," http://www.couponsinc.com/new-research-explores-attitudes-and-behaviors-of-digital-coupon-users/, accessed August 22, 2014.
2. "Digital Coupon Redeemer: Shopper Trends," GfK, May 2013. http://marketing.gfkamerica.com/050813-1516/Digital-Coupon-Redeemer-Shopper-Trends-2013.pdf, accessed September 25, 2014.
3. Visit https://www.inmar.com/Pages/Resources/Research.aspx to access all of Inmar's research. Once you register, the report titled "2013 Coupon Trends" may be accessed at https://www.inmar.com/Communications/Pages/2013%20Inmar%20Coupon%20Trends.pdf, accessed September 27, 2014.
4. Rajkumar Venkatesan and Paul Ferris, "Unused Coupons Still Pay Off," *Harvard Business Review* (May 2012).
5. Chip Bayers, "The Inner Bezos," *Wired* 7, no. 3 (March 1999).

Chapter 10: The Power of Stuff

1. Clive Hamilton, *Requiem for a Species* (New York: Earthscan, 2010), 66.

Chapter 12: Coach Burgess and the Brainiacs

1. A. Selin Atalay and Margaret McCoy, "Retail Therapy: A Strategic Effort to Improve Mood," *Psychology & Marketing* 28, no. 6 (June 2011): 638–59.

2. "Dopamine Jackpot," *The Guardian* (August 11, 2011), http://www.theguardian.com/science/punctuated-equilibrium/2011/aug/11/1, accessed July 17, 2014. This site also includes video of Sapolsky's fascinating lecture from the California Academy of Sciences.
3. Brian Kutson et al., "Neural Predictors of Purchases," *Neuron* 53 (January 4, 2007): 147–56.

Chapter 13: Two, Four, Six, Eight, What Do I Appreciate?

1. Martin Seligman, *Authentic Happiness* (New York: Atria, 2002).
2. Marilyn Elias, "Psychologists Now Know What Makes Someone Happy," *USA Today* (December 8, 2012), http://usatoday30.usatoday.com/news/health/2002-12-08-happy-main_x.htm, accessed September 21, 2014.
3. Daniel Gilbert, *Stumbling on Happiness* (Toronto: Vintage Canada, 2006).
4. Martin Seligman et al., "Positive Psychology Progress: Empirical Validation of Interventions" (unpublished paper, April 22, 2005), http://www.ppc.sas.upenn.edu/articleseligman.pdf, accessed September 17, 2014.

Chapter 15: True Confessions

1. Henry Chu, "Pope Francis Takes Vatican Trappings to a New Plain," *Los Angeles Times* (March 15, 2013), http://articles.latimes.com/2013/mar/15/world/la-fg-pope-trappings-20130316, accessed August 13, 2014.

Chapter 16: The Worst Parents Ever

1. "Who Is at Risk?" http://www.stopbullying.gov/at-risk/index.html, accessed September 22, 2014.

Chapter 17: Yoga Pants and Jock Straps

1. "Expenditures on Children by Families 2012," United States Department of Agriculture Center for Nutrition, Policy and Promotion, Miscellaneous Publication no. 1528-2012 (August 2013), http://www.cnpp.usda.gov/sites/default/files/expenditures_on_children_by_families/crc2012.pdf, accessed September 24, 2014.

Chapter 18: Naked in the Flat

1. "Naked in the Flat," promotional video, https://www.opendemocracy.net/transformation/%C3%B3l%C3%B6f-s%C3%B6ebech/naked-in-flat, accessed September 7, 2014.
2. Meg Sullivan, "Trouble in Paradise: UCLA Book Enumerates Challenges Faced by Middle Class L.A. Families," UCLA Newsroom (June 19, 2012), http://newsroom.ucla.edu/releases/trouble-in-paradise-new-ucla-book, accessed September 25, 2014.

3. "Self Storage Association: Your Not-for-Profit Trade Organization for the Self Storage Industry," http://www.selfstorage.org/ssa/content/navigation menu/aboutssa/factsheet/, accessed September 25, 2014.
4. Phillip Brickman, Dan Coates, and Ronnie Janoff-Bulman, "Lottery Winners and Accident Victims: Is Happiness Relative?" *Journal of Personality and Social Psychology* 36, no. 8 (August 1978): 917–27.
5. Claudia Dreifus, "The Smiling Professor," *New York Times* (April 22, 2008), http://www.nytimes.com/2008/04/22/science/22conv.html?pagewanted=all &_r=0, accessed September 24, 2014.
6. "Naked in the Flat."
7. "Stumbling on Happiness," Mindful: Taking Time for What Matters, http://www.mindful.org/in-body-and-mind/psychology/stumbling-on-happiness, accessed March 18, 2015.
8. Patricia Greenfield, "The Changing Psychology of Culture from 1800 through 2000," *Psychological Science* (August 7, 2013), 1722–31, http://pss .sagepub.com/content/early/2013/08/07/0956797613479387, accessed February 17, 2015.

Chapter 20: Good-Bye Nana Claus

1. Derek Thompson. "What Is the Secret to Happiness and Money?" *The Atlantic* (March 23, 2011), http://www.theatlantic.com/business/archive/2011/03/what -is-the-secret-to-happiness-and-money/72874/, accessed September 25, 2014.

Chapter 21: Our Discipline Problem

1. "Saudi Arabia: Retail Rising," Oxford Business Group (March 14, 2012), http://www.oxfordbusinessgroup.com/economic_updates/saudi-arabia-retail -rising, accessed September 25, 2014.
2. Jaymie McCann, "No Time for Family: You Are Not Alone," *The Daily Mail: The Mail Online* (July 14, 2013), http://www.dailymail.co.uk/news/article -2363193/No-time-family-You-Parents-children-spend-hour-day-modern -demands.html, accessed September 25, 2014.
3. "Free Printable Family Dinner Questions," http://blog.chickabug.com/2013 /02/free-printable-family-dinner-questions.html, accessed September 28, 2014.

Chapter 22: The Most Awkwardly Awesome Prom Ever

1. "How to Make Crepe Paper Flowers–DIY Flowers," http://www.martha stewart.com/893987/how-make-crepe-paper-flowers, accessed March 17, 2015.

Chapter 25: Gala People?

1. *Merriam-Webster Online*, s.v. "gala," http://www.merriam-webster.com /dictionary/gala, accessed March 19, 2015.

Chapter 28: Brainiacs Revisited

1. Sara Konrath et al., "Motives for Volunteering Are Associated with Mortality Risk in Older Adults," *Health Psychology* 31, no 1 (January 2012): 87–96.
2. Ben Gose and Emily Gipple. "Rich Enclaves Are Not as Generous as the Wealthy Living Elsewhere," *Chronicle of Philanthropy* (August 19, 2012), http://philanthropy.com/article/Rich-Enclaves-Are-Not-as/133595/, accessed September 24, 2014.
3. F. Warneken and M. Tomasello, "Altruistic Helping in Human Infants and Young Chimpanzees," *Science* 311 (March 3, 2006): 1301–3.
4. A. Genevsky et al., "Neural Underpinnings of the Identifiable Victim Effect: Affect Shifts Preferences for Giving," *Journal of Neuroscience* 33, no. 43 (2013): 17188–96.
5. Ibid.
6. Paul J. Zak, Angela Stanton, and Sheila Ahmadi, "Oxytocin Increases Generosity in Humans," *PLOS One*, Public Library of Science (November 7, 2007), http://www.plosone.org/article/info%3Adoi%2F10.1371%2Fjournal.pone.0001128, accessed September 25, 2014.

Chapter 29: Filling

1. Jean C. Buzby, Hodan Farah Wells, and Jeffrey Hyman, "The Estimated Amount, Value, and Calories of Postharvest Food Losses at the Retail and Consumer Levels in the United States," United States Department of Agriculture, Economic Information Bulletin No. (EIB-121), February 2014, http://www.ers.usda.gov/publications/eib-economic-information-bulletin/eib121.aspx#.VCeQ5xas3gU, accessed September 25, 2014.

Chapter 30: A Homemade Halloween

1. Rebecca Dube, "'Pinterest Stress' Afflicts Nearly Half of Moms, Survey Says," *Today Parents* (May 9, 2013), http://www.today.com/parents/pinterest-stress-afflicts-nearly-half-moms-survey-says-1C9850275, accessed September 21, 2014.
2. Ethan Kross et al., "Facebook Use Predicts Declines in Subjective Well-Being in Young Adults," *PLOS One*, Public Library of Science. doi: 10.1371/journal.pone.0069841, accessed September 25, 2014.
3. Hui-Tzu Grace Chou and Nicholas Edge, "'They Are Happier and Having Better Lives than I Am': The Impact of Using Facebook on Perceptions of Others' Lives," *Cyberpsychology, Behavior, and Social Networking* 15, no. 2 (February 2012): 117–21, doi:10.1089/cyber.2011.0324.

Chapter 32: The Santa Clause

1. Check out the Advent Conspiracy and get involved. Interesting stats and ideas can be found at http://www.adventconspiracy.org/, accessed September 24, 2014.
2. World Bank GDP Tables, http://data.worldbank.org/data-catalog/GDP-ranking-table, accessed September 24, 2014.

About the Author

Scott Dannemiller is a writer, blogger, worship leader, and former missionary with the Presbyterian Church (U.S.A.). He and his wife, Gabby, reside in Nashville, Tennessee, with two very loud children.

Scott makes his living as the founder and president of LifeWork Associates, a leadership development consulting firm focused on building more trust and fostering authenticity in corporate America. Most weeks, he can be found delivering a workshop or keynote speech somewhere in the United States.

As a musician, Scott has performed and produced an album of original songs and stories called *What Would You Do*, based on the year he and his wife spent serving in Guatemala. These days he posts his regular writings on his blog, The Accidental Missionary at www.theaccidentalmissionary.net. Follow Scott on Facebook at www.facebook.com/theaccidentalmissionary or on Twitter @sdannemiller.

We would love to hear how you have found peace and connection through simplifying your lives and getting back to what's important. Visit our online community to share your story: www.facebook.com/theaccidentalmissionary